Organizational Dynamics and Intervention

Tools for Changing the Workplace

Seth Allcorn

M.E.Sharpe
Armonk, New York
London, England

In memory of Lt. Savik,
Maine Coon Cat,
1987–2003
My friend, my companion, my teacher

Copyright © 2005 by M.E. Sharpe, Inc.

Library of Congress Cataloging-in-Publication Data

Allcorn, Seth.
Organizational dynamics and intervention : tools for changing the workplace / Seth Allcorn.
  p. cm.
Includes bibliographical references and index.
ISBN 0-7656-1519-3 (hardcover : alk. paper) ISBN 0-7656-1520-7 (pbk : alk. paper)
1. Organizational change—Psychological aspects. 2. Organizational
behavior. 3. Leadership—Psychological aspects. 4. Behavioral assessment.
5. Management—Psychological aspects. 6. Quality of work life. I. Title.

HD58.8.A6776 2005
658.4'063—dc22

2005002773

Printed in the United States of America

The paper used in this publication meets the minimum requirements of
American National Standard for Information Sciences
Permanence of Paper for Printed Library Materials,
ANSI Z 39.48-1984.

∞

BM (c)	10	9	8	7	6	5	4	3	2	1
BM (p)	10	9	8	7	6	5	4	3	2	1

Organizational Dynamics and Intervention

Contents

Preface

This book has its origins in the school of hard knocks. Its content is the product of hard-won insights that seem to consistently apply to most organizations, managers, employees, and organizational consultations. These insights have provided me a way of understanding my work as an executive and organizational consultant. They are in many ways my bag of cognitive tools, tools that permit me to discern the nature of organizational life and events as well as to analyze them and consult about and manage them. My twenty years of part- and full-time consulting and twenty-five years of management experience in the large complex organization that is the academic health sciences center have provided me many challenging learning opportunities that I have embraced whenever possible. I have learned from my successes and my mistakes, and time has allowed me to gradually organize and contextualize this continual learning process.

The notion of a compound perspective that examines a dozen different types of insights into organizational dynamics also creates the potential for integrating these understandings into a whole much like the compound eye of a fly, which makes sense of its multilensed panoramic view of the world. The insights gained from each of the twelve perspectives are unavoidably synthesized in one's mind into an interactive whole that contributes to understanding self, other, and organizational experience. This understanding is nurtured along in my case by a twenty-five-year exploration of how psychoanalytic theory informs one's understanding of the workplace. Each of the twelve perspectives implicitly contains many different psychologically oriented aspects that must be taken into account. This is done, it is hoped, not so much by belaboring the technical language of psychoanalytic theory as by using it to look deeply within each perspective for its underlying psychological core, where meaning and psychological defensiveness coexist.

In sum, this book represents an effort to bring together a myriad of first-hand workplace experiences and endeavors to apply psychoanalytic theory to the study of organizations. It is a compendium of inklings gathered as an executive, consultant, and organizational theorist and researcher. As one might expect, this is a work in progress; however, it is always useful to take an occasional time-out to inspect one's progress. In this regard, the book serves to create a capstone of my learning to date as well as point the way for progress to follow.

Acknowledgments

Learning and every effort to write about it contains an intellectual heritage that permeates the presence. This book contains these intellectual markers contributed by colleagues and friends. Michael Diamond has throughout almost three decades contributed to my learning by introducing me to new theoretical perspectives and striving to use them in practice. The same holds true for Howard Stein who, when looking upon the world and workplace, sees a rich tapestry to complex cultural interpersonal influences that must be discerned and heard. In particular Michael and Howard contributed a great deal to Chapter 10. A third friend who has made a contribution is Arnold Mandell. Our weekly walks on Sunset Mountain in Asheville, North Carolina, were filled with theoretical pondering that served to explore new ways of understanding life and the workplace. Others, including Harry Levinson, Howell Baum, Yinanis Gabriel and Manfred Kets de Vries have contributed insights at a distance through their writing. I must also acknowledge experiential learning opportunities provided by the A.K. Rice Institute that explore the boundaries of group dynamics under stress and many members of the International Society for the Psychoanalytic Study of Organizations. My acknowledgments have also historically included a deeply felt appreciation for the constant presence of Lt. Savik. I, as her person, was the constant focus of her attention during many thousands of hours of manuscript preparation over nearly two decades. Her passing is a true loss. Not to be forgotten is Jean who allows me the space and time to work.

Organizational Dynamics and Intervention

1

Introduction

The workplace often does not fit well within the notion that "If you can't measure it, you can't manage it." Putting aside the fact that in many instances the measures are not available or, if available, they are not put to good use, there is the world of the workplace that lies beyond this pseudo rationality. Employees in many ways create their place of work every day that they come to work. They shape and reshape their work, job descriptions, and interpersonal relations. At the same time, they are influenced by the organization, its leaders, and their colleagues. There is a rich complexity to daily work life that lies well beyond the best efforts of engineers and accountants to quantify the workplace. The development of a better understanding of this workplace beyond the numbers is as essential in terms of better managing others and operations as any number-filled financial statement or analysis. Understanding people and relationships is important.

This book is devoted to exploring a gradually developing literature that examines organizations, organizational dynamics, leaders, followers, groups at work, and organizational structure from a psychoanalytically informed perspective. This theory, while far from monolithic, provides many useful insights into what amounts to a vast complexity that lies below the surface of organizational life and awareness. Many aspects of this theory are drawn together in the following chapters to provide insights that, when taken together, raise fundamental questions about what we have occasion to accept as the nature of organizations and their daily functioning. The intended purpose of this book is to advance this new way of understanding organizational life and work experience to permit a more informed and proactive approach to management. It is not, however, my intention to suggest that a comprehensive workplace theory is being put forward. At the same time, the development of inter-linking insights can inform theory building, organizational study, consultation and organizational analysis, and most of all executives, managers, and employees.

The topics of the chapters are linked. Each informs the other. In particular, it is noteworthy that Chapter 2 on organizational resistance to change is echoed throughout the book. Psychological resistance may take many forms. Goals may be resisted. Incentives may be resisted. Leadership styles may be resisted. Power, control, and authority may be resisted. In general, psychological resistance is a factor in many interpersonal, group, and organizational dynamics. All of these resistances, it may be appreciated, are also frequently combined to create an overarching resistance to many aspects of the organization. Poor leaders may create perverse incentive systems and set unachievable goals that lead to their subsequent rejection and modification by employees. It is therefore important to appreciate that an inspection of the workplace through one lens of a metaphoric compound eye must be integrated with the others to look upon the entire organizational scene.

A second consideration, pertaining to the use of language and theory, bears mentioning. Psychoanalytic theory is not one unified theory but many theoretical perspectives that have been developed throughout the past several centuries. Object relations theorizing is primarily relied upon here. This theoretical perspective is translated into understanding organizational dynamics in what I hope is an accessible manner. Complicated uses of theory and jargon are avoided or, if resorted to, defined and discussed.

A final introductory consideration is the diversity of the twelve perspectives (lenses) discussed here. Some are familiar, such as planning and goals and performance incentives. Others are more abstract and explore important aspects and experiences of the workplace that may be so commonplace and accepted as to go unnoticed. These aspects lack a suitable context-setting perspective that encourages their recognition and exploration. This diversity of perspectives, while not exhausting the possibilities of the metaphoric compound eye, point to a set of sweeping interactive considerations that must be integrated to form an accurate image of the workplace. It is also the case that some of the twelve perspectives challenge conventional thinking. In these cases, this book sets forth an opportunity for reflection and critical thinking. Is what is being said really true? And, if in some measure it is true, what can be done to avoid the problems sighted?

I now turn to an outline of the book's organization and contents. Of particular interest is the concluding section of provisos. It provides helpful cognitive organizers for the chapters that follow.

The Book and Its Organization

Chapter 2 examines the widespread phenomenon of organizational resistance to change. Our large, complex, invariably hierarchical organizations contain a deeply embedded quasi-scientific reliance upon bureaucratic methods. These are not very easy to change, and many times they defy change, especially in the short run and many times over the years. Resistance to change resides in all types of organizations, including the general categories of for-profit, not-for-profit, and governmental units. The significance of this resistance lies in the eye of the beholder. Rapid change driven by a charismatic leader who pursues many different directions within a short period of time may ultimately destroy the organization if the leader is not contained in some way. At the same time, resistance to change can lead to a loss of adaptation in the ongoing struggle for organizational survival. This chapter explores the nature of this resistance to change and the effects of change upon those who are dependent upon adaptive change for work and personal and family survival.

Chapter 3 explores the all-too-common aspect of organizational life that pits "us against them." It is devoted to understanding organizational fragmentation and how it affects self and group experience and organizational performance. Our organizations invariably contain specialization that is driven by the professionalization of work and the hierarchical organization structure that creates divisions and layers. The unique characteristics of workers (ethnicity, age, sex, interests, and union membership) that are expressed within the informal organization also contribute to the fragmentation of the workplace. As a result, small and large organizations alike end up with divisions, layers, and individual and group differences that contain an "us versus them" view of each other and the workplace.

Chapter 4 examines the role of goals within the workplace. The setting of goals is a commonplace aspect of work. However, the setting of goals does not always imply that they are rationally selected or that they necessarily contribute to fulfilling the larger mission of the organization. In fact, why particular goals are set can be one of the more puzzling aspects of one's work experience. It is also the case that, while goals presumably provide clear direction that allows employees to voluntarily coordinate their work to achieve them, they may also be stated in unclear terms or not communicated at all. Once set, they may then be subsequently manipulated to raise the bar or lower it to better fit actual performance. It is also the case that a goal, like achieving profit by increasing revenue and reducing costs, may not create the superordinate direction that is implied. Organizational goals are most often subject to change within the organizational hierarchy or they are minimally followed by employees—"lip service." In sum, inspection of the setting and achieving of goals within organizations reveals a great deal about how certain organizations operate and what it is like to work for them.

Chapter 5 is devoted to inspecting the nature of incentives in the workplace. The leaders of many of our large organizations in the public and private sectors frequently resort to using incentives in the hope of controlling employee behavior. The use of all types of incentives (carrots) is often accompanied by disincentives in the form of progressive discipline, including threats to continued employment (sticks). The carrot-and-stick approach to controlling what employees do is an established feature of organizational life. Employees may, for example, be incentivized with a bonus to increase sales in the last two weeks of a quarter to "make the numbers" or threatened with a loss of their job if they do not. Another contemporary incentive is the use of stock options that, at least in theory, link management performance and increases in personal wealth with corporate success as evidenced by rising stock values. Incentives and disincentives all fall under the heading of *behavior modification*. It is the fundamental nature of these workplace manipulations that is demeaning to employees, often producing unintended outcomes. Incentives are, therefore, frequently not the sought-after "silver bullet."

Chapter 6 takes a hard look at the darker side of executive leadership. Especially when under pressure, leaders may resort to less-than-scrupulous management and interpersonal methods that introduce what I call leadership pathology into the workplace. Those who assume the mantle of leadership are, above all else, human beings. A leader does not magically cross a line in time and space to become one who is not dominated by his or her human qualities, not the least of which are thinking, feeling, and unconscious psychological processes. Leaders bring to their roles and work all of their humanity, which may include aspects that make them feel anxious and vulnerable, thereby introducing psychological defensiveness. Leadership pathology has many origins, takes many forms when acted out at work, and produces a vast array of outcomes, some of which end up making the executive in question more anxious, psychologically defensive, and pathological. It is also the case that executives work within the complexity of a larger milieu of organizational and interpersonal variables. Others who support dysfunctional, dishonest, and destructive organizational leaders may be said to enable the behavior. How else might the leaders of WorldCom, Tyco, and Enron have carried out such vast conspiracies against their employees, stockholders, and communities? Much the same can be said of brutal dictators who starve their people and conduct genocidal warfare. Those who do not support the leader's vision, actions, and narcissistic needs may find themselves banished to a gulag in an organizational Siberia or outplaced (executed). This chapter provides insights into leadership pathologies that harm the world, organizations, and employees.

Chapter 7 underscores the importance of locating and acknowledging the presence of many forms of violence in the workplace. Our organizations contain cultures of organizational violence that are not frequently recognized as violent or seldom formally addressed in the literature. We are most familiar with workplace violence that erupts into the national news in the form of mass shootings. We are also familiar with aspects of the workplace that contain a violent nature that may not be so apparent: contemporary management methods that include organizational downsizing, reengineering, and restructuring not only wreak havoc upon those who are terminated but also upon those who remain. These distressing aspects of the workplace are so common as to be taken for granted. We are encouraged to "grin and bear it" and to "soldier on." Sexual harassment, excessive interpersonal competition and undermining, backstabbing, rumor propagation, threats to people's career and wages, and inter-group rivalries all contain violent qualities. In particular, we may be readily made to feel marginalized, disposable, replaceable—a human resource to be managed.

Chapter 8 explores the nature and role of the human psyche in the workplace. *Psyche* as used here is defined as the soul or spirit in the secular sense, where our spiritual nature is the center of thought, feeling, and behavior. Masterson (1988) notes that Freud's work was not correctly translated and that when he used the word "soul" it was translated into "mental organization." This led to an understanding of Freud's work as more mechanical than spiritual. It is, therefore, important to appreciate that psyche, soul, spirit, and self all reflect an innate human quality that interacts with our experience of others and the workplace. The psyche is metaphorically the vessel that contains the sum of all of the parts. In this regard, there are two lines of inquiry about the interaction of the psyche and the workplace that are not sufficiently differentiated in the literature. One line of inquiry examines the confrontation of organizational structure with psychic structure. Each may be described as *structuring* the other. Do we unconsciously create organizations in our own likeness, or does the organization create us in its likeness? The second line of inquiry speaks to the conscious and unconscious reaction of self and organization to this encounter, where organizational membership promotes anxiety and concomitant psychological defensiveness that may lead to the *restructuring* of self and the workplace.

Chapter 9 directs attention to another workplace phenomenon that incessantly shapes organizational functioning, culture, and our experience of the workplace. The workplace may be thought of as filled with those who stay or, conversely, is *not* composed of those who leave or are terminated. The process of selecting in and out creates in a manner that is not discussable and most often not appreciated, an organizational homogeneity that may severely limit the diversity that breathes life into organizational survival. Organization members slowly become more alike as those with contrary thoughts and feelings gradually leave or are pushed out. This process of selecting in and out is largely masked by efforts aimed at hiring the right person for the right job and by natural attrition (selection) in the form of employee turnover. In particular within the senior ranks of management, there is a strong tendency to support and promote those executives who fit the image of being a team player, resulting in a senior management team whose members are much more alike than different. This outcome accounts for what can become a complete turnover in top management (an epoch of extinction) if organizational performance is bad enough.

Chapter 10 introduces what may at first appear to be a theoretical perspective that is hard to relate to the workplace. The "surface of organizational experience," however, speaks to our most fundamental experience of the workplace in terms of organizational silos or stovepipes and glass ceilings. Are they really there? They seem to be because these metaphors illustrate a very real sense of concrete organizational experience. More importantly, the experience of these types of organizational psychic artifacts is a social phenomenon. Many employees, out of immediate awareness, share these same fundamental experiences of the workplace. These experiences are ultimately hard to articulate and may be described as possessing autistic qualities. Employees feel that they cannot safely interact directly with another department or division, or skip layers when they send communications up and down the organizational hierarchy. These surfaces of workplace experience are very real, limiting, and forbidding. While not being directly observable or measurable, they clearly serve to affect our experience of ourselves, each other, the organization, and organizational viability.

Chapter 11 explores the presence and nature of mysticism in the workplace, which may take many forms. Mysticism amounts to not thinking things through but relying upon intuition and gut reactions when it comes to how we manage our organizations. The decision "feels right." There are also many aspects to the workplace that contain mystical qualities that are supposed to magically motivate employees (incentives, motivational speakers), create a convergence of behavior (mission, goals, and objectives), and containing clear and undisputed meaning (financial statements and performance reports). Some leaders may also believe that they have received divine guidance in their decisions. The rational workplace may then not be so rational after all. Closely related to mysticism are such things as mystification, mystique, and workplace myths. Enron and WorldCom illustrate well that financial statements and operations may be subjected to mystification in the service of executives earning their incentives. These same executives, after appearing on the cover of *Fortune* magazine, may also acquire a mystique, all of which may be captured in organizational mythology. This chapter explores fuzzy systems of beliefs, intuitive processes, and gut feelings that are hard to know and understand and most often contain individual and group dynamics that we may not be aware of.

Chapter 12 inspects the uncommon commonality that exists within our organizations. Beyond the sameness created by selecting in and out, there exists a quality to organizations that is familiar to those who consult with organizations or have worked for a number of different ones. The commonalities, while differing in their specifics, contain pervasive similarities. If all organizations are different and all leaders are different, why do organizations and leaders so often seem to be the same? Why are marginal and bad management and mediocrity so pervasive? Why is clearly communicated strategic direction so often lacking or not followed when provided? Why are organizations thought of as data-rich environments so often poorly understood and their performance so poorly monitored? Why are these commonly found features of organizations so common? In the final analysis, the one thing they all share is human nature. Human nature is the ultimate commonality that must be appreciated for its effects on the workplace.

Chapter 13 examines yet another underappreciated aspect of the workplace, the narrative of workplace histories. All organizations have a history. In general, that history begins with the organization's creation, followed by growth in size and changes in direction and leadership. This appreciation is most often lost in the crush of trying to conduct daily business and making the quarterly numbers. Organizational history is often ignored, or used for political purposes. There is, nonetheless, an experience of meaningful organizational life that is shared by many but also in many different ways. This appreciation is especially important for those who endeavor to create organizational change guided by the plotting of two points. One point is "Where are we?" The other point is "Where do we want to be?" The line between the two is the opportunity for change and the path change must take. The notion of organizational history contains all three of these perspectives, that is, the two points and the line between them. "Where are we?" asks the question "How did we get here?" Where we want to be in the future is informed by organizational history in terms of appreciating how future points have been located in the past and, more importantly, achieved. Organizational history and culture also guide the process of change, showing how some types of leadership and change processes have worked better than others. This chapter explores how organizational history may be uncovered in such a manner as to heal working relationships and direct attention to the need for timely and adaptive organizational change.

Chapter 14 assembles the perspectives discussed in the previous twelve chapters into a consolidated approach: "Organizational Diagnosis and Intervention." These unique and often underappreciated aspects of the workplace constitute lenses through which we can view, understand, interpret, and respond to a vast array of work experiences and organizational dynamics. This compound–eye–view of the workplace creates an opportunity to assemble the views through the twelve lenses into an integrated model for organizational diagnosis and intervention. This chapter is devoted to advancing the notion of organizational diagnosis implicit within the compound eye's panoramic view of organizational life.

Chapter 15, "The Final Analysis," looks back upon the many ways to examine, understand, and intervene in organizational life. The best of theory building and implementable ideas would wisely be placed within a larger context that includes the past, the present, and the future. As organizations change, so must our ways of understanding them and their place in society. Our twelve lenses will not, ultimately, reveal everything that is important about understanding and changing the workplace. They do, however, reveal the complexity of the workplace and give insight into the underlying undiscussable and unconscious processes and dynamics that serve to frustrate the best of intentions and even the hardest driving of efforts to change organizations. The perspectives formed in the organization also inform one's life outside of work. This book provides insights into our interface with "organization" outside of work. We are a part of a vast landscape of large and small organizations that we must deal with on a daily basis. Understanding them permits us to understand our successes and failures in dealing with organizations and those who staff them. This fact may have already been encountered, when we ponder each chapter's content and locate similarities between workplace experience and experience outside of work.

In Conclusion

Each chapter contains a perspective that must be blended with the others. Each chapter provides multiple insights and learning opportunities, and each is grounded in psychoanalytic theory. Concrete examples are provided to anchor the content within the realm of everyday workplace experience. In sum, this book challenges its readers to think about the workplace and its many pressures that too often are taken for granted. Reflection is a critically important part of acquiring insight and this understanding.

The Provisos

Before proceeding, a time-out should be taken to review a few provisos. The first proviso is that psychobabble is all too common these days. Radio and TV talk shows and many self-help books contribute to the perception that popularized psychology is mush for profit and self-promotion. This book is, however, firmly grounded in psychoanalytic theory and particularly in theories of object relations. There is little here that can be thought as "lightweight fare." At the same time, the use of this theory to inform the discussion is not intended to dominate it.

The second proviso is that every effort is made here to make complicated psychological concepts and terminology accessible to the reader. This content is expressed in plain English. However, it is impossible to completely avoid the use of psychoanalytic terminology. In these instances, attention is paid to providing definitions that are anchored in workplace experience. The third proviso is that the twelve perspectives or lenses do not exhaust all possibilities. They are, however, a start at creating a gaze through the compound eye. The lenses and their integration into a diagnostic tool are intended to promote critical thinking and build toward a better understanding of work life.

The fourth proviso is that the reader may well discover linkages between chapters not discussed here. The twelve lenses are part of a systemic whole in which the interactions that are possible between our lenses and other lenses is limitless.

Finally, this book underscores that the world of the workplace is filled with a diversity and complexity that most often defies ready understanding, although a good sense of what may be going on can be had via a careful organizational diagnosis. In this regard, embracing workplace complexity has many advantages over the more frequently encountered slash-and-burn, cookbook, do-it-by-the-numbers management and consultant–driven interventions.

2

Organizational Resistance to Change

Knowledge of human nature, whether or not it be what is called intuitive or however it be acquired, is important. This ability to understand the probable reactions of people and to judge of individual differences is an indispensable quality. Executives differ in the amount of this quality that they bring to their work. But that it can be improved and cultivated by thought and study has been shown again and again.

[T]he underlying contention of this entire volume is that modern psychology points unmistakably to this conclusion: that the true means of permanently influencing others lie in the direction of fostering conditions in which people in and through their own inner desires come to see the results which the leader also comes to desire.

—Ordway Tead, *Human Nature and Management* (1933)

Large organizations are notoriously hard to change to any great extent in a short period of time. Many times they actually seem to defy change. This point of view may be particularly fitting when it comes to national and local government. Depending on one's perspective, this may not be all bad, or it can be interminably frustrating. In the sense that it may not be all bad, citizens depend upon a steady state for governmental services where gradual and measured change is preferred. In particular, there seems to be a genetic wisdom to this when one considers the ever-blowing political winds that vary in direction and magnitude from one election to the next. At the same time, large public bureaucracies also often seem to not change at all despite a clear need to do so in response to poor service and changes in public policy.

Much the same can be said for many large corporations, as well as small to middle-sized businesses. There are, in fact, few exceptions. Despite the belief that the profit motive should provide clear direction, it is more often the case that, while profit is not ignored, it is also not the dominant influence in how private sector organizations are operated. In this case, if the profit motive was so strong, we would have to ask why so many businesses fail. Individuals who have bright ideas for new products and services or develop concepts to improve organizational performance and productivity are all too often simply ignored (Allcorn 1991; Allcorn et al. 1996).

Charitable organizations may also be resistant to change. Large charitable organizations are frequently encumbered with unresolved operating problems that compromise the good that they may do. In particular, large national charity organizations often seem to not be able to steadfastly avoid excessive salaries and inappropriate spending. Religious organizations may also be resistant to change even if it is demanded by their members.

In sum, resistance to change in all types of organizations is a common problem. Diamond (1996, 226) notes,

> Human energy (cognition and emotions) that otherwise might be channeled into the correction of errors and actual problem solving is often displaced by the influence of anxiety into substitute objects (which can include new technology), promoting the illusion of safety and security without substantive reflection and change. Under the stress of uncertainty and anxiety, form (e.g., procedures, regulations, impersonal rules, red tape, etc.) takes precedence over organizational mission and substantive output (e.g., problem solving, provision of services, personal responsibility, and the quality of product). Managerial control and accountability take priority over organizational learning, collaboration, and problem solving.

Resistance to change is such a pervasive theme in organizational life, and so predictable, that one must necessarily wonder why. The balance of this chapter is devoted to exploring its omnipresence in the workplace. Resistance may take many forms. Some commonly found types of resistance will be described in order to locate and define organizational resistance to change. The reasons for these resistances will then be discussed from a psychologically informed perspective. These appreciations lead to considering how resistances can be avoided or overcome by executives, managers, and consultants. Last, the implications of organizational resistance to change for theory building and those who lead organizational change will be explored.

It is important to note that this chapter relates to the remaining chapters in one key way. Human nature influences not only individual and group resistance to change but also resistance to goal setting, less-than-desirable leadership styles, the use of incentives, and the design of the workplace and work. Resistance is, therefore, a common theme that is either explicitly or implicitly a part of the balance of the book. Conversely, it should also be noted that the following chapters illuminate the main facets of human nature and its connection to resistance to change. These informative interactions underscore much of the complexity that resides within any examination of how human nature affects the workplace.

What Exactly Is Organizational Resistance to Change?

Everyone in the workplace has witnessed and likely experienced resistance to change. Perhaps you made a much-needed suggestion for change that went unheeded. Possibly it was blatantly clear that some form of change was needed in order to avoid major operating problems or to correct existing ones. Nonetheless, even when the likely solution was known, nothing happened. There are also those instances in which a need for change was acknowledged, a plan for change developed, and efforts to implement the plan made. However, unaccountably, the change failed or was ultimately compromised, or it left significant problems untouched or created new ones. Resistance to change can take many forms, and it may morph between one form of resistance and another, making it that much harder to overcome. These resistances share the common result that nothing happens, or, if it does, it turns out misshapen and ineffective, or worse, unintended consequences arise that were not anticipated and not responded to in an effective way. Many are the times that "Oh yes, we tried that once" has been heard. Some organizations seem to be so ineffective at fomenting and managing change that most employees are demoralized and do not believe successful change can be accomplished even if it is crucial to the success and the survival of the organization. A few concrete examples are informative. Each illustrates a different way resistance to change can occur.

Nothing Happened

Several business graduate students were able to convince a plant manager to allow them to observe its operation for a class project. The students noticed a number of ways in which production work could be improved. These were outlined for the assistant manager, who patiently listened but ultimately did not take any action. A year later, a second class project encouraged several of the students to revisit the plant to see how things were going. They were surprised to find that many of their suggestions had been implemented, and even more gratifying, seemed to be working. Why did the assistant manager wait until they left to make the changes? One might speculate that receiving and acting on the suggestions of these students threatened the assistant manager's ego.

Shown the Door

A new sales representative went to work for a small company that manufactured candles. She was invited to the factory for an orientation. Manufacturing candles, it was clear, was more difficult than pouring paraffin into molds. In fact, getting the colors, scents, and finishes right could produce a lot of waste. During her walk-through of a huge warehouse, she noticed many familiar products that were in the catalogue and also a large number that were not. A meeting with the owner revealed that he was worried about coming up with a considerable amount of money to build a second warehouse since the one she had been shown was almost full. It occurred to her that she might walk through the warehouse and measure the number of linear feet of shelving filled by products that were not in the catalogue. She also learned that the unlisted items were batches of candles not suitable for sale to customers. Some had the wrong wicks and burned either too fast, too slow, or not at all. Others had surface or internal defects. Some had scents that were either not appealing or deficient. The total amount of these products added up to approximately 40 percent of the total warehouse capacity. The sales representative suggested to the owner that he sell the defective candles at a low cost to a nearby discount store to recover his raw material costs and clear out the warehouse. The owner promptly acted on the suggestion. Upper management, however, was not amused. They had missed discovering this possibility. As a result, the new employee was marginalized in her role and eventually pointed toward the door (Allcorn 1991).

Change the Hard Way

The chief executive officer (CEO) of a fairly large company appropriately mandated an update of the information systems that drove sales, service, shipping, and accounting for a major mail order supply division. As fate would have it, the large consulting company designing and overseeing the system changes sponsored the products of vendors that the company was partnered with. This consulting company belatedly discovered that their effort to adapt the vendor's software to the application would not readily work. Not only was the software marginally suitable, but nonintegrated software (order taking, shipping, billing, accounting) was involved at every turn. Connectors of various types had to be either created or purchased off the shelf and programmed to fit specific needs. All of the added complexity led to the conclusion that the deadline would be missed. What was the CEO's response? He ordered implementation on time and without running the old system parallel. Just as important, he had cut corners to reduce costs. His IT staff was to write all the code for management and operating reports—something that had not yet been started. "Go live" led to the immediate collapse of all other work. Employees were pressured into working seven-day weeks to manually cope with the problems. The cascade of software glitches was almost unlimited. Fixes to one programming error often created new ones. Sales and service were seriously compromised. Operating, programming, and opportunity costs were soaring out of control. How could this have happened? Why had reasonable advice been resisted and ignored? It appeared that saving face was more important than the bottom line. As a final insult, the CEO learned about a year later that he had purchased obsolete software that would no longer be supported by the vendor. It would need to be replaced much sooner than planned. Most recently the division was sold. It never recovered from this fiasco.

Unintended Consequences

A division within a state was developing a major new software application as part of a massive redesign of its services. This change was federally mandated, and not achieving it would lead to dire fiscal consequences. The change process was, however, $50 million over budget and five years behind schedule. The loss of federal funding was an imminent threat. A consultant offered a number of suggestions that were embraced by the division director. The director hired an experienced chief information officer (CIO) and a consulting company experienced in managing software vendors. In short order the software design was completed and ready to implement. While this was occurring, the consultant had the opportunity to interview county administrators currently responsible for the program's operation to be centralized. They were skeptical and worried about failures that would have a negative impact on their citizens. They also felt left out of the planning and design of the changes. It was obvious that a lot of effort needed to be put into planning the implementation. This advice was not heeded and the consulting engagement ended shortly thereafter. Approximately nine months later, a follow-up call to see how things were going was made. Everyone in the leadership team of this division had been fired. The implementation had failed when the counties challenged it, and it became a major media event.

Some Resistance to Change May Have Merit— A Counterpoint

It is also the case that not all change is necessarily prudent or needed. Perhaps a senior executive comes up with a pet project that is pursued despite every indication that it is an expensive and time-consuming waste of time. In other instances, an executive may sponsor rampant change. He may see a threat or marketing opportunity behind every headline and door, or seem anxious to show others up by trying to outdo colleagues. He may also be a creative thinker or a perfectionist. For whatever the reason, the direction, speed, and frequency of change may be inappropriate and poorly conceived, planned, implemented, and subsequently managed. The following two vignettes illustrate the effects of this kind of organizational change.

Excessive Fine Tuning

A CEO who had risen through marketing continually expanded the number of products offered and created many variations on existing products. Employees pointed to a large, new, and expensive piece of equipment that had been purchased to do one project to close one deal. The equipment had not been used again. These same employees were also burdened with an excessive and continuous expansion of the number of products they had to produce. Small variations abounded and were proving to be hard to manage in production. Waste, delays, and performance problems were increasing along with customer complaints. These problems led to rapid and misinformed interventions by the CEO, who ordered changes after a quick inspection of the situation. This quick-fix strategy led to a predictable cascade of additional problems that revealed to all concerned that the CEO had little insight into business process reengineering. Employees were constantly being blamed and blindsided, and this made them overly defensive and resistant to accepting the CEO's directions. They often listened attentively and then used their own judgment to fix the problem.

Marketing Perfection

Yet another example of dysfunctional change is the development of a new staff in a marketing department that continually modified direct mail advertising right up to the last minute. One story illustrates the adverse outcomes. The mailing division had purchased millions of custom envelopes designed to fit a mailer. At the last minute, the marketing staff changed the mailer and its size. It was now bigger than the purchased envelopes. This necessitated having to pay a premium for a rush delivery of new envelopes accompanied by the indefinite storage of the original inventory—a combined cost in the hundreds of thousands of dollars.

Perhaps enough has been said about excessive change. We can acknowledge that ill-conceived, rampant change can increase the likelihood of organizational resistance to change. Therefore, not all resistance to change is bad. However, this appreciation does not eliminate the need to further explore the kind of resistance to change that introduces comprises, failures, and threats to organizational survival.

Why Does Resistance to Change Occur?

The examples thus far provided should make clear that resistance to change is a common feature of the workplace that may take many forms and have just as many reasons for occurring. Bungling, top-down, poorly conceived, and out-of-touch ideas for change may be accompanied by equally bad analysis and planning in which sufficient time and resources are not provided. In fact, the process of change can sometimes seem designed to make employees feel anxious, alienated, and set upon.

The aspects of organizational life that promote resistance to change are a product of the foibles of human nature—foibles that are accentuated in management roles. Yet the personal dynamics that work against change are almost universally the underrecognized, and in most cases undiscussable, elephant in the room. It is also the case that faddish, quick-fix, one-minute type thinking is so common in this arena that it is labeled as psychobabble, ready to be discarded from consideration or embraced without any real insight. My purpose in the following section is to thread my way between the psychobabble and the well-established but hard-to-understand psychoanalytically informed theory to acquire insight into the interaction of human nature and the workplace.

The Nature of Psychological Resistance to Change

During a vacation at the beach, I met a former New York City Fifth Avenue psychotherapist-turned-artist. We discussed his metal sculpting and the nature of his former practice. Eventually I asked why he had changed professions. He reflected a moment and said, "I guess it is easier to change the shape of steel than to change people." He was speaking about the problem of psychological resistance to change. His patients, while presumably seeking his help, were most often steadfast in their resistance to developing personal insight or changing their thinking, feeling, and behavior even though change was logically indicated to achieve better personal and social adjustment. The notion of not being able to teach old dogs new tricks is a metaphor that reflects the difficulty of getting people to change to benefit themselves and others.

Psychological resistance to change has been explored by a number of authors. One of the more informative discussions that links clinical resistance to change to organizational resistance to change is that of Kets de Vries and Miller (1984). They note that psychological resistance to change comes from one's desire to avoid the psychic pain associated with confronting the state of one's self, and the tendency instead to maintain a familiar equilibrium regardless of how dysfunctional, self-defeating, and self-destructive that equilibrium may be. There develops a defensive resistance to knowing what would happen if one's inner structure of conflicts and defenses and self-inflicted suffering were confronted. Any sense of this balance being destabilized threatens change and the foreboding loss of one's carefully created and balanced psychological defenses and self-images. The possibility of acknowledging that change is needed also threatens a distressing personal disorientation in which the individual faces mourning the loss of the false self, a state that may be described as peering into the empty void of the self (Masterson 1988). The notion of the false self amounts to a lifelong psychologically defensive construct that distorts accurate reality testing and blocks personal change to improve adaptation. The individual finds it much too painful to call into question this well-established pattern of self-modification and the accompanying carefully developed defensive structure that most often produces an unhappy, depressed, and possibly self-destructive existence. The false self epitomizes what resistance to change is all about. Diamond (1996, 224) notes, "Asking people to approach their work differently requires cognitive shifts in the naming and framing of problems . . . and places emotional demands on their feelings of self-competence and self-confidence: their self-esteem at work." In a therapeutic setting, Kets de Vries and Miller (1984) note that defensive resistance must be confronted, clarified, interpreted, and worked through in such a way that working through contains elements of mourning.

The workplace implications of psychological resistance and defensiveness are straightforward. The workplace is saturated with our humanity. We do not leave our human nature in all of its complexity and vulnerability at the portal to work. It is also the case that the workplace introduces many stressful experiences that threaten our sense of being valued, competent, successful, likable, and attached to something larger than ourselves such as an idealized leader, a group, or an organization. Organizational change that threatens to alter carefully balanced work experience and relationships is distressing. Our relationships, work, office, and employment status could be abruptly changed by remote authority figures who hand down orders for change from on high. A sudden reassignment, a missed promotion, or the loss of one's job can readily evoke feelings of fear and anxiety, guilt and shame, and envy and hatred (Baum 1987). We may feel set upon and paranoid, deficient, useless, engulfed by the power of the organization (or CEO) or, alternatively, abandoned by it and alone. Certainly almost everyone working within large organizations has had these experiences or witnessed them in others.

An executive who hands down a unilateral order for change may not only evoke feelings of paranoia, loss, and anger; she could provoke an individual or group response aimed at undermining her career and affecting her ability to perform work, provide direction, and be accepted as a member of the "team." She could be seen by others to be a horrible person without redeeming qualities. Psychological splitting and projection aid this process. This refers to a defensive mental process in which opposing parts of the self (good and bad or desirable and undesirable) are separated. The individual retains one of the parts (often the good part) and projects the bad part onto another person. Thus the individual experiences herself as all good and the other as all bad. Instructions may be reinterpreted (rationalized and changed), not communicated to others (withheld), or ignored to the point that it is as though the instructions were never issued (denial). Foot dragging and explosions of anger may slow movement. Outbursts such as this are not unlike childhood temper tantrums and are referred to as psychological regression. The individual accesses childhood coping mechanisms that have historically worked but may be out of place in the moment. Such responses to the mandated change can ultimately block it or make it unworkable, thereby leading to the logical conclusion that the old way was better.

Workplace resistance to change can therefore be understood to consist of individual and group defenses that serve to forestall change. Overcoming or, better yet, avoiding it is important.

Interpreting and Responding to Resistance in the Workplace

Resistance to workplace change can take many forms within various organizational contexts, in the presence of leaders with many different personal characteristics and leadership styles. This appreciation leads to consideration of how to successfully manage organizational change.

Managing Organizational Change

Managers often lead, support, and are subjected to change in the workplace. Each of these types of experience creates new learning opportunities. It is fair to say that anyone with more than a few years of work experience has encountered these experiences. It is also the case that many executives, managers, and supervisors have been exposed to horrific examples of management failure to create effective change (Allcorn et al. 1996). What seems to work is to approach change as a process rather than a product or event. It is not a question of how fast change can be rammed through the organization but rather how it can be designed as an inclusive and participatory process that creates a reasonably safe holding environment for discovery, analysis, planning, implementation, and response to unintended consequences.

An overview of the literature and offerings of consulting groups from the Internet reveals general agreement. The development of an open, inclusive, participative, listening, and respectful setting invites employees (or stakeholders) to not only participate and contribute but also to ultimately accept changes even though they may not entirely agree. If agreement is lacking, at least objections were heard, which is an important part of building consensus. Employees, in order to contribute to the design of change, must also learn more about why change is necessary and how to plan for its implementation. Many of the feelings associated with resistance to change can be avoided or minimized by everyone joining in the work. It is also the case that an open process invites inspection of feelings of anxiety—"How will this affect me?" The development of cross-functional change management groups also serves to break down internal barriers and promote better understanding and empathy across layers of management (see Chapters 3 and 10). This outcome promotes trust that facilitates the discovery of variances from plan and timely responses to unintended consequences. This permits responses before the problems become critical. If managers approach change in this manner, resistance to change can be avoided or, when encountered, more readily worked through.

Managers charged with implementing change may feel a loss of direct control, misgivings about group processes that may seem to drag along, and the sense of "I am not sure I would do it that way." These discomforting anxieties are, however, much easier to deal with as a manager than being confronted with deeply felt and highly mobilized resistance to change that is frustrating, time-consuming, and hard to overcome. The old phrase "an ounce of prevention is worth a pound of cure" comes to mind.

Managers should not only appreciate the importance of avoiding resistance to change but also recognize it when it arises. In particular, they must learn to be aware of its presence in terms of their inner experience. In clinical terms this amounts to acknowledging and interpreting countertransference. Countertransference is one's unconscious response to what another person is saying and doing that is fueled by prior life experience. In clinical terms, this phenomenon contaminates the therapist's understanding of the patient. However, if the countertransference is spotted, it provides insight into the other person. In a sense, this insight consists of the realization "if I felt this perhaps the other person felt it or is feeling it." In sum, I have to understand my self-experience, thoughts, and feelings, and be able to observe my own behavior, which is a response to what is going on around me in the workplace.

All CEOs, executives, and managers have these experiences, thoughts, and feelings. What is important is what we do in response to them. Are we open to experiencing them, and, if so, how can our response promote organizational effectiveness?

This consideration raises a fundamental question. If I feel anxious, frustrated, unsure, pressed for time, and even angry, do I merely act or not act on these feelings or do I use them to inform myself about what is going on? If a manager is having some of these feelings, it might be the case that others around her are also experiencing them. Everyone is in the same experiential boat. An appreciation such as this raises the possibility of empathy and interpersonal group process insights into the dynamics of the moment. It also raises the possibility of the manager's testing her assumption: "As I sit here, I do not know if any of you are feeling frustrated by our lack of progress, but I surely am." Some may acknowledge sharing this experience, and others may remain silent and listen. Discovering the cause of the feelings of frustration is the task at hand. When placed back in the hands of the group or organization, this process leads directly to the possibility of identifying the problem and doing something about it. Problem solving is obviously a contributor to organizational success. My ability to speak of my own experience regardless of whether it is feelings of anxiety, being blocked or sabotaged, unsupported, under-resourced, or set upon by unrealistic expectations of superiors permits me to explore whether others are also having the same experience and feelings. We do not have to unwittingly stew in our own juices. If we can locate in ourselves the experience that is most likely shared by many, we can then locate the cause of this experience and a way to correct or deal with it even if it sometimes feels dangerous and foreboding. This might be the case within an organizational culture where "the messenger" is often annihilated. In this case, a group is usually harder to kill off than an individual.

The point being made is that although it can seem that self-awareness and sensing our own experience is illusive and off task, if we are open to the possibility of doing so, it invariably reveals actionable knowledge that might not otherwise be available as an organization resource. Leaders who are able to do this hard work are frequently the most respected and admired in the workplace.

Consulting to Change

Organizations always need to change—some more than others, depending upon how fast-paced change is within the given industry and how successful the organization has been at keeping pace with the change. Consultants and executives who become agents of change are usually hired to locate problems, find solutions, and facilitate change. In this regard the consultant many not only be greeted by organizational resistance to his presence (a hatchet man?) but also resistance to fundamentally questioning what is going on, testing out of new ideas, problem recognition, preparation of analyses, and the planning and implementation of change.

Consultants inevitably become filled to overflowing with a confusing and frequently distressing array of thoughts and feelings as they begin work. They are frequently greeted with fear, competitiveness, avoidance, manipulation, withholding of support and resources, as well as direct challenges to their expertise and authority. Consultants are, it seems, most often lumped altogether. Executives, managers, and employees assume that all consultants are the same. If employees have experienced consultants who are arrogant and indifferent and use harsh and ineffective methods, these experiences are seldom forgotten. It is then expected that all consultants will be much the same.

It is therefore essential that consultants attend to their own experience and try to interpret the underlying nature of that experience for meaning, including the interpretation of countertransference (Diamond and Allcorn 2003). This is especially challenging when working alone. Consultants can expect to be confronted with a wide variety of resistance that will vary between groups, departments, divisions, and sites, since organizational change is not a uniform experience across an entire organization. Some are excited about it (possibly the sponsors) and others are threatened by it or feel defeated or neglected and left out. The possibilities are limitless. Not being aware of the presence of resistance and the many reasons for it can lead to the insensitive ramming through of change on the part of management that promotes further resistance and defensiveness. The psychologically informed consultant, however, has the luxury of being able to travel through the organization to locate resistance and its underlying experience, thoughts, and feelings, as well as being able to address these dynamics, thereby encouraging an open discussion and working through.

Part of this work, much like that of the therapist, is recognizing the various forms defenses may take as well as the ability to better understand them via the interpretation of countertransference. Does a black-and-white world exist in some places within the organization that is fueled by splitting and projection? Are there areas that seem completely out of touch and even unaware of operating problems and plans for change (denial and rationalization)? Is there overthinking of the problem, a preoccupation with data collection and analysis, or excessive planning for change and implementation (intellectualization)? The ability of the consultant to label these experiences is an important part of understanding the resistance. Labeling, however, must be accompanied by the inspection of one's own experience as well as insights into transferential processes that take place within the organization among executives, managers, and employees (Diamond and Allcorn 2003).

In sum, consultants, while possessing many fine technical and analytical skills, also need to develop the skills required to understand the interaction between human nature and the workplace as well as the connection of employees' self-experience to their experience of the workplace. This consideration encourages a further inspection of the implications of resistance to change for successful organizational adaptiveness.

The Implications of Organizational Resistance to Change for Management, Consulting, and Theory Building

This chapter has underscored the not always obvious. Resistance to change is a difficult aspect of organizational life to avoid and overcome. Every new idea and initiative may well be greeted with skepticism and varying degrees and types of resistance to change. I have discussed how to avoid resistance and to work through change from a psychological perspective. Those leading change and those theorizing about it must more openly address the psychological considerations involved. It is critical to be able to locate and work through resistances, many of which are based in individual psychology, and others in shared social defenses. Embracing this perspective directs our attention to the need to design change methodologies that avoid promoting these defensive responses. Incorporating openness, transparency, inclusiveness, communication, reflectiveness, and trust and respect into the dynamics of change seems to be essential. However, more is at stake than merely avoiding or working through resistance as a part of implementation.

A well-designed change process also contributes additional value added in two ways. The pinpointing of the need for change and the location and design of change will both be enhanced. Change may well occur sooner and be better thought through. A nondefensive change process promotes the early identification of unintended consequences and problems as well as the rapid location of solutions to them. If most employees feel included, they will feel engaged and committed to making the work of change a success. It is much better to have a thousand pairs of eyes looking out for unintended consequences than trying to spot consequences by using reports or hearing about them only after they have created operating problems. In sum, taking the time to avoid and overcome resistance to change offers value added throughout the change cycle. Effectively dealing with human nature in the workplace can then be understood to transform costly resistance to change into a cost-effective and value-adding change dynamic.

The implications of this perspective also evoke the need for a well-conceived process of organizational diagnosis and intervention that can be used primarily by new executives and consultants. Chapter 14 provides a basic outline of how this work might be accomplished. It is important at this point to appreciate that complexity, ambiguity, and not-so-rational interpersonal, group, and organizational dynamics must be effectively reckoned with. This is best accomplished by developing a carefully conceived and systematic process of delving into organizational life. Often, an understanding of the human side of organizational life leads to a much greater appreciation of how to gain employee acceptance of the need to create change.

In Final Analysis

Resistance to organizational change and its many repercussions is costly for organizations; the substantial value added by avoiding and working through resistance is essential for improving organizational effectiveness in the twenty-first century. This fundamental acknowledgment reminds me of a conversation I had with an engineering consultant on one of those long coast-to-coast flights. He had just finished a major project and shared with me a bit of what he had been working on. A large manufacturing concern wanted to have its production lines tuned up to improve operating efficiency. He and his colleagues found a variety of opportunities to accomplish just that. I inquired how his clients usually responded to the completion of these research projects and the summing up of the findings in a polished and nicely presented report. Did his clients tend to embrace the proposed changes and proceed with implementation? He fidgeted a bit in his seat and then turned to me and said "no," and that bothered him. Why was it that these huge companies were willing to pay large sums of money to receive his analyses if they did not have any real intention of acting upon his recommendations? Herein lies the significance of this chapter for consultants and those who hire them, for executives who lead change, and for the organizational researchers who theorize about organizational resistance to change.

Resistance to change and psychological resistance are evidence of the omnipresence of human nature in the workplace. This consideration is a fundamental part of the rest of this book. Implicit and explicit resistance to goals, incentives, and leadership must be factored into our understanding of the workplace. This chapter puts in place a foundation from which insight into human nature at work can be gained. Chapter 3, which discusses the inevitability of horizontal and vertical organizational fragmentation, underscores this appreciation. Fragmentation arises, in part, from human nature and as a result, is extraordinarily resistant to change.

3

Organizational Fragmentation

Splitting of self and other occurs in psychological responses to stress and anxiety at work. What happens? Individuals experience critical incidents (change in the organizational status quo) very personally—that is, as damaging to their core sense of self (their self-identity). In some instances, otherwise whole, integrated self-images split into two opposing views of self: good versus bad, loved versus hated, accepted versus rejected, idealized versus despised self-images.

—Michael Diamond, *The Unconscious Life of Organizations* (1993)

Modern-day organizations are almost invariably specialized to some extent. The amount of specialization and the degree of potential specialization is limited only by the number of professions that exist within the workplace, the size and complexity of its hierarchical structure, and by the characteristics of workers, which, while not a part of the formal organization, introduce further division among organizational members. A few examples serve as informative reminders of these many divisions, layers, and individual and group differences.

A department of human resources (HR) management can be constituted of those who specialize in recruiting, training, compensation, benefits, internal consulting, performance problem resolution, and so on. These specialties within the HR profession may also be further specialized. Benefits may be broken down into health insurance, dental insurance, life insurance, death and disability insurance. Specialization may also occur within these, such as health insurance being broken down between active and retired personnel and types of programs—managed care and preferred providers. There may also be direct contracting with local providers, and some health care delivery issues may be outsourced to hot lines or chronic care organizations (disease management). Manufacturing may be split into divisions that are themselves broken down into detailed processes, each overseen by specialized engineers. Marketing may be divided up in many ways that take into account products, product groups, and regions (local, state, regional, national, and international), and by marketing methods such as managing a sales force, telemarketing, and advertising, each requiring special knowledge.

These traditional types of organizational specialization are accompanied by the notion that organizations are divided into hierarchical layers of power and authority. A small team of experts will usually have a supervisor who reports to a manager who reports to a more senior executive and so on, up the chain of command and control. The larger and more complex organizations become, the greater the number of layers. This layering contains its own unique properties and dysfunctions that serve to divide one layer from the next and the top of the organization from the bottom.

These formal organizational divisions and levels that are so familiar are most often matched by an equally complex informal organization that is driven by the creativity of human nature and individual and group differences. Employees may see fit to divide themselves up in many different ways. Some of the most common informal divisions are male/female, generational (age), ethnic, and by neighborhood, type of position held, religion, politics, athletic teams, and recreational and social interests. It is, of course, likely that several of these informal subgroupings apply to every individual.

These types of organizational differences might be thought of as existing within an overarching social matrix where formal organizational differences are arrayed across the top and informal differences arrayed down the side. A human resources department may contain many informal groups, and the informal groups may contain individuals from all parts of the formal organization. This socially complex matrix underscores the true diversity of the workplace, which can make entry a stressful experience and maintenance of good relations across these many subgroups challenging.

This chapter is devoted to exploring the significance of this rich tapestry of interpersonal and intra-organizational divisions, layers, groups, and subcultures. One way of approaching this inspection is to examine the two-dimensional nature of organizational charts. Organization charts reveal the specialization and divided nature of work that contributes to horizontal fragmentation as well as the many layers of power and authority associated with controlling and coordinating work (vertical fragmentation). These columns and layers and the informal divisions become the basis for organizational splits that are contributed to by psychological splitting and projection. Understanding the relationship between organizational fragmentation and psychological splitting and projection is a critical first step in responding to their presence in the workplace. The chapter concludes with a discussion of the challenge of managing and healing these splits that create some of the worst outcomes of organizational fragmentation.

Organizational Fragmentation

Organizational fragmentation is such a pervasive workplace phenomenon that it is taken for granted: it is the way that organizations are designed and operated. Or is it? Organizational fragmentation can be thought of as existing in two dimensions within our organizations. There are a great many aspects of organizations that exist on a horizontal plane. This plane is filled with the departments, divisions, and groups mentioned. There are also vertical divisions commonly referred to as organizational layers. Within twenty-first-century organizations these layers are composed of an ever-ascending array of job titles that contain formal organizational power and prestige and preferably, but not inevitably, responsibility. The individual employee reports to a supervisor, who reports to another supervisor, who reports to a manager, who reports to a general manager, who reports to a regional manager, who reports to a divisional vice president, who reports to—well, you get the picture. Implicit with this hierarchy of positions is the notion of the pyramid, where the amount of power and authority amassed gradually becomes all-inclusive in the position of the chief executive officer (CEO). Understanding the dimensions of organizational fragmentation is, therefore, a prerequisite to understanding, managing, and changing organizations.

Horizontal Organizational Fragmentation

A vast array of potential organizational problems is embedded within the presence of what is commonly referred to as organizational silos or smokestacks. These silos are visually discernable in organization charts that have columns for operations, marketing, finance, accounting, design and development, human resources, legal affairs, and public relations divisions, to list but some of the possibilities. The columns will differ by the type of organization. In contrast to a corporation manufacturing a wide variety of paper products for the international market, hospitals will have some similar and some different columns. Hospitals will have columns for human resources, finance, and accounting, but also for divisions based on clinical specialties such as cardiology, pediatrics, surgery, and family practice, with subspecialties within these specialties. Even though there are highly noticeable differences in how any given organization is divided up into specialized silos, the bottom line is that the silos themselves are essentially the same. They contain the same types of self and "other" experience, introduce the same problems in coordinating work among the silos, and create unique subcultures that may not always contribute to the work of the larger organization.

Organizational silos can have a profound effect on how work is accomplished. A case example is informative.

The Case of the Invisible Barrier

During a visit to an office within a large division of state government, I was walked through the office space. At one point I was shown a room with two rows of desks on either side of an aisle. There were two offices for supervisors at the back of the room. The office layout seemed to be unremarkable. A number of employees were subsequently interviewed as to their work experience, and these interviews included staff from this room. The image revealed from the interviews of what the organization of the space and the organization in the room really meant for accomplishing work was unexpected. In particular, one employee provided an example of a routine problem that she had encountered. She was working on a case that involved trying to resolve family discord involving children. She said that she was responsible for the welfare of the children and that a colleague across the aisle was responsible for dealing with the parents. She went on to say that she had overheard a telephone discussion her colleague had had with the parents. Some of the content of the conversation would have permitted her to do a better job of working with the children. She said, however, that she was forbidden from interacting directly with the employee speaking to the parents. More specifically, she could not formally use what she had learned. The only valid information was that provided by her supervisor. Although she had overheard the conversation, she was obliged to disregard what she had heard. This remarkable state of affairs prompted further probing. In particular, how was it that these rules had come into existence? The employee shared information about how the legislation that drove the work was interpreted as creating two divisions, one for the parents and one for the children. Each division had its own supervisor and operating procedures. This information accounted for the presence of the two supervisors' offices at the back of the room. These supervisors were held accountable for enforcing this division of the work, and each had mandated that her employees could not voluntarily coordinate work across the aisle. Rather, all requests and information had to flow through the supervisors, who were overwhelmed by the work flow and unable to, in a timely manner, pass information between each other to keep employees on either side of the room informed. Enough said.

This example highlights what can happen when the mentality of organizational silos is taken to its logical extreme. It also introduces the problem of vertical organizational fragmentation discussed below. It is not ultimately possible or meaningful to consider one dimension in isolation from the other.

Vertical Organizational Fragmentation

The notion of vertical organizational fragmentation is a derivative of the equally familiar and often unquestioned nature of hierarchical organization designs that answer the question, "Who is in charge here?" at every level of an organization. In fact, it is so difficult to envision organizational life without the many hierarchical layers of power and authority that we may think of organization structure as being locked within the hierarchical paradigm (Allcorn 2003). Its omnipresence, while providing the CEO and others some measure of control, also introduces a great many well-documented organizational dysfunctions (Baum 1987; Blau and Meyer 1971; Downs 1967; Hummel 1982). These dysfunctions create a sense of organizational fragmentation. One layer may not know what another layer is doing. The top of the organization may be out of touch with what is going on at the bottom. This eventuality is contributed to by each layer modifying communication up and down the organization to defend against being held accountable. A supervisor might conceal a major problem generated by one of his decisions. Middle management might modify upward reporting in such a manner as to conceal operating problems and create an impression of outstanding performance for bonus, salary, promotional, and tenure considerations. The CEO might, in turn, speak of organizational performance in glowing terms to appease a governing board and stockholders. Conversely, downward communication can be equally compromised, making an instruction given by a CEO problematic in terms of implementation and intended outcomes. Intervening management layers will see fit to interpret, add to, omit, and customize instructions from on high to fit their perception of what should be done. It is also probable that instructions from the CEO may in part be based on a false impression created by compromised information flowing upward through the organization. In sum, the bi-directional nature of communication in a hierarchical organization is always problematic.

Organizational Fragmentation Within the Informal Organization

Managing the performance of a roomful of automated machines is easier than managing a roomful of people. The presence of employees introduces the challenging aspects of managing human nature. We continually divide ourselves up into groups of all kinds based on personal attributes, interests, thoughts, and feelings. Already mentioned are such common informal divisions as sex, age, ethnicity, religion, and where one lives. It may also be the case that we just do not like another person's personality, mannerisms, attitude, or system of beliefs. These groupings and likes and dislikes inevitably lead to problems in working together as individuals and among groups including formal organizational divisions and layers. Two supervisors who must share information but do not like or trust each other will intentionally and unintentionally create communication lapses and backlogs that compromise organizational performance and the delivery of suitable and timely products and services to those who depend upon the organization to have their needs met. Dysfunctions arising from the informal organization can also yield excessively competitive outcomes, where defeating the other individual or group takes precedence over organizational well-being. Much the same can be said for competition for resources, raises, and promotions. Virtually anything is possible.

Organizational Fragmentation as a Function of Boundaries and Experiential Surfaces

Those who study and write about organizational fragmentation most often refer to the fragmentation as an outcome of organizational boundaries. Just as nations have boundaries around their land, divisions and layers within our organizations are also set apart by boundaries that are rigorously defended by those inside of them. The presence of these boundaries is observable because the transactions across them render them locatable, discussable, analyzable, and changeable (Diamond, Stein, and Allcorn 2002). These conceptual boundaries are created in many ways and are designated by a wide variety of markers. The experience of getting off the elevator at the executive office suite contains many signals that may evoke anticipatory anxiety for those who seek entry. Divisions often exist behind guarded doors. Gatekeepers (receptionists) often control boundary-crossing points. No appointment, no access. Much the same can be said for all manner of telephonic, electronic, and paper-based communication. Anyone familiar with organizations will have encountered these vertical and horizontal boundaries so often as to understand that they are in many ways the essence of organizational life.

There is, however, more to the notion of boundaries than meets the eye. While boundaries are often as clear as a line in the sand that can only be crossed at some personal risk, it is also true that one is more than merely stepping over this line. The notion of a boundary line must be extended to include its full experiential significance, which leads to considering such lines as having three dimensions (length, width, height). The boundary is not so much stepped over as stepped through. Getting off the elevator to enter the executive suite signifies a great deal more in an experiential sense that merely stepping off the elevator and across a boundary. One's experience of boundary crossing is often filled with an experiential richness that belies the simplicity symbolized by the line in the sand. Arriving at the closed door of the office of a senior executive who has unexpectedly summoned you for no apparent reason evokes feelings that unconsciously link backward in time to past workplace experiences, childhood, and confrontations with a remote authority figure such as a teacher.

The point is that the presence of the silos and layers in our workplaces, while observable in organizational charts and at the doors to divisions and executive offices, contain their ultimate meaning in our minds, which adds exceptional substance to their presence. If we fear walking through a door, it is not the door and the boundary it signifies that frightens us. It is the significance, conscious and unconscious, of the door that we create in our minds that contains the threat that fosters the anxiety that can lead to primitive fight/flight responses such as an elevated heart rate (Diamond, Stein, and Allcorn 2002). This experience is, I suggest, an experiential and symbolic surface that may envelope us with security or insecurity (see Chapter 10). Touching the door exposes this experiential surface that we create. Turning the knob can be terrifying.

There are, therefore, critically important experiential and theoretical elements that reside within the notions of horizontal and vertical organizational fragmentation. The creation, maintenance, defense of, and meaning associated with organizational fragmenting boundaries and surfaces ultimately contain a vast array of unconscious individual and group processes that give them their ultimately primitive psychological meaning.

Psychoanalytic Theory and Its Contribution to Understanding the Underpinnings of Organizational Splits

Psychoanalytic theory teaches us that psychological defenses can take many forms. One form involves the process of denial, splitting, and projection, and an accompanying notion of projective identification (Grotstein 1985; Tansey and Burke 1989). In the simplest of terms, an individual may, when confronted with a difficult task, feel anxious and defensive. This person may feel up to the task or not. In the event he feels up to the task, there may ensue a process of minimizing and doing away with those parts of self that feel insecure, ineffective, and unable to cope with and master the task. The denial of these parts of the self leaves the individual feeling masterful, expert, and in control—the self-experience a CEO would surely like to have. Once these less desirable aspects of the self are denied, they may also become split off from the self to make them separate from self-experience. This process of splitting off undesirable parts of the self permits the individual to attribute them to others who possess some recognizable personal flaws (Shapiro and Carr 1991). This results in the projection of the rejected, denied, and split-off aspects of the self onto others, thereby creating a deficit within these others that is compensated for by the projector (hereafter the CEO), who may now experience himself as powerful, authoritative, and in control. He certainly has to be all these things, because those around him are not only seen to be inferior and requiring firm direction, but also are known to be deficient beyond all reasonable doubt (pathological certainty).

It is important to note that the reverse phenomenon also exists. Parts of self that are effective and able to master a situation may be denied, split off, and projected onto someone else, possibly the CEO, thereby making her in one's mind into someone who is powerful, masterful, and in control. As a result, the CEO is known to be able to take care of the person making the projections, who consequently experiences herself as ineffective and needing to be taken care of. In sum, this unconscious defensive process and its two outcomes can lead to the creation of an idealized leader and unworthy followers—something that often appears to be the case in organizations.

Many possible insights are raised by this theoretical discussion. For example, less likely but still possible is the outcome of the leader projecting onto followers power and mastery so that he may be supported, nurtured, and taken care of by them. In this case, the leader may be seen as bumbling and incompetent and waiting for someone to take charge. At the same time, the leader may also be thought to be a caring and wonderful person who should be taken care of by his followers. In this case of what amounts to a role reversal, followers are encouraged to project those parts of themselves that are sensitive, ineffective, and unmasterful onto the leader, further reinforcing the outcome. Running the business is taken care of by high-task, take-charge employees who are cared for by their leader.

The notion of projective identification as used here refers to a process by which the "other" onto whom the projection is made takes in the content of the projection and actually feels more powerful and masterful (or weak and ineffective). An individual may, for example, be encouraged to feel that she is unable to get the job done by a senior executive. Frequent nervous inspections of the individuals' work in a mistrusting manner accompanied by criticism and many suggestions all serve to encourage her to feel uncertain and unsure of her ability to do the work. Since everyone contains the possibility of this self-experience, being treated in this matter encourages the tapping of self-doubt, leading to the feeling of needing the executive's help: If "I" did not feel this way before, "I" do now. I have taken in (introjective identification) and realized the executive's projections that were reinforced by the way she treated me. "I" will be much more vulnerable to this process if "I" unconsciously link this experience to similar childhood experiences (a small helpless child). If I was not much good then, I must not be much better now.

These unconscious intrapersonal and interpersonal dynamics can be observed to take place to some extent in virtually every situation. These dynamics may also be shared among group members. During times of war, the opponent is turned into a lip-smacking baby eater or a filthy, diseased-ridden varmint that deserves to be killed, thereby creating a good. This phenomenon can also be found within organizations where conflict and competition consume organizational resources and detract from performance. A headquarters in a large city might see a plant in a small town or rural area in an unflattering light, as though they could not know anything about running a business.

Organizational fragmentation can therefore be understood to be influenced by psychologically defensive processes such as denial, splitting and projection, and projective identification. This underscores the problematic nature of prying the lid off of these undiscussable and unconscious dynamics. Doing so calls for inspecting these processes, and this can be exceptionally threatening to those involved. Psychological resistance may also feed the organizational resistance to change discussed in Chapter 2. This somewhat theoretical discussion can be readily anchored in one's experience at work. The insights inform the answers to the questions that follow.

Responding to Organizational Fragmentation in the Workplace

Thus far, the notion of organizational fragmentation has been explored for what it is—something that can be understood from a number of perspectives, all of which explain the separation of members of an organization from one another. As described, organizational fragmentation in all of its complexity should be familiar to anyone who has work experience. Given the problems that organizational fragmentation introduces into the workplace, it is essential that we locate ways to minimize it. Recognizing it is the first step.

How Is Organizational Fragmentation Spotted?

Organizational fragmentation is an omnipresent part of our daily lives. This omnipresence often makes it difficult to see the forest for the trees. Spotting fragmentation requires us to experience and acknowledge its presence. In addition to noting geographically based boundaries such as doors, floors, and buildings, organizational fragmentation may be spotted in other ways. Fragmentation is frequently found within the use of language and ways of thinking. An experimental particle physicist and an accountant may well encounter language barriers driven by education and professional orientation. Instances of lapsed or poor communication, "us versus them," and failure to articulate and coordinate work processes are often important signals that organizational fragmentation is at work. We all have to be open to the possibilities of seeing and experiencing the boundaries that dominate our lives. This taking of a mental time-out to spot their presence is a critical first step that must be accompanied by reflection as to why the fragmentation is there and what the boundaries and experiential surfaces mean to organization members. In addition, reflecting upon our experience can also reveal the experiences of others within the organization's boundaries and layers. We create them. Only we can know them.

What Does Organizational Fragmentation Mean?

Anyone entering an organization for the first time must be respectful of what is already in place. What is encountered might be thought of as "innate organizational intelligence." There is very often a good reason for what is in place, even if it does not appear to be rational or contribute to organizational success. In order to avoid vigorous resistance to change, all of the elements of organizational fragmentation and the way in which they have evolved within an organization must be appreciated for their stabilizing and anxiety-reducing effects before consideration is given to changing them (see Chapter 2). In this regard, their true meaning resides in the unconscious psychologically defensive aspects of the interpersonal world encoded in the form of organizational history and culture (see Chapter 13) (Allcorn and Diamond 1997). How exactly an organization is divided up by its members has clear meaning to them in terms of being able to work together. It is also important to appreciate that attempts at changing these familiar relational and knowledge-creating paths will be resisted. In effect, they have "always done it that way." In sum, understanding the pattern of organizational fragmentation and how exactly it is relied upon to accomplish work is one of the keys of figuring out how to locate operating improvements and avoid or overcome resistance to change.

Organizational culture and history create meaning (Schein 1985). Organization members come to understand that problems of a certain type are to be dealt with in a well-established manner. There is often no serious questioning of this response, except by the occasional foolish new hire who has not had time to understand the wisdom of the approach. Much the same can be said for aspects of work such as work processes and flows, service designs, accounting and reporting, and managing styles. These are usually deeply entrenched aspects of organizational life that, if called into question, create anxiety and defensive responses. There are also often stories of past failed attempts to change things and the lesson learned is to be careful when changing anything.

In sum, the meanings of these many hard-won and well-established patterns of interpersonal, interdepartmental, and intra-organizational dynamics that foster fragmentation are so taken for granted as to be hard to bring forward for inspection. Their meaning to organization members is so deeply embedded in members' experience of the workplace and each other that they are taken for granted and, if questioned, are usually vigorously defended. In short, how work is divided up provides anxiety-reducing meaning for organization members that, if disrupted, threatens a collapse of history and culture. Organizational history, cultural meaning, and familiar patterns of relating contain a quality of possessing a great, hard-to-move mass. Overcoming inertia and organizational resistance to change can be challenging.

What Are the Implications of Organizational Fragmentation for Working Together?

Organizational fragmentation and the polarizing underlying defensive splitting and projection that creates a black-and-white world of "us versus them" introduces a great many workplace dysfunctions. Many of these have already been touched upon. These outcomes can be readily documented, measured, and explained. However, doing so taps into only one of their dimensions. The other dimension is how organization members experience these many dysfunctions. The following list is provided as shorthand for bringing forward these experiences without further elaboration; none is likely needed. These experiences are so omnipresent in the workplace that everyone has encountered them:

- frustration and anger
- lack of teamwork
- excessive competition
- a struggle for resources

- time-consuming struggles for power
- compromises that suboptimize performance
- being blocked and tied up in red tape
- being or feeling inhibited
- cut off from getting the work done
- bureaucracy (impersonal, regimented, etc.)
- alienation from self, others, and work
- combativeness
- turf battles
- endless looping defensive patterns
- threat
- danger
- unresolved problems
- mistrust
- a lack of cooperation and teamwork
- vendettas

Unfortunately this is not a comprehensive list. It is, however, indicative of the experiences associated with organizational fragmentation and splitting.

What Are the Implications of Organizational Fragmentation for Organizational Change and Adaptation?

The implications of organizational fragmentation are clear when it comes to improving organizational performance. Organization members are not eager to give up what is familiar, especially when it is thought to have worked up to this point. This helps to account for the many unintended consequences of failed efforts at change that are so frequently encountered. In particular, the means and methods discussed for overcoming resistance to change in Chapter 2 are an effort to access the meaning contained in history and culture as, in part, represented in concrete terms by the elements of organizational fragmentation unique to each organization. It should be reasonably clear that top-down change that is rammed through an organization usually violates this familiar steady and predictable state, thereby creating resistance to change. Taking the time to develop an inclusive and participative process for improving operations, as also discussed in Chapter 2, adds value and reduces resistance to change. Embracing not only organizational members but also their history and their culture, including its fragmenting aspects, is a prerequisite for successful organizational change. This may be recast in terms of managing and consulting to organizational splits.

Managing Through the Splits

Organizational splits can take many forms. Some of the most destructive are those associated with horizontal and vertical organizational fragmentation (silos and layers). It is not uncommon to encounter organizations in which employees are blocked from working with peers and colleagues in other departments. Communication may flow only up and down the hierarchy, never across divisions. In other instances, departments, divisions, and geographically dispersed sites may be pitted against one another for resources and approval in the form of promotions and increased budgets and compensation. There may be a long and colorful history of "us versus them" that becomes the starting point for change.

Much the same can be said for organizational splits of a vertical nature. It is not uncommon to find layers such as top, middle, and lower management engaged in an unending struggle for career development by taking credit for desirable outcomes and avoiding responsibility for less-than-desirable outcomes. These are some of the common workplace elements that contribute to vertical organizational fragmentation and can make it appear that no one is in charge and make CYA ("cover your ass") so common as to be regarded an undiscussable institutionalized pattern that is known to everyone.

Healing Horizontal Splits

We are approaching this discussion from the point of view of a new leader or executive who has the responsibility of managing a large and complex organization or division. We assume that organization members want to do a good job and that achieving this outcome requires working together. For sure, there may also be a few areas and individuals that just thrive on confrontation and promote rivalry, competitiveness, and hostility in their daily course of conducting business. A second assumption is that some of these folks can be salvaged and some others are not going to be open to personal change.

In general, the leader can set the tone that the us/them attitude is not contributing to performance and that more collegial, collaborative, and cooperative modes of intra-organizational relations are in order. Establishing this tone and drawing the leadership of all of the areas together into one or more interdisciplinary or cross-functional work groups is a start. Usually there is an impressive degree of organizational resilience and adaptability that emerges if a safe enough context (holding environment) is created by the leader. In fact, some of the most remarkable turnarounds I have observed have been driven by the ability of a new leader to collapse the horizontal fragmentation. The following case vignette illustrates this outcome.

Catharsis in the BAT Cave

A large clinical department within a school of medicine had a long history of its ten major divisions operating autonomously. There had also been a leadership vacuum at the department level that spanned several decades. The strong divisions and weak departmental presence created exceptional mistrust and conflict regarding the functions of each division. In this case, the department managed a centralized professional fee-billing system. Division leaders and their billing staff had a long history of attacking the billing office for its deficiencies. A new department chairman and administrator were hired to create a stronger departmental administrative capability. The new administrator called together a boundary-spanning task group that included division administrators and billing staff and the leadership of the central billing office. The task assigned was to locate new billing opportunities and improve upon methods and processes. The name assigned to the group was the Billing Assault Team (BAT).

The first few meetings of the team were torturous, although it gradually become clear that they could make progress by working together. During a subsequent meeting, there occurred a cathartic event that reportedly left many in tears. The culture of constant attacks and aggression suddenly collapsed when those participating realized that they did not have to act this way in the future. They realized that, as a team, they could change their group dynamic and, figuratively speaking, put down all the stones that were being hurled about. Following this meeting that created a new sense of inclusion and ownership, some team members hung rubber bats from the ceilings of their offices (Halloween was a few weeks away). The results of this work more than doubled the professional fee billing based on the same amount of clinical work being done by faculty. Some of the competition between the divisions gradually abated as the division administrators got to know one another and found opportunities to better cooperate on shared work.

Beyond setting the tone and drawing people together, the leader can further contribute by adopting a management style that promotes a sense of everyone being in this together. Walking around and visiting areas and employees is a boundary-spanning activity that is most often welcomed by everyone. Creating interdisciplinary teams to locate systemic solutions to operating problems is another excellent way to encourage thinking about the whole rather than defending one's turf. It is also important to examine past incentive systems and allocation patterns for built-in favoritism created by past leaders who rewarded supporters and punished those that may have questioned their style, decisions, and methods. Finally, the new leader must be open to receiving input and feedback even if it is negative. This becomes a model for open and nondefensive communication patterns that can be liberating to everyone.

Healing Vertical Splits

Overcoming vertical splits requires much sensitivity involving careful information collection, close observation, and a vision of what is reasonably possible. At the same time, tilting at windmills, while at times threatening, should not be entirely avoided. One must find a balance and comfort level regarding how to challenge dysfunctions embedded within the hierarchy; this includes the building of new bridges. There are so many possibilities and nuances in this realm that providing concrete advice will surely fail. Appreciation of the organizational performance problems driven by vertical splits permits the development of a gradual, interlayer teasing-out process that lays them open to inspection and change. There are also those serendipitous opportunities where a new manager is hired who replaces a hard-to-deal-with senior individual, or possibly the building of a coalition that challenges the status quo.

In sum, new executives as well as those who have been in place for a while must be willing to find ways to point out instances where vertical splits have created a problem in such a manner as to be heard or, conversely, not be killed off as the messenger. It is not always easy to point out that a senior executive is not entirely informed about what is happening in the trenches. Nor is it easy to confront one's peers, who may be contributing to lapses in performance by ignoring instructions and pursuing their personal agendas.

Consulting to the Splits

Management can also put the expendable nature of the consultant to good use. Consultants offer the opportunity to somewhat safely reveal the presence of horizontal and vertical organizational splits by documenting the problems they are causing. In fact, the problems are often well known. Documenting them in a setting that draws together departments and divisions as well as layers of management is an important first step in consensus building. To the extent that the problems and issues are agreed upon, it is usually possible, with a little coaching, to have the management group bring out into the open such things as bidirectional communication and coordination problems that arise from organizational fragmentation. Once again, if this work can be entered into within a safe enough context (a holding environment that offers transitional space and time) created by top management and the consultant, a great deal of good work and organizational healing can ensue.

It is critical to revisit our earlier discussion of the psychological nature of splitting and projection and its contribution to organizational fragmentation. The splits themselves can be carefully confronted, and by doing so, a psychodynamically informed consultant can gradually erode the psychologically defensive underpinnings of the fragmentation. At the same time, it is important to recognize that these defensive dynamics will be defended. Attacking them will create a self-fulfilling prophecy—resistance to change.

It is, therefore, essential to combine documentation of the operating problems created by organizational fragmentation and stories and images acquired during interviews that point to the underlying defensive splits. In sum, performance issues, splits, and organizational fragmentation can be held up for inspection if the consultant has data to share and provides a psychodynamically informed context for interpreting them.

In Final Analysis

This chapter has introduced the importance of acknowledging organizational fragmentation that is often driven by unconscious individual and group dynamics. Recognizing these splits and fragmentation opens them up for inspection and change. Also to be appreciated is that human nature is the underlying driver of the presence of psychological and social defenses that take the form of denial, splitting, and projection. Those planning and leading organizational change must be prepared to be open to the not-so-rational possibilities that human nature introduces into the rational, economic-man model of the workplace. The questionable nature of this rationality is further highlighted by the equally questionable nature of planning and goal setting in the workplace, to be discussed in the next chapter.

4

Goals Within the Workplace

An effective goal focuses primarily on results rather than activity. It identifies where you want to be, and in the process, helps you determine where you are. It gives you important information on how to get there, and it tells you when you have arrived. It unifies your efforts and energy. It gives meaning and purpose to all you do. And it can finally translate itself into daily activities so that you are proactive, you are in charge of your life, you are making happen each day the things that will enable you to fulfill your personal mission statement.

—Stephen R. Covey, *The 7 Habits of Highly Effective People* (1989)

This chapter is devoted to the proposition that the reason we are working so hard is not as clear upon close inspection as perhaps we would like. In contrast to the belief that the profit motive provides an invisible guiding hand that directs our actions in the workplace, a close examination of the workplace most often reveals a confusing and even chaotic quality to work. Are we always striving to do an outstanding job to achieve excellence in the service of profit (Allcorn 1991)? Is the public announcement of a major organizational downsizing on a Friday at the end of a quarter an organizational strategy calculated to create espirit de corps and improve organizational performance? Or is it an effort by an anxious chief executive officer (CEO) to look powerful and in control while striving to improve stock value? Is staffing a public department such as child support enforcement with primarily divorced women necessarily the best way to achieve the goal of enlisting men in the support of their progeny? Might an organization staffed in this manner work at cross-purposes to fulfilling its larger social mission?

Many executives begin their careers with the idealistic perspective that the pursuit of worthwhile goals and objectives can be accomplished on a more or less rational basis supported by quantitative and analytical tools acquired in MBA programs. It often does not take long to discover that much of what is happening in the workplace does not make sense at all. The goal of one group to finish a street-paving project on time might yield a month later to the dismantling of the project as another group buries new water and sewer lines in the same street. Organizations do not run like machines in the pursuit of fulfilling worthwhile goals and objectives. The workplace contains a broad spectrum of irrationality that makes the best laid plans at times almost irrelevant (Schwartz 1990). Things are happening. Decisions are made. Work is being accomplished. Products and services are delivered. Profit and keeping to budget are achieved. Yes, all of this can be observed to be taking place. However, a deeper understanding of "the work" reveals that it is most often not accomplished in the best manner dictated by rationality. The balance of this chapter is devoted to understanding how this can be the case.

The nature of goal-oriented behavior will be explored first, followed by a review of the theoretical nature of goals, and espoused goals versus goals in practice. The presumption of rational goal setting is explored from a number of vantage points, such as outsourcing planning and goal development to the weekend retreat approach in which a few senior executives are supposed to get most of the work done in a few intense days. There are also many aspects of strategic planning and goal setting that must be inspected for the true degree to which they achieve rationality.

Goal-Oriented Behavior

Experimental psychologists are fond of running rats through mazes to receive a food reward. The notion of receiving a reward is the basis for behavior modification systems such as stock options and pay for performance. Workplace incentives are examined in Chapter 5. Here the focus is on better understanding goal-oriented behavior. Our goal might be to achieve a certain handicap in golf, run ten kilometers in a certain time, or defeat an opponent at chess or ping-pong. We might also set weight-loss goals, the goal of reading a chapter a night, or cleaning the house once a week. We might be a member of a group such as a family, athletic team, or work group that has goals that range from clear and communicated to only vaguely known and acknowledged. Is winning everything or are we just trying to have fun? We are also members of larger groups, such as corporations, and citizens of communities, towns, cities, counties, states, and nations. Goals are implicit within all of these different contexts. Goals are, therefore, an omnipresent aspect of our lives that influence our allocation of time and energy. Some are worthier than others, and some remain for the most part out of our conscious awareness.

Goals can also have many different qualities. We may have secret goals or well-articulated ones that everyone knows about. Some of our goals might have a narrow and immediate focus (winning a game), and others might be extremely broad, taking many years or decades to achieve. Certain goals might narrowly benefit one individual or group; others could advantage just about everyone (such as developing a highway system). They might have noble social qualities, such as curing a disease, or conversely, contain elements that are highly destructive to individuals and property (war and corporate raiding). Goals may also be set for us as well as for our groups. Some externally set goals can be challenging and stimulating, and encourage everyone to rise to the occasion. In other instances, goals can be subject to gradual change and manipulation in the service of those who set them. We might find we are never quite good enough in the eyes of a perfectionist. Research I conducted a number of years ago on what contributes to a sense of well-being and happiness yielded only one noteworthy finding: having goals for living one's life is important for creating self-direction, self-worth, well-being, and happiness. Goals provide purpose for our lives, but they can also be harmful and self-defeating.

Goal-oriented behavior and goal setting encompass what is, without a doubt, a more complex topic than just saying the word or setting a few goals. This complexity fills the workplace with a great many influences that direct work. Often, however, what seem like clear goals that provide precise direction are not communicated, poorly conceived, not kept current, or are ever-changing to take advantage of opportunities. Some goals may contain implicit harm to customers and clients as well as the environment, and the notion of corporate ethics and service for the greater good can be lost in the fever to make the numbers, achieve profit, and drive up the value of stock options.

In sum, the notion of setting and achieving goals contains a great deal of complexity and with it the likelihood of the train derailing. In fact, concepts that rely upon goal setting and achievement, such as management by objectives (MBO) and strategic planning, may be more of an act of faith than a meaningful way to operate an organization (Stacey 1992). At the same time, I do not want to throw the baby out with the bath water. However, in order to embrace the value added by the coordinative aspects of goals, one must avoid the use of goals in ways that compromise their utility.

The Theoretical Nature of Goals

There are a number of theoretical perspectives for examining the notion of goals. The following discussion can be informative in terms of understanding where goal setting succeeds and where it does not. It is also important to again mention that the setting of goals, in addition to providing direction and creating a context where employees can coordinate their efforts, contains a motivational element. The rat does not run the maze for fun. Vision and mission statements are ideally motivational and inspiring. Challenging but achievable goals create a psychological thirst to achieve them, and some employees may pursue them compulsively once they are set. It is therefore problematic to strive to separate the rational, directional, and coordinative aspects of goals from their rather more irrational motivational aspects.

Espoused Goals Versus Goals in Practice

An espoused goal does not always inform subsequent management decision making, thereby creating a noticeable difference between the espoused goals and the goal in practice (Argyris and Schon 1982). For example, an organizational goal of creating profit for shareholders or revenue for state government by increasing sales and improving margins would seem to provide clear direction. Such quantifiable goals and their subgoal measures may be developed to monitor progress. However, despite the seeming clarity of declarations of tactics, it is not difficult to find instances where management behavior seems to be directed toward achieving other goals that are inconsistent with achieving profit. These goals can be theoretically cast as "basic assumption goals" that unconsciously direct behavior (Bion 1961).

A typical example is that of a marginally skillful senior executive or CEO who is more concerned with improving his resume and chances at career advancement than with the long-term health of the organization. A university that operated a television station hired a new station manager to turn around what had been a losing effort to make money. Shortly after his arrival the station was running in the black. Everyone was pleased that the drain on university resources was over. The profitability of the station extended for four or five years and led to substantial raises for the manager. He was eventually recruited into a much better position at a larger television station. A true success story. The goal of a profitable bottom line had been achieved and the manager suitably rewarded.

However, after his departure a darker side emerged as to exactly how he had achieved his goal. The station had, since his arrival, systematically cut back on equipment maintenance and upgrades. Key maintenance staff had been laid off. This manager's goal achievement left the station in a position in which costly refurbishing was necessary. A similar story could be told about a CEO who wants to make the quarterly numbers broadcast to Wall Street analysts. Difficulties within a quarter might be covered up by hiring freezes, layoffs, rescheduled purchases, and rushed order taking that puts the next quarter's sales into the present quarter and so on. These examples underscore the fact that the noble and, I suggest, somewhat mystical notion of a goal such as profit as an important determinant of executive behavior may not be all that it is made out to be. In fact, reliance upon such notions as profit and sales goals can actually contribute to organizational failure. There is, then, a problematic aspect to the belief in profit as an overarching organizing goal (mysticism is discussed in Chapter 11).

Much the same can be said for governmental organizations. The CEO of a large state lottery who, when presented with many innovative and implementable ideas for increasing sales by his staff, responded by saying that he did not want to rapidly increase sales. Rather, he wanted to be able to show his board that he was creating a smooth trend line of ever-increasing sales. A major increase in sales in a one- or two-year period would suddenly raise the trend line and create what was in his mind a threat to his tenure if he could not then continue growth at the same pace. Achieving the goal of increased sales and revenues was, therefore, a threat rather than a desired outcome.

The point has, I hope, been made. Saying that the for-profit sector has profit as its goal is not entirely true and many times is exceptionally misleading. In reality, the notion of a clear goal such as increased profit is perhaps more of an illusion than anything else. Much of the balance of this chapter is devoted to exploring this proposition from a number of perspectives.

The Psychology of Goals

Setting goals, whether we do it ourselves or others do it for us, not only directs our attention to them but also creates an intrinsic motivation to achieve them. Goal setting may also be accompanied by extrinsic incentives (discussed further in the next chapter). However, if we look beyond these aspects of goals to embrace what I suggest is an almost magical belief in their relevance in the workplace, we encounter a system of underlying beliefs supported by myths, irrationality, and even a quality of mysticism regarding their creation, pursuit, and fulfillment. This section focuses attention on this unconscious system of beliefs (basic assumptions), which is supported by denial and rationalization when it becomes apparent that efforts to achieve the goals may actually be compromising organizational performance.

It is not hard to find instances where, once the decision to take an action is made by top management, the basis for the decision and the decision itself are not open to discussion. Offering of comments or suggestions may seem threatening, and the messenger might be sacrificed. In this regard, goals, once set, can become dogmatic. The notion of dogma applies to the profit motive, whose significance borders on the magical. Making the quarterly numbers in order to demonstrate profitability at almost any cost to the organization's longer-term ability to sustain itself may seem irrational, but it is also common. The underlying psychological nature of organizational goals may also create a difficult-to-acknowledge and hard-to-understand organizational dynamic that irresistibly leads an organization over the cliff. One could say that they made their numbers every quarter right up to when they declared bankruptcy. They may have won every battle in Vietnam, but the brass and their civilian controllers lost the war. The presence of goals can promote immoral and unethical business decisions that cover up or fudge the numbers to conceal the unattainability of the declared goals.

Goals must, therefore, be inspected for their psychological underpinnings. I have already mentioned the notions of extrinsic and intrinsic motivation. These are different workplace phenomena that share some of the same psychological underpinnings. Intrinsic motivation arises from within each of us. We may find work on a particular goal-oriented task exciting, fulfilling, and rewarding, regardless of what others think. Yet this does not address the origins of our internal motivations. These arise from our earliest development as a child. It is natural to want to play a certain way as a child. The child self-initiates and then enjoys her play. However, her parents may not always approve of the play and may limit or unilaterally change it to better suit themselves. Herein arises the possibility that less-than-rational internal motivations can grow to dominate the balance of our lives (Masterson 1988). As an adult the individual may always be anxious when it comes to self-expression or taking the initiative to accomplish something.

It is not my purpose here to delve deeply into the nature of distorted inner images and thoughts, feelings, and actions. What is important is to appreciate that none of us has passed through life unencumbered by damaging parental actions and their role in developing our irrational motivations. We might strive for mastery, control, and perfection in our work in order to earn the approval of critical, perfectionistic, and vindictive parental figures. We might tenaciously cling to the pursuit of control, admiration, love, and power to compensate for an inner emptiness and a deficient, powerless, and unlovable self—one formed from parental neglect and abuse. We might also feel that we are in a constant competition with others where winning is essential. We might constantly compete against others for the sought-after parental responses. Not to be overlooked are competitive responses that lead us to aggression arising from deeply felt personal injury and concomitant anger about being hurt; such impulses may know few limits. We may not only feel bad about ourselves due to parental failings; we may feel deeply enraged about how we were treated. This creates a lifelong reservoir of rage that can be tapped at the slightest provocation from others. Intrinsic motivation is therefore in part, if not largely, filled with unconscious processes and irrationalities that are part of human nature and not particularly open to inspection or analysis.

If intrinsic motivations are a problematic aspect of goal achievement, then extrinsic motivation takes this problematic quality to a new level. In addition, intrinsic and extrinsic motivations interact. Throughout our lives, starting with our parents, we receive extrinsic motivation from those who want to control and direct what we think, feel, and do. This is so obvious that it does not bear mentioning. Yet within the realm of extrinsic motivation lies considerable psychological conflict and consternation. Many of the parental and workplace failings evoke psychological coping mechanisms that play into a predictable pattern of being controlled and manipulated.

Starting with the notion of others striving to control us (dominance and submission are the issue) we are immediately confronted with the behavior-modifying carrot and stick. We may be rewarded with TV viewing, cookies, or a raise or promotion for doing what is requested of us. We make a trade-off by giving up what we want to do for what is requested in order to receive a reward or avoid punishment. We are therefore coaxed, encouraged, promised, and threatened in the service of others. In the workplace, we are constantly controlled, directed, and manipulated by rewards and the threat of punishments that put us in touch with how we were treated as a child. The workplace is often thought to contain infantilizing characteristics. Naturally, all this pushing and shoving to modify our sense of self leads us to defend ourselves by possibly developing a false sense of self (Masterson 1988). Our work experiences range from true enjoyment of our work to a much more robotocized existence in which we are not only alienated from ourselves but also from others, from our work, and from the workplace. Our responses to control by others can be thought of as ranging from a masochistic, morbid submission to withdrawal, avoidance, and resistance, including overtly and covertly fighting back. All of this should sound familiar when we reflect upon our lives within organizations.

In sum, the setting of goals by others, including their attempts to direct our behavior, is heavily influenced by if not dominated at times by unconscious, irrational, and undiscussable intrapersonal, interpersonal, and organizational dynamics. Goals that are set too high or too low, that are constantly manipulated, or seem to be self-serving many times have psychologically based underpinnings that arise from unconscious and irrational motivations.

A discussion of strategic planning as it relates to goal setting and achievement in the workplace is in order. The point to be made is that strategic planning should involve the careful use of logic to lay out a plan of action based on the setting of goals and objectives. It is, however, not necessarily logical or rational.

The Presumed Rationality of Strategic Planning, Goals, and Objectives

Thus far, a number of different aspects of the nature and psychological significance of goal setting and planning have been discussed. From this point forward the focus changes toward the inspection of the concrete aspects of strategic planning. Some of the methods used are not necessarily logical or rational. In particular, there are potential and frequently encountered pitfalls that are driven by psychodynamics and resistance to change. Before proceeding, due respect must be paid to Lewis Carroll, for any discussion of strategic planning should start with the much quoted wisdom of his book *Alice's Adventures in Wonderland*.

> The Cat only grinned when it saw Alice. It looked good-natured, she thought: still it had very long claws and a great many teeth, so she felt that it ought to be treated with respect.
>
> "Cheshire Puss," she began, rather timidly, as she did not at all know whether it would like the name: however, it only grinned a little wider. "Come, it's pleased so far," thought Alice, and she went on. "Would you tell me, please, which way I ought to go from here?"
>
> "That depends a good deal on where you want to get to," said the Cat.
>
> "I don't much care where—" said Alice.
>
> "Then it doesn't matter which way you go," said the Cat.
>
> "—so long as I get somewhere," Alice added as an explanation.
>
> "Oh, you're sure to do that," said the Cat, "if you only walk long enough."

Anyone who has worked to support strategic planning initiatives for an organization has developed a respect for how difficult it is to do a good job of this work. Indeed, many roads are often traveled with no particular purpose in mind. In particular, there are aspects of this work that militate against understanding strategic planning as a carefully thought through, articulated, and resourced pursuit of goals and objectives. There are a number of reasons why this conclusion seems appropriate. Before proceeding it should be noted that a primer on strategic planning is not being provided here. Anyone unfamiliar with the terminology will benefit from a review of the literature (Goodstein, Nolan, and Pfeiffer 1993; Schwartz 1996).

Weekend Planning

Many organizations approach the development of a strategic plan as a weekend retreat that will then supposedly direct the destiny of the organization for the next three, five, or more years. Exercises such as developing internal and external analyses and engaging employees in the work are forgone in favor of senior-level executives developing these perspectives. A planning consultant usually facilitates. The end product is most often seen to be a plan created and published by top management that must be packaged for sale to the organization. The plan is also usually heavily influenced by the CEO's desires, since everyone at the retreat is dependent upon her for promotions, raises, and tenure. Due to their rushed development, these plans lack sufficient specificity to be readily implemented. They may also be distorted to focus upon but a few areas of concern. In this case, ideas are developed without a systemic view of the workplace and the effects of the plans upon it.

In sum, a considerable amount of what passes for strategic planning is of this little pain and quick-fix flavor. When such plans are rolled out to the rest of the organization, resistance to change is predictable, since no one has a stake in the plans' success other than a few executives. This can be appreciated by anyone who starts work in an organization by asking about the existing strategic plan:

"Oh yes, we have one."

"May I see it?"

"It is somewhere on my bookshelf (or filed somewhere)."

Glancing through it—"Tell me, how has it been working out?"

"Well, frankly, we followed it for a few months and that was about it."

"Have you tried to measure progress in accomplishing the plan?"

"Initially we set out to do that, but we found we did not have the information, and efforts to develop it were just going to be too time-consuming and expensive."

"Would you say then that the plan has not been followed to any great extent?"

"That is basically true with a few exceptions that the CEO insisted on."

"Do you think developing another strategic plan or tuning up the old one is a good idea?"

"You know, I would like to think so. But really, it is just going to be a waste of time."

This script may sound familiar. If strategic planning and the setting of goals and objectives is so logical, why, then, is it so often either not done or only minimally so, and if a document is created, why is it not followed, monitored, and kept up to date?

You Write the Plan

Another excellent example of why strategic planning and the setting of goals and objectives is not so logical can be found in those organizations that hire an industry-specific expert to write their plan for them. This planner is expected, in a few weeks, to produce a comprehensive plan that everyone will implement. This work might be informed by interviews with a few key people as to their views on what should be included in the plan. However, implicit within this approach is the fact that many of those in charge likely do not have a clue as to how to run the business and are outsourcing the management expertise. Two not unexpected results of this approach are that the executives, who have no ownership in the plan, simply put it on the shelf or, even if they attempt to follow it, lack the management and leaderships skills to implement it. The above script thus applies equally well here.

Layering Goals and Objectives

Planning is above all else a logical process that creates a coordinated step-wise course of action. Creating a vision for an organization leads logically to designing a number of specific goals that, when taken together, can be explained to fulfill the vision and mission. Similarly, the setting of goals leads to many tactical considerations that break the goals down into clearly stated, actionable, and measurable objectives. These objectives can be assigned to one or more individuals for achievement and the progress monitored. The ability to get this work done is time and resource limited, which is discussed next. However, having to lay out a logical series of steps that break goals down into implementable and measurable increments is not so easy to do in practice. One reason is that there is a geometric increase in complexity. Ten objectives may have developed for each of ten goals (100 total). Each objective calls for the development of detailed plans on how to achieve it that take into account working on several objectives at the same time (parallel process); in other instances, the achievement of one objective is followed by the achievement of another (serial or linear process). Resources such as staff, equipment, and space must be found and a planning coordinator designated to track all of this effort.

This discussion points not only to the real complexity that good planning implies, it also demonstrates how rigorous the logic has to be. It is, however, at this point that the work can gradually break down if not "bird-dogged" by internal planners. In particular, executives, managers, and employees may not see all the possibilities implicit in accomplishing an objective, nor may they be particularly resourceful in working around sticking points and overcoming unintended and unforeseen consequences arising from implementation. If these problems are avoided, what emerges is an implementable plan and accompanying process.

In sum, planning—the setting of goals and the identification of tactical objectives—while a logical process, can become a swamp if not carefully managed. Organizations most often find individuals who are devoted to carrying out the plan and keeping it current (planning as an ongoing process). It is also not uncommon to find instances where planning has been used by middle and upper management to keep the organization vital and profitable despite the best efforts of an ineffective or dysfunctional CEO to derail it. These successes basically used planning as an institutionalized defense mechanism. There are also those instances where the planning process may have gradually decayed with the arrival of new leaders who had no stake in its development. We can thus appreciate that the worthwhile aspects of goal setting can encounter all types of problems and resistances that can degrade them over time, even if they are well conceived at the start.

Time Lines and Matching Resources

These are the last steps in the planning process. At this point, "organizational reality testing" happens. Can all the goals be accomplished within a reasonable time frame? Do we have the people and resources to accomplish them? Are some goals and objectives more important than others, thereby revealing the need to prioritize? Do some contribute greater financial gain than others—more bang for the buck, as revealed from a cost/benefit analysis?

If developing a logical set of objectives to achieve each goal was a true test of attention span and the ability to think about the possibilities, then the placing of all of this work on a time line matched to the resources further raises the bar. Accomplishing this work, however, may be thought of as some of the best organizational development that can be had. The attention of many is directed to thinking about the associated costs of each objective and what the organization stands to gain by making the investment. There also develops a true test of scheduling ability that not only examines the subevents, data capture, and progression toward achieving an objective, but also examines the need to plan across all of the objectives that have been placed on the time line. For example, many times there are choke points that will block the achieving of some objectives. There may be too few programmers to tackle all of the information needs that have been identified, thereby creating the need for either more resources or for a much longer time line.

Resistances of various types often compromise the logical nature of this work. The plan's implementation occurs at this point; oxen may be gored and sacred cows sacrificed. Time-consuming and arduous work meets resistances when people's jobs are already hard enough to do without their having to contribute information, analyses, and time to this process.

In sum, those who develop a plan of action will encounter a true test of their skills and their ability in completing all of the steps toward all of the objectives that fulfill the goals. This underscores what may not be so logical after all. Some may eventually feel that winging it is just as good: after all, "Have we not gotten this far without a formal plan?"

A Note on Chaos

Neither the past nor the present is a predictor of the future. What will happen in the future cannot be perfectly predicted, and the degree to which it is unpredictable, some suggest, makes strategic planning and the pursuit of goals a less than logical and possibly a self-defeating and futile strategy (Stacey 1992). Just as our ability to predict accurately is limited, so is our control over what might happen. Embracing unpredictability leads directly to the need to view planning and goal setting as a process requiring continuous reality testing and renewal. Goals and objectives should be constantly adjusted and changed. It is therefore important to acknowledge relying heavily upon strategic planning, as a written plan that must be followed will not survive its encounter with reality. Rigidly following a plan is neither logical nor a rational management methodology.

Goal Setting and Achievement Pitfalls

Another way to understand the problematic nature of planning, goal setting, and tactical implementation of goals in the form of objectives is to examine some of the pitfalls that are encountered along the way in this rational pursuit of strategic direction. Goodstein, Nolan, and Pfeiffer (1993, 1) note, "our experience as consultants to a wide variety of organizations has convinced us that most strategic planning processes are poorly conceptualized and poorly executed; the process is often not very creative and it is tactical rather than strategic in nature; and the so-called strategic plan rarely impacts the day-to-day decisions made in the organization." The problematic nature of goal setting is echoed by the following vignette.

The Case of the Shrinking Bottom Line

A major hospital encountered fiscal hard times, not unlike every other hospital in the United States. Revenues were shrinking and with them, the operating margin. Managed care, competition, changes in government reimbursement, and laws and regulations had all contributed to this problem. The CEO, chief financial officer (CFO), and chief operating officer (COO) of the hospital assembled all levels of management and supervision within the hospital—more than 100 people. After a greeting by the CEO, who then promptly left, the CFO presented a number of financial analyses and trends that indicated that the hospital's long-term ability to continually upgrade and improve its equipment and services was being threatened. This was not particularly new information for those in attendance. They were well aware of the local and national situation.

The CFO then proceeded to define the problem as one of the hospital having too many expenses. Costs, primarily labor costs, had to be reduced. Layoffs had to occur. The COO followed by announcing a new stress-management training program for those in the room. As the meeting approached its end, a question-and-answer period was announced. "Does anyone have any questions?"

A variety of clarifications were sought regarding the numbers, timing, training program, and cost-reduction process. A final query, however, fundamentally called into question all that had gone before. "Why is it that the problem has been defined as one of only cutting costs? Would it not be just as logical to develop an aggressive program of revenue enhancement?" Most of the managers and supervisors in the audience were eager to follow up on this line of inquiry, which promised to reduce the number of layoffs. Why was the goal of cutting many millions of dollars out the budget the only answer to the problem? The CFO and COO had no ready answers and retreated to the analyses, insisting that the goal was stated correctly. However, a few weeks later another new program was announced. Revenue enhancement would indeed by sought. This vignette illustrates how powerful management can be in terms of first defining a problem and then setting what are presumably logical goals to deal with it.

Who Sets the Goals?

The advent of management by objectives and its subsequent downfall in terms of delivering on its promise is a good place to start this discussion. Advocates of MBO offered many approaches and techniques, but they all seemed to share in common the tension between subordinates setting their own goals and negotiating their setting with management. It does not take a rocket scientist to understand that no one wants goals to be set so aggressively that exceptionally hard work is required to meet them. Nor should goals be set that risk failure, nor should the goalposts be constantly moved as goal achievement nears. The question of who sets the goals and how they are agreed upon and subsequently administered is one that again challenges management control and its manipulation of employees to squeeze out more productivity. There is, then, perhaps more than one pitfall associated with this question and its related issues. How much direction is optimal? How hard do we press ahead? Who benefits, why, and to what extent? Related questions are: What measures will be taken? What data will be collected? How and when? How will data be manipulated, and in what manner, to assess performance? In the end, it may not be feasible to actually measure the pursuit of some goals that are not adequately described, defined, and operationalized so as to permit accomplishing or measuring them. Goal setting therefore has to be understood as a complex topic filled with superior/subordinate tension, anxieties, interpersonal issues of feeling demeaned, losses of autonomy, and inevitable resistance.

How Can Goals Be Achieved?

Everyone has thought, "I would not have done it that way." Reasonable people can differ on many things, not the least of which, putting aside the problem of deciding what to do (the goal), is how exactly the work should be performed to achieve a goal. If an employee or group of employees agrees on a goal that management concurs with, getting the job done can result in endless unilateral interventions by top management. It can also result in manipulations regarding resource availability ("you can use this but not that") that serve to direct the work. There is also, of course, the not infrequent outcome of reassigning people to different projects or reassigning the project to another individual or group. Even the best thought through, documented, and communicated plan of action will, as battlefield generals have been heard to say, not survive its encounter with the enemy. How exactly the goal will be achieved is therefore infused with problematic aspects, uncertainties, and even chaos, all of which generate unintended consequences. This inevitability leads to reactions that range from giving up to incredible persistence beyond any reasonable expectations, from dogged adherence to the plan to rampant innovation and creativity in the service of wiring around but not necessarily solving the operating problems and the unintended consequences created. Getting the job done can once again be considered to be quite complex, and fraught with superior/subordinate tensions, anxiety, and interpersonal issues about the loss of personal autonomy.

How Will Progress Be Measured?

I have alluded to the problem of pinpointing, agreeing upon, and acquiring the data to measure progress. This process, however, is so fraught with difficulties and problematic outcomes as to merit additional discussion. What seems like a perfectly clear quantitative goal that is fundamentally easy to measure might, upon close inspection, have its clarity and ability to be quantified evaporate. A mandate to a call center to obtain 40,000 orders per month seems clear on the surface. A close inspection of this goal and its achievement, however, can reveal that things are not so straightforward. Employees are creative, and, once aware of what is being measured, they will find ways to circumvent the intent. They may take one order and break it down into two, or knowingly omit an important item from an order that will necessitate a second order to be initiated by the purchaser or the telephone marketer: "When I took your order last week, we overlooked the fact that you need this item to go with that." If shipments are being used to measure orders, an order might be broken down into multiple shipments. Also to be considered might be the size and frequency of orders per customer and software glitches and failures associated with data capture and reporting. Canceled orders may count as an activity thereby creating a count of two when zero is correct. Issues can also arise as to how often the data sets are collected and how the data is compiled into information that is then further manipulated into some form of understanding. Here again, the possibilities of creating erroneous, manipulated, and untimely outcomes is omnipresent. The rat in the maze is above all else resourceful in finding the shortest path to the cheese.

The ability to measure exactly what is going on can become so important as to determine what goals can be set. This backward engineering effect is often implicit in goal setting, but not often appreciated. Holding employees accountable for meeting a goal is, therefore, no easy task.

How Do We Respond to Variances from Plan?

The answers to the above question yield substantial insight into how an organization is run. A plan that has quantifiable goals and measurable objectives encourages progress inspections that may yield variances from plan—either falling short or exceeding expectations. In fact, if a plan is encountered that is almost exactly on target, one has to wonder how this could be. A good example is the use of budgets to control rates of expenditure in designated categories. A hospital struggling with financial management published a monthly variance report. Significant variances required a written response. It was almost invariably the case that expenses co-varied with volume. More patients meant more testing, more supplies consumed, and more revenue generated. Variances above and below expectations required only one explanation—changes in volume. Executives who paid no attention at all, or minimal attention, to cost per unit of production (test or service) reinforced this. The reporting process ate up a lot of time and paper and produced little insight. No change in the budgeting methodology, such as using a flexible budgeting approach, was considered. Worse, a computer could have more readily located variances that were not driven by changes in volume, permitting everyone to focus on variances that had a different explanation. This is but one example. In other instances, there might be no effort made to collect data to calculate variances or, if made, it is too late to make any difference. Efforts to collect timely data not available from the information system invariably generate parallel manual data bases. In other instances, the vagaries of what exactly constitutes a variance and how it is explained are overlooked by CEOs or senior executives who merely condemn poor performance or congratulate performance above trend without any real insight into what is going on. Heads could roll and bonuses be handed out, but in the end, there is no clear understanding of what is driving the numbers or, for that matter, what is really driving operations.

How Are Plans and Goals Kept Current?

The answer to this question is often shaped around the idea that a plan was written and is being followed as though the task environment were caught in a time warp. Worse, to the extent that the elements of the plan are falling behind current events, it may be observed that the idea of making a better buggy whip or icebox is never questioned. It is essential to continually monitor the chaotic and unpredictable nature of what is going on within the organization's task environment that might necessitate a response not heretofore anticipated. Nonetheless, many times a plan is adhered to by all concerned with a religiosity that forecloses organizational learning (Argyris 1983; Argyris and Schon 1982). No one wants to have to tell the CEO that his plan needs to be changed.

In sum, there are many pitfalls to successful planning, goal setting, goal achievement, mid-course corrections, and long-term performance monitoring. They are often resisted due to extra work involved and the organizational change implied. An additional consideration is the embedded issue of power, authority, control, and dominance/submission. These considerations can be depended upon to make planning and goal setting difficult and unnecessarily threatening to individual, group, and organizational experience.

In Final Analysis

This chapter has confronted the problematic nature of the setting and accomplishment of goals. The entire process of setting goals and working to achieve them is filled to overflowing with illogic and, indeed, unconscious and irrational dynamics. Goals, as well as the larger context of strategic planning, can be and most often are compromised by this consideration. This makes an unquestioning reliance upon goals as a magic management bullet untenable. Doing so, I suggest, evokes a realm of dogma, magical beliefs, and managerial mysticism in which what management is doing becomes unquestionable and to some extent unknowable. A soldier must, in the end, have faith in the general who sends him or her into battle.

The next chapter continues to examine to the rational workplace, where logic is used to create employee incentives and finally tuned performance enhancement systems, yet where unfortunately the results are driven by processes that are not necessarily so logical. Reliance upon incentives to influence workplace behavior may, I suggest, seriously detract from organizational performance.

5

Incentives

Get the incentives right and productivity will follow. If we give people big, straightforward monetary incentives to do right and work smart, the productivity problem will go away.

—Tom Peters and Robert Waterman,
In Search of Excellence (1982)

We found no systematic pattern linking specific forms of executive compensation to the process of going from good to great. The idea that the structure of executive compensation is a key driver in corporate performance is simply not supported by the data.

—Jim Collins, *Good to Great* (2001)

America is hooked on incentives or, more specifically, extrinsic motivation. Incentives are an omnipresent aspect of our daily lives at work and at home. Advocates of behavior modification principles are surely proud. These days there are an endless array of incentives, carrots, and sticks, both within and outside of the workplace.

The federal government consistently tries to manipulate citizens, groups, and organizations by creating incentives to act one way versus another, or by introducing disincentives to discourage undesired behaviors. Tax shelters are provided to encourage the development of housing for the poor. Funds are made available to educate ever-more physicians. One type of research is funded, another is not. Tax laws are changed to encourage or discourage investment in the stock market. The number of government programs, laws, rules, and regulations that have been developed to influence behavior in one direction or another is truly impressive. Incentives are a large part of American public and foreign policy.

Not to be outdone, the private sector has also focused attention on incentives to influence employee behavior. These incentives take as many forms as the imagination can conceive or the "operating problem of the day" or quarter appears to dictate. Some of the more infamous examples are stock options, executive loans, lavish expense accounts, and, on a more mundane note, pay for performance and bonuses for making the numbers. Executives most often think nothing of using incentives to control their employees.

Anyone familiar with government and the workplace will have encountered incentives in many forms. The fundamental question is why. Why are incentives in the form of rewards so frequently relied upon? Conversely, we frequently encounter just as many disincentives.

Disincentives can take many forms. In the workplace this may be an understatement. Employees are routinely faced with a vast assortment of negative outcomes if they do not conform. To list but a few: low or no raises, shunning, reassignment to less desirable, dead-end jobs, geographic transfers, public humiliation, bullying and threatening behind closed doors, and progressive disciplinary measures driven by human resources procedures that may culminate in "outplacement" or, less euphemistically, termination. These disincentives and others are an omnipresent threat when what we say and do are deemed unacceptable to the powerful members of the corporate hierarchy. Whistleblowers beware. Organizations are usually filled with stories about people who used to be rising stars or used to be employed. It is not hard to find stories of people who have been sent to organizational Siberias such as windowless basement offices or undesirable geographic locations. In other cases, meaningful work may be withheld, sending a message that one's career progression is at an end. Experiences like these are often accompanied by other negative workplace occurrences such as downsizing, restructuring, and reengineering, where entire sections may be reshaped or eliminated.

The removal or containment of already present aversive stimuli is equally important. Executives who are anxious about marginal organizational performance that will reflect poorly on them can become agitated, demanding, and threatening, and resort to micromanagement and unrealistic demands for organizational performance accompanied by implicit threats of punishment if they are not met. Keeping the executive happy can become the not so hidden agenda of his or her employees. An undiscussable interpersonal contract gradually emerges where everyone knows that the executive's denigrating and threatening behavior is distressing and that almost anything would be better. As a result, employees may be willing to work long hours to overcome a problem or bend their moral and ethical principles to get the job done as it is specified. In a sense, much like an alcoholic family member, organization members may devote themselves to a strategy of codependent behavior (Allcorn 1992). They prefer to change themselves in order to change the executive's behavior and remove the negative experience.

In sum, incentives hold out rewards (carrots) for conformity and doing as requested; disincentives (sticks) promise some form of punishment if the desired behavior is not forthcoming. The use of rewards (reinforcements) is not repugnant to most executives who presume to set the goal and reward its achievement. This closely resembles operant conditioning (stimulus/response), where the reward is linked to the appropriate behavioral response. However, executives and managers are not averse to the use of workplace punishments or, more often, the threat of their use. These efforts represent aversive conditioning in which undesirable behavior is extinguished. A less direct approach is the rewarding of behavior that approximates the desired behavior. This may occur as one goal and reward are replaced by successively more demanding goals to achieve the ultimate goal. This approach, in its purest sense, will result in a reward for employees who volunteer behavior that contributes to goal achievement—the one-minute manager reduced to its essence. Underlying this discussion are a number of important questions that have to be addressed: Do incentives really work? What are the psychological underpinnings associated with their design and use? How do employees respond to them? Is their use ethical? These are the questions discussed in this chapter.

A Brief Review of Incentives in Practice and Their Meaning to Employees

We modify our own behavior and that of others many times without really thinking about it. We respond positively to some of the thoughts, feelings, and actions of people around us, and not at all or negatively to others. Positive reinforcements used to change our behavior may take many forms, from financial rewards and gifts to verbal approval. They can be found in schools (gold stars) and other places that use a system of merits and demerits, such as a therapeutic setting or military school. A child may get a hug for putting away her toys.

Negative reinforcements are aimed at discouraging or extinguishing less desirable behaviors. We may punish others through words (criticism), emotionally by withdrawing love and affection, and by physical discipline (spanking, go to your room, prison confinement). We may also see fit to remove a privilege or desired product or service (restricted use of a car).

The workplace is also filled with many forms of behavior-modifying influences. Most basically, we must perform specified work in a specified manner in order to remain employed and receive compensation. Although this is the fundamental underlying nature of work, it is not saturated with moral, ethical, and psychological problems. Executives seeking to control human behavior may, however, modify the nature of this contract. This problem is not new. Daniel Yankelovich (1978, 47) made much the same observation:

> Today, millions who do hold paid jobs find the present incentive system so unappealing that they are no longer motivated to work hard. As a consequence, not only do they withdraw emotional involvement from the job, they also insist upon steady increases in pay and fringe benefits to compensate for the job's lack of appeal. The less they give to the job, the more they seem to demand—a process that cannot continue for long without breaking down. A deep flaw in the incentive system, signified by the failure of the old incentives to catch up to the new motivations, leads inexorably to deterioration in the workplace.

In sum, incentive systems reward those whose behavior is consistent with management desires and punish those whose behavior violates management directives, even when the directives are poorly conceived and managed. In fact, when one encounters frequent reliance upon incentives such as bonuses to make a target, it is important to look for management problems, not employee performance problems. This sounds cynical, yet other authors have also characterized behavior modification incentives and progressive discipline as being immoral and unethical methods relied upon by ineffective executives.

Incentive programs are designed to manipulate almost all aspects of employee life, from controlling employees' work and safety to determining when they retire. The fact that much of the time employees do not fulfill expectations is most often thought to be a problem of fine-tuning incentive programs. The use of these programs is seldom questioned (Argyris and Schon 1982). Incentives take many innovative forms, such as pay for performance, stock options, and various types of monetary bonuses as well as nonmonetary rewards like favored parking spaces, employee-of-the-month designations, gift certificates, and company dinners, picnics, and sporting activities. The range of possibilities is endless. Almost any type of behavior can be incentivized (reinforced). Alfie Kohn (1993) notes that these programs are often packaged in such a way as to encourage employees to embrace them without thinking too much about what is being imposed upon them or how exactly they feel about it. This packaging may include partnering, goal setting, performance management, pay for performance, and labeling everyone as an "associate." All of these include some form of rewarding employees for doing what they are told. This chapter asserts, consistent with Kohn's views, that all such programs are experienced by employees as controlling and degrading. Many executives pursue these frequently dehumanizing methods, revealing the belief that their use makes them feel powerful and in control. If these are their only tools, they are neither.

Incentives in the form of rewards and punishments signal the desire on the part of others (parents and superiors) to control what we think, feel, and do. Executives frequently resort to these methods without much hesitancy in the hope that employees will embrace them without much reflection. This loss of reflective capacity, however, promises that little organizational learning will take place. This failure leads to the introduction of additional incentives when the first round fails to yield the desired outcome. It is important to appreciate that not all incentives are bad per se. Not throwing the proverbial baby out with the bath water is discussed below.

Beyond the psychological and moral questions attached to the use of incentives, they may be ineffective for other reasons as well. In fact, to call them ineffective understates the problems that they introduce into the workplace. A few workplace examples will underscore this point.

Be Careful—You Might Get What You Ask for

The theoretical basis for the use of incentives has been discussed. It has also been noted that, contrary to theory, their actual use in the workplace can be less than constructive. They introduce a manipulative, dehumanizing atmosphere that employees are aware of and may well resist. Extrinsic motivation, at least in part, presumes that people are readily manipulated by behavior modification principles. However, if we look past the moral, ethical, and philosophical nature of incentives, we might question whether they really work at all.

An executive in charge of a large telephone marketing call center recounted a story of incentives gone awry. He said, "Be careful, you might get what you ask for." He had, in an effort to increase the number of orders being taken by the call center, provided an incentive to take orders. In this case, the information system kept track of the orders shipped by each employee. Based on the dependable availability of this information, the executive provided a monetary incentive for every order taken above a baseline. The employees were quick to figure out that the incentive was being computed on orders shipped, not on the size of the order or the number of orders taken. The logical response to the incentive was to create more shipments by breaking each order down into multiple shipments. It was not long before the executive discovered that the average value of a shipment had decreased. Employees were breaking orders down so that various supply items were being shipped separately to the same address. An example he gave was a $2 shipment of batteries that cost $2 to ship. The result for the bottom line is not hard to figure out. More money was being paid to the employees than prior to the incentive. The total number of orders taken remained the same. The cost of shipping and postage increased in some instances to the point that for every shipment that went out the door the company lost money.

An additional example is a story about a new division president who was seeking to make targeted quarterly sales figures and instituted incentives when the numbers for total sales were running behind at the end of the quarter. Once again, employees responded in a logical manner and a trend developed in which, predictably, during the last few weeks of every quarter sales began to lag. The executive, as anticipated, would respond by instituting an incentive to increase sales. The employees, having stalled their sales work, were able to increase their sales given that they had set aside a pool of clients to contact. One might reasonably ask the question, "Who was managing whom?" This same executive, while chief executive officer (CEO) of another facility, had relied on an incentive program to motivate an MBA responsible for cleaning up a multi-million-dollar pool of health-care-related billing that for one reason or another had not been entered into the billing system. The MBA's response was to locate what is traditionally referred to as "the low-hanging fruit." He analyzed the tens of thousands of invoices to locate the ones that were more readily cleared up for entry into the billing system. The CEO was pleased with his outstanding progress and paid out incentives to this manager for work that was easily accomplished. Gradually, however, the low-hanging fruit was all picked and the going got tougher. The manager's outstanding performance lagged. The CEO predictably responded by increasing the incentive and becoming more demanding. Progress remained slow and the manager began to be criticized by the CEO. The manager responded by allowing billing to be entered into the system that was incomplete, incorrect, and lacked sufficient documentation to be reimbursed by insurance companies. The CEO was pleased to see his numbers going back up and was more than happy to provide a bonus beyond the incentive. Scrutiny of this billing by the manager of the billing system, however, revealed a garbage-in, garbage-out problem that was much more expensive to deal with than having done the work correctly on the front end. A complaint led the CEO to take back some of the bonuses. However, the incentive remained in place with predictable results: eventually the billing system became clogged with unbillable and incorrect invoices that were rejected for payment and a vast amount of mail that had been misaddressed and returned, increasing postage and handling costs.

Extrinsic incentives can take many forms. The avoidance of being disciplined (punished) is one. A large division of a state served the citizens using a case-based approach. The information system, although somewhat rudimentary, did keep track of who had each case file. A new director and leadership team reviewed how fast cases were being handled and decided it was not fast enough. Given the limitations of the information system, they made a rule that employees could not work on a case longer than a week. It was thought that if their work were closely monitored, increased productivity would result. Assumptions like these are not entirely unfounded. However, creating a blanket incentive to avoid being held accountable is not the best way to go about tapping people's potential. Good supervision is. The employees quickly figured out how the information system was being used to monitor their work. The grapevine had also uncovered some instances where employees had been disciplined in order to "send a message." The employees responded by reviewing all their case files on Friday morning. Those that they had had for the full week were passed to another section even if their work was not complete. This cleared the case from the information system, thereby avoiding having it counted as delinquent. The new section received the incomplete case and held it for much of the following week, returning it on Thursday or Friday to the former section to complete. This once again cleared the case from the system. Senior management was thrilled to see their performance measures improve.

Wherever performance incentives are relied upon, they introduce unintended consequence. As a result everyone loses. These executives assumed employees could be routinely manipulated, like rats. Employees, however, prefer to be trusted, respected, and adequately resourced and supervised. Senior management does not ultimately improve performance and might become even more suspicious of employees. Employees lose respect for management and feel justified in resisting its efforts to control and manipulate them. Reflecting on these examples leads to a better understanding of the psychological implications of using incentives and disincentives to change the behavior of employees.

The Psychology of Incentives

We discussed the motivational aspects of goals in Chapter 4. Some of these points will be revisited here, but recast for incentives. Incentives and behavior modification, however, raise different issues regarding their use in controlling and changing human behavior.

The Psychological Side of Setting Incentives

Anyone with management experience has very likely had the opportunity to sit in on discussions of the use of incentives as well as to observe their effects upon employees. When it comes to setting incentives, I have been continually struck with how often the CEOs and senior-level executives who use them are out of touch with or do not have a clear understanding about how their organization works. Understanding operations (ops) is not often a strength of many executives, who may have risen to the top from marketing and finance. They do not have hands-on work experience in ops, and they may be thought of as not having personal characteristics that make them effective at managing ops. When the numbers are not headed in the right direction, they most often feel that it is a question of getting people to do more rather than working smarter.

If we overlook for the moment that incentives may be more consistently relied upon by those who do not understand ops, the internal motivations for their use raise a number of issues. To start with, the creation of an incentive is implicitly a powerful act imposed in a unilateral, top-down manner that demonstrates beyond any reasonable doubt who is in charge. If the numbers are not looking good, it is most often the case that CEOs want to believe that they are powerful and in control (the alpha male or female). Creating and imposing incentives conveys this message. Psychologically this process can be viewed in a number of ways. Before proceeding, it is important to note that a number of these perspectives may be involved at any one time and that the same executive may rely upon different ones depending upon the context and upon her perception of threat.

When the numbers are headed in the wrong direction, the CEO and senior level executives may feel threatened. Taking charge by setting an incentive, therefore, serves to compensate for feeling vulnerable, threatened, and, at some level of awareness, ineffective. Many times the immediate response is to create a quick fix to make the numbers by the end of the quarter, since changing operations takes longer and costs more. Employees are expected to do more with equipment and systems that may increasingly limit their performance the harder they work.

Another way to view the use of incentives is to suggest that management is involved in splitting and projection. Employees are seen to be deficient, foot dragging, slow, incompetent, passive-aggressive, resistant, not properly trained, inefficient, undependable, not devoted to the organization, slackers, abusers of sick leave, lazy, and so on. They are seen to be bad and the cause of the problem. Management, by comparison, is striving to make a success of the organization. They are good. Any time these good/bad organizational splits are found, psychological splitting and projection are involved. This psychologically defensive and unconscious process involves denying undesirable self-experience and attributes (incompetence) and then splitting this experience off and locating it in others. This is the same powerful unconscious process that during wartime creates an entirely evil enemy who merits annihilation. In the workplace, employees are attributed undesirable characteristics that are the cause of the performance problem. They must be whipped into shape. Employees may then find themselves being motivated by the carrot-and-stick approach by management.

The setting of incentives to control others may also include characterological defenses such as perfectionism, arrogance, and vindictiveness. These three traits are reaction formations in which the individual is responding to the inner-self experience of not being valued, powerful, and in control that most often first arises during infancy and childhood but that may have also been reinforced throughout life. Employees are seen as imperfect. They must not only be micromanaged, but also encouraged along in their work to achieve perfectionistic standards and goals that may not ultimately be achievable, thereby reinforcing the view of them as imperfect. Arrogance is often revealed when a CEO, beyond any reasonable doubt, knows exactly what the goal should be and how to get there. A reckless indifference to information that does not support the CEO's views is combined with a self-imposed ignorance of operations. "I am the CEO. I am in charge here. Do as I say." Arrogant pride is often accompanied by a willingness to be vindictive toward any person or group that threatens this inflated, false, and unfounded sense of self-importance. The messenger may be slaughtered and naysayers and opponents attacked to such an extent (an all-out win/lose struggle for dominance) that personal and organizational survival may even be called into question. In this case, the stick is out in plain view.

One additional perspective may be added. In the movie *Forrest Gump*, the main character, portrayed by Tom Hanks, says at one point, "Stupid is as stupid does." Unfortunately for me, this statement is either so self-evident or so profound that I am too stupid to get it. However, I am often reminded of it as I observe the use of incentives in the workplace. Stupidity is not a psychological defense mechanism, yet the consistent reliance upon incentives by some executives despite a great deal of evidence that they are yielding dysfunctional and expensive outcomes seems to point to an exceptional level of stupidity. However, also to be considered are psychological defenses such as denial and rationalization that block and distort knowing what is going on. They inhibit accurate reality testing, perhaps in the support of stupidity. This consideration raises the issue of reflective practice discussed below (Schon 1987).

The Psychological Side of Responding to Incentives

Top management, by acting powerfully to set incentives, sets the psychological context for employees to feel dominated, controlled, and manipulated, and not trusted or respected. Employees are not, however, powerless. They may resist the use of incentives by turning the incentives against the executives who use them. Employees are thus using management's energy and force against it, as is the case in some Eastern martial arts. These intentional acts of resistance on the part of employees are motivated by many unconscious forces, most often in response to feeling disrespected and manipulated. Yet there are some employees who, for unconscious reasons related to morbid dependency or possibly masochism, readily submit to these management interventions. They want to be valued team members. They also want to stay employed.

Frequent reliance upon incentives is also a likely indicator of marginal management of many aspects of workplace that further limit employee morale. The organization's equipment may be old and in need of repair or replacement. The raw materials and supplies used may be inappropriate or defective. The information systems may not always work and may not be designed to make work efficient or effective. Training may be poor, rushed, or not done at all. Leadership styles may be abusive throughout the management hierarchy.

In sum, in a context such as this it is not unusual to find a deeply felt alienation and rage generated by dehumanizing and devaluing management methods. Anyone who has worked with groups drawn from middle and lower management to explore organizational performance has likely encountered outraged employees who are angry about how they and those they supervise have been treated by upper management and the CEO (Allcorn 1994). This much anger has to be somehow psychologically neutralized in order to avoid a workplace meltdown (Allcorn and Diamond 1997). Psychological mechanisms such as denial, rationalization, and intellectualization serve to avoid and shut out events that fuel the anger. These defenses must also be assumed to be at play when employees resist being manipulated and controlled by intentionally compromising the intent of incentives or avoiding being punished by concealing adverse performance information. Individual defenses might also be viewed as shared by others, thereby becoming a social defense (Menzies 1960). As strange as it may sound, marginally competent CEOs and executives should be thankful for these psychologically defensive responses that avoid, contain, and displace employee anger and aggression about their treatment.

Some of the Moral and Ethical Issues in the Use of Incentives to Control Employees

Moral and ethical issues are linked to the problematic nature of imposing behavior-modifying incentives and disincentives upon others. Who has a right to not only change the behavior of others, but also to decide what that behavior should be? In the workplace, many of the motivations behind the use of unilaterally imposed incentives are linked to self-interest: bonuses, promotions, and driving up the value of one's stock options are some examples. Why should the executives be empowered to influence what others think, feel, and do? Does the cloaking of the use of incentives in social science, or in the fact that everyone uses them, remove the presumptive and arrogant nature implicit in designing and imposing them upon others? I suggest that the answer is no. There is a moral and ethical problem of imposing one's will upon others through a mechanism such as workplace incentives. The moral and ethical issues associated with the use of incentives must be taken into account in order to avoid crossing a line where their use is hard to reconcile morally or ethically. This consideration informs the following discussion of using incentives in a meaningful, moral, and ethical way that incorporates trust and respect for others.

Don't Throw the Baby out with the Bath Water

Thus far, the darker side of incentives and disincentives has been discussed. We have acknowledged that they can be used for the wrong reasons and in dehumanizing and illogical ways, resulting in resistances, unintended consequences, and self-defeating outcomes. These considerations provide insight into what to avoid when designing incentives. This, of course, is no easy matter. As pointed out, resorting to incentives and disincentives (rewards and punishments) is frequently driven by deficiencies on the part of the executives who rely upon them. In this regard, there exists many times a quality of hopelessness about weaning these individuals off their automatic and unthinking reliance upon their crutch. CEOs and senior executives who might reasonably have been expected to have learned from concrete examples about some of the negative consequences of their use when pointed out, nonetheless frequently reintroduce incentives when the going gets tough. This compulsive and unthinking resort, if challenged on a timely basis, often results in an equally quick change of heart that, it can be conjectured, points to some awareness on their part that they usually choose to ignore. In these cases, CEOs and executives are ambivalent about the use of incentives, but also do not seem to have any other ideas on how else to deal with the problem at hand. Argyris and Schon (1978, 29) write, "In organizational single-loop learning, the criterion for success is effectiveness. Individuals respond to error by modifying strategies and assumptions with constant organizational norms. In double-loop learning, response to detected

error takes the form of joint inquiry into organizational norms themselves, so as to resolve their inconsistency and make the new norms
more effectively realizable." CEOs and executives, then, either continually improve their current methods (tighten things up) or step back and
ask themselves if their methods and even their goals are the best way to
go. In either case, learning is taking place. However, as noted, when it
comes to incentives, and for that matter the content of many of the remaining chapters, CEOs and executives frequently do not seem to be
learning at all, even when self-defeating outcomes of the use of incentives are pointed out. This underscores the problem that if they do not
use incentives (single loop), what will they do (double loop)? It also
underscores the fact that things are not so logical and rational in the
workplace (Diamond 1986). Argyris (1983, 80) offers an additional insight when he introduces the notion of psychological distancing:

> Distancing occurs when people act to reduce their awareness of, and their
> actual personal causal responsibility for, creating the very conditions that
> they criticize. One source of distancing is the state of being disconnected
> from the reasoning process. Another may be that people are programmed
> to produce the self-fulfilling prophecies, self-sealing processes, and es-
> calating errors. . . . A third cause is that if the first two are valid, then it
> follows that human beings create cultures and systems that reinforce and
> protect the first two causes.

Distancing produces the outcome that the learning loops are no longer
available and the organization's culture becomes sealed off from learning, reflection, and change. In many ways the unthinking and even compulsive reliance upon incentives appears to fit within this insight. No
matter how dysfunctional incentives may be, they are continued. This
unthinking resort to incentives, however, does not entirely negate their
potential value if properly used.

Incentives, I suggest, can be successfully used without violating ethical values and common sense. In the short run, the challenge is almost
invariably one of better managing the situation at hand and redesigning
systems and processes to be more effective. The use of incentives and
disincentives can yield favorable results only when all of the prerequisites for good organizational performance are in place, *although I note
that incentives may not then be needed.*

To begin with, incentives must be used reflectively by executives where
employees are not only treated with trust and respect, but also encour-

aged to reflect upon the incentives' design, presentation, and use in practice. Chapter 2 underscores the necessity of respect, trust, and including employees in creating change. The development and use of incentives is equally benefited with this approach as incentives can be fundamentally aimed at changing how the worker experiences work. There is then an important role in not only planning and implementing change but also in creating and implementing systems of incentives and disincentives for reflective practice.

The Role of Reflective Practice

Reflective practice is an important aspect of being an effective leader, manager, supervisor, or employee. The unthinking use and acceptance of workplace incentives leads directly to many of the unintended and costly outcomes mentioned. Reflective practice encourages each of us to think about what is going on in the workplace in contrast to merely accepting or ignoring it. Indeed, reflective practice might have avoided the infamous corporate scandals that have been uncovered as we start the twenty-first century.

When applied to the use of incentives, reflective practice requires many of the psychological, moral, and ethical issues mentioned to be open to inspection and discussion. Doing so taps the potential of reflective practice by opening the use of incentives to the respectful give-and-take of dialogue with all those responsible for their design, implementation, and monitoring, including those who must embrace them—the employees. Not only is their design and use then open to discussion, so are the outcomes of adopting them. In sum, an open and participative process of incentive use promotes the development of insights that lead to their acceptance. Nonetheless, an open and participative process is no guarantee that an incentive or system of incentives will work. In this regard, good management and supervision might better achieve the desired outcome.

In Final Analysis

"I am not smart enough to create an incentive that will actually work." I have offered this statement to executives to try to get them to think about what they are doing. I have also advocated "manage it first and incentivize it later." If anything can be said in final analysis, it is that executives who consistently rely on incentives as a fix-all patch are many times the least informed about how to manage operations. Incentives become a crutch. In addition, the creation of incentives that work consistently across time is problematic. The time, effort, and money invested in creating, imposing, and paying for incentives, when combined with the waste that they generate, should lead to a time-out to reflect. Might not these resources be put to a better use, such as hiring competent managers, developing adequate systems and processes, and purchasing the proper equipment? Chapter 6 continues to explore the role of management in the workplace. Managerial roles of leadership may well become distorted by deeply embedded personal propensities and unconscious interpersonal and group dynamics that led to the development of toxic leadership styles and outcomes.

6

Leadership Pathology

The entrepreneur is a man under a great deal of stress,
continuously badgered by his past, a past which is experienced
and re-experienced in fantasies, daydreams, and dreams. These
dreams and fantasies often have a threatening content due to the
reoccurrence of feelings of anxiety and guilt which mainly
revolve around hostile wishes against parental figures or, more
generally, all individuals in a position of authority. Distrust and
suspicion of everyone in a position of authority force the
entrepreneur to search for non-structured situations where he can
assert his control and independence.

—Manfred Kets de Vries, *Organizational Paradoxes* (1980)

Our elected leaders and those who claw their way to the top of the corporate ladder are, as a group, represented by a bell-shaped curve. A few
are very good and lead their organizations to great success that includes
creating good employee morale by their having a true sense of compas-
sion and humanistic values. The vast majority of leaders can be described
as neither the best nor the worst. They are basically average. They are
able to lead their organizations to success, but not infrequently they produce less than successful and occasionally disastrous outcomes. Employee morale varies under such leaders. Some of them may be
compassionate and place humanistic values at the forefront of their work.
Others may be indifferent to the needs, thoughts, and feelings of the vast
sea of humanity that they manage. In all, within this average group there
are some leaders who are better than others, and some that tend consistently to not meet reasonable leadership expectations, thereby gradually
introducing a pervasive harm to their organizations. The bell-shaped
curve also contains leaders who lead their organizations to great success
that is ultimately socially destructive (Hitler, Stalin, Saddam Hussein)
and to massive failures (Enron, WorldCom, and famine in Africa and

North Korea). These leaders introduce a true sense of foreboding pathology into their work. Their ambitious personal and organizational goals, and the means by which they seek to achieve them, are driven by personality-based pathologies. They bolster their fearful, paranoid, and empty sense of self by developing expansive self-images (egos) that are dependent on having their way and controlling others. In the organization setting, those who are not supportive of their agenda may find themselves deported to an organizational gulag or, euphemistically, outplaced (terminated).

This chapter provides insights into leadership pathologies that harm the world, the community, and organizations and their employees. Some of the more familiar organizational outcomes fueled by these pathologies are downsizing, reengineering, and demands for loyalty and conformity (team players). Additionally, pathological leadership behavior may be concealed and obfuscated by periodic uses of quasi-democratic and participative group processes. These leadership outcomes are often the result of leadership pathology driven by psychological regression, low self-worth, anxiety, and psychological defenses such as splitting and projection and withdrawal. These tendencies may be accentuated by group dynamics. The intertwining of these two perspectives not only helps to explain workplace experience, but also provides direction for avoidance and remediation.

The Advent of Downsizing and Reengineering as Suitable Management Strategies

Michael Hammer and James Champy's book, *Reengineering the Corporation* (1993), examines how large, sweeping organizational change displaced continuous and incremental improvement. The 1990s saw many leaders embrace these methods, which were called into question by the *Newsweek* cover article "Corporate Killers" of February 26, 1996, for which many chief executive officers (CEOs) who had called for massive downsizings were pictured on the cover in mug shots. The severity of the image drove home the point that what had come to be considered as state-of-the-art management was, in fact, a fad causing social, organizational, and employee destructiveness (Micklethwait and Woolridge 1998). A longitudinal case study I developed in the 1990s with three colleagues led to the conclusion that downsizing and reengineering were so widespread as to have affected everyone in the United States (Allcorn et al.

1996). No one had escaped either directly experiencing downsizing (sometimes multiple times) or observing it in organizations around them. The pervasive use of this management methodology created a vast population of shell-shocked and disbelieving employees. Upon close inspection, it was hard to tell who the victims were. We might think it was those who were "outplaced" after decades of loyal service. However, those who stayed often felt guilty about still being employed, mournful for the many friends they had lost, fearful that they would be next, and frequently overloaded with work to the point that they no longer felt that they were doing a good job.

The Quest for Loyalty and Conformity

Downsizing, restructuring, and reengineering have left a shameful legacy. Yet there are many other aspects of leadership pathology that, while not so sweeping, can also adversely affect organizational performance. One of those aspects of workplace experience that manifests leadership pathology is the demand for unconditional loyalty to the leader. Hitler is a good example. He required all members of the military to pledge an oath of loyalty to him as he and many others thought of him as symbolizing Germany. Refusal to do so, I am sure, was not an option. Stalin, and more recently Saddam Hussein, purged those whom they suspected of disloyalty. When you rule by the sword, loyalty becomes the key ingredient to avoid dying by the sword. We do not, however, have to look to these horrific leaders for examples of the quest for loyalty. The Bush presidencies are a more benign example in which unquestioning loyalty to the president and the Bush family is seen to be a prerequisite for affiliation and employment. One may be expected to "fall upon one's sword" to protect the president, as evidenced by George Tenet's acceptance of responsibility for erroneous statements made by the president. This expectation of and demand for loyalty, it must be appreciated, sets the stage for policies and protocol that some have described as having fascist overtones.

In the corporate world, leaders can become all-important, often spawning a personality cult, such as when CEOs who appear on the cover of *Fortune* magazine come to be seen through this lens as possessing grand qualities. The leader is perceived to be all-powerful and godlike, or at least royal. His power is sweeping and may be used to provide glorious rewards for those who follow. He may also wield a terrible, swift sword against those who do not obey unquestioningly. When challenged, this leader frequently slaughters the messenger and weeds out those who are threatening, thereby creating a loyal band of followers.

The group of loyal followers (sometimes referred to sycophants) usually in turn expects high levels of loyalty from their own followers. Any doubters are identified and also weeded out as not really having "the right stuff" (see Chapter 9). Self-differentiation within this group presents a problem to the whole group. In particular, if the leader tends to have favorites, this threatens everyone else. It is also critical that those who report to the members of this group of insiders are loyal to the leader and willing unquestioningly to conform. This is how the leader's preoccupation with loyalty and conformity gets transmitted downward through the organization (Allcorn 2003). Everyone becomes a member of the same team and is expected to make personal sacrifices to fulfill the leader's vision.

Team Players

The notion of teams is a sports metaphor that directs our attention to working together toward a common goal. A team may be said to have accomplished a great feat, such as the American Olympic ice hockey team—The Team on Ice. The notion of a team conjures up a sense of team spirit—being joined together, sacrificing together, supporting one another and coordinating actions to optimize team performance over individual achievement and recognition. What can be wrong with this world view? It sounds great. We should all be so lucky to be a member of a team that has these attributes. However, reality is often different. Teams do not actually have all of these attributes all of the time, and much of the time, they may be severely lacking some or many of them. A losing team may not demonstrate many of these attributes. In other instances, individuals might have been drafted onto the team and not share the team's history, culture, and values. Some teams have star performers; this distorts the benefits of being a member of the team. Team members may consciously and unconsciously seek to join with this star and by doing so bask in her bright shining light. It might also come to pass that some team members sabotage and undermine the star out of a sense of envy, threat, and competitiveness. Indeed, team membership can be a stressful and unrewarding experience filled with intrigue, threat, and occasional intra-team rivalry and violence (Allcorn 1991).

The team metaphor invariably conceals the hierarchy of power and control within an organization. Team as metaphor implies a sense of interpersonal equality and egalitarianism: We are all in the same boat. We either work together or hang separately. However, inevitably the team metaphor empowers those in control. Teams have captains and co-captains. They may have a variety of coaches who plot strategy and direct team members. These coaches report to a head coach, who reports to a general manager, who reports to a team owner, board, alumni, supporters, donors, and stockholders. An athletic team is, therefore, a hierarchy of power and control. When applied to the workplace, the notion of team serves to conceal a hierarchy of power and control. The development of work teams and the use of the word itself conjure up good fantasy imagery to conceal the true experience of dominance and submission that lies within the metaphor. In particular, autocratic, dominating, unilateral leaders often rely heavily on the notion of teams to conceal their need to feel in control and dominate what others think, feel, and do. Not being a team player is not an option. This concealment of power and control can take many forms, such as appeals for open participation on the part of all employees.

Round-Table Quasi-Democracy, or the Quasi-Participative Approach to Concealing Hierarchical Power and Control

The team metaphor can be raised to a higher level. Leaders who want control often develop a group of insiders sometimes referred to as a kitchen cabinet. These individuals are intentionally recruited to work with the leader but within the context of co-equality as represented by King Arthur's round table of knights of the realm. Work life becomes infused with a romanticized idealism that pervades membership at this conceptual round table. Everyone is regarded as co-equal; however, there is only a limited sense of a team. There is no hierarchy among the knights. Everyone's opinions and insights are, in theory, treated equally. This serves to conceal not so much a hierarchy of power and control but rather the absolute control of the king or CEO, who is the individual who is empowered to assemble the round table. The king's power is seldom disputed, since the metaphor implicitly provides for the king's control and imposes the obligation of loyalty and submission upon the good knights. They, in return for maintaining their membership in the round table, acquire status, promotions, increased wealth and power, admiration, and control over others. Everyone at the table is a winner. The reader is also reminded that the members of the round table are handpicked by the leader, and anyone who does not prove to have the "right stuff" is eventually displaced (see Chapter 9). A brief illustration of how this works in practice is helpful, as it is not always obvious that the round table is at work.

A new CEO assembled a small group of handpicked individuals whom he described as the best people in the organization. This was flattering to everyone in the group and predisposed them all to think favorably of the CEO. Being supportive would be important in order to maintain this special status in his eyes. The CEO presented the group with a major but not overly complicated problem that required an immediate decision. After explaining the problem, he then went around the table asking each person what he or she would recommend he do. It was clear that the CEO would be making the decision. The group was merely there to advise and counsel him. As each person provided a recommendation, the CEO showed more interest in some aspects of each recommendation than others. This interest was of a nature that it appeared that the CEO had already made up his mind and was selectively evaluating each person's point of view for those elements consistent with his unannounced point of view. The CEO concluded the meeting by thanking everyone for his or her time and opinions. He said that he would take into consideration everything that he had heard before announcing his decision. It was clear that he would be able to say that most everyone agreed (at least in part) with his decision, although it might be a decision that no one in the group proposed or would necessarily support. Subsequent meetings of the group excluded several individuals who were critical of the process and did not always endorse the CEO's decision. Others were added in their place, gradually creating an ever-more-homogeneous group in support of the CEO (for more on homogeneity, see Chapter 9).

It is easy to see that within this context the leader's power, control, and influence can fulfill his narcissistic needs. Absolute power, it has been said, corrupts absolutely. The round table magically creates and reinforces a dynamic which assures that the leader's role is secure and that his narcissistic deficits are filled to overflowing from without. At the same time, interpersonal threat and paranoia are minimized. This consideration encourages a further exploration of the unconscious and darker side of workplace experience.

The Undiscussable Nature of Workplace Experience

Powerful leaders may think nothing of using their power to disadvantage or dispose of unsupportive others. Because of this, no one is willing to venture forth to convey criticism, thus assuming the role of the disposable messenger. To the observer of organizational life, this leads to a context in which the elephant in the room must be steadfastly ignored. The notion of the emperor having no clothes comes to mind. Organization members, regardless of whether they are part of a team, a round table, or an out group (a dispossessed individual pushing a pencil in an organizational gulag), find the leader at some level to be dangerous and unpredictable. She is thought to be sufficiently willing to kill off messengers or otherwise diminish, neutralize, and dispose of anyone perceived to be a threat. The outcome is that even thinking about saying something to others much less the leader is so personally threatening that no further thought is permitted. In these cases, organizational history is replete with instances of narcissistic rage on the part of a leader who is willing to risk destroying the organization along with herself in order to defeat and dispose of a threat to her grandiose self-image (see Chapter 13). The pathological narcissism invested in maintaining a grandiose self creates a self-experience in which almost any type of operating problem, articulated idea, or group position may be experienced as a threat. This individual's grandiosity amounts to a house of cards. It is fragile and potentially unstable and must be defended at all costs. Since acknowledging this aspect of the self is not in the cards, the external world must be bent to the service of sustaining this hard-to-maintain sense of self.

It is within this intra- and interpersonal psychodynamic context that the true essence of the undiscussable nature of fear and anxiety arising from unavoidable threats to self, career, others, groups, and the organization lies. The organizational historical narrative (Chapter 13) contains stories and mythology about the leader's vindictive actions in the service of his or her grandiosity and control. There are stories of individuals and groups that were surreptitiously vanquished and their work outsourced, reallocated, or eliminated. The telling of organizational history is not unlike the telling of ghost stories. Some past organization members live on within the hearts and minds of organization members. There may also be a caché of those who walk the halls without any real work or respect from the leader. In the news recently were stories of a

National Institute of Health (NIH) employee who had for years shown up for work but was not assigned anything to do as a result of calling into question some of the leader's methods and decisions.

Thus far we have discussed aspects of the workplace that often have a dark side created by pathological leaders. This leads us to delve into the nature of leadership pathology.

The Psychodynamic Nature of Leadership Pathology

The psychodynamic nature of leadership pathology focuses on understanding individual psychology. Before continuing, several provisos have to be mentioned. First, the leader is not an island. A pathological leader is, upon closer inspection, enabled by many members of the organization for many different conscious and unconscious reasons (Allcorn 1992). Second, no amount of psychologically informed discussion can capture the true diversity and perversity of the flaws that human nature may contain. The focus here will be on a few instances that are frequently found within organizations. Similarly, the diversity of the motivations of a large number of organization members is equally beyond the reach of easy explication. The following discussion focuses on familiar aspects of the workplace in order to explore the darker side of human nature.

Leadership pathology has historically produced some of the most exceptional outcomes. Hitler, Stalin, and Mussolini are prominent world leaders who, with their group of enabling supporters, brought terror, destruction, and death to their countries and others. Corrupt political and corporate leaders have consistently contributed to this history, albeit on a less lethal level. When one examines leadership pathology, one must enter the realm of individual psychology with all of its ambiguity and lack of traditional rigorous, empirical measures. Leadership pathology has been examined from many perspectives by many authors (Allcorn and Diamond 1997; Czander 1993; Diamond 1993; Kets de Vries 1980, 1984, 2001; Kets de Vries and Miller 1984; Stein 1994, 1998). Of particular interest is *what* rather than *who*. What are some of the personality trends and aspects of the workplace and self-experience that contribute to the leadership pathology encountered in the workplace? In this regard it is important to appreciate that this list is not exhaustive, nor is each item exclusive of the others. Human nature is complex. It is almost always the case that a single factor of analysis is insufficient for understanding a leader's internal dynamics and behavior. The reader is encouraged to explore these further by reading some of the referenced authors.

Psychological Regression

Psychological regression is an always present potential when leaders are placed under a great deal of pressure to perform (Kernberg 1979). It is defined as a return to an earlier stage of development. In particular, the notion is associated with poor impulse control, acting out, temper tantrums, and otherwise childlike behavior that is marginally adaptive (Rycroft 1973). This appreciation is further illuminated by Kets de Vries (1984, 130), who writes,

> Any leader will act or react in ways consistent with his personal style and will resort to his habitual modes of managing internal and external conflict. I cannot offer a definitive answer to the relative weight of situational and personal factors in determining decisions. However, I believe the personality factors have been underestimated in their capacity to determine how a chief executive acts upon the constraints and opportunities available to him. In fact, many leaders discover themselves in trouble when shifting events place a burden on their defensive apparatus because these events demand modes of action which lie beyond the leader's personal style.

Leaders are particularly vulnerable to regression, especially when their personalities contain certain key pathological elements. Much of the sense of pressure leaders feel is prompted by the need to feel in control and to achieve mastery of the situation. When these needs are not sufficiently met, anxiety ensues to create an intrapsychic cocktail of influences that encourage leaders to resort to well-established but not always effective or adaptive behaviors. It is not uncommon to find executives who become irritable, aggressive, loud, demanding, and argumentative, and who are more than willing to scapegoat others. Anyone can be suddenly attacked. I recall a senior physician executive who, as I passed by a door he was coming out of after a bad experience in a meeting, displaced his anger onto me by verbally attacking me. This attack continued without my saying anything until I turned left down a hallway and he continued straight. This is an example of displaced aggression in which a safer object is attacked (kicking one's dog) rather than the meeting group or its leader. Discussed below are four psychological concepts that function together to create pathology.

Low Self-Worth

Low self-worth is frequently referred to as low self-esteem. Low self-worth introduces the basis for considering compensatory defenses and behavior aimed at bolstering this self-experience. If I feel worthless and not worthy of love and respect, if I feel powerless, helpless, ineffective, and unable to deal with my anxieties in the workplace, I may respond in several ways. Narcissistic deficit is a psychological term that describes self-experience driven by childhood and adult experiences that have stripped the person of a sense of self that is effective, valued, admired, and loved. The inner self is diminished and in search of narcissistic "feel-good" supplies. The individual responds in one of two ways: In one response, she can fight back against these feelings by trying to acquire love and admiration, or by dominating those who do not support her personal needs for external aggrandizement. Everyone has encountered others who have an overinflated view of themselves and their abilities. These individuals may think nothing of using the power that they have in the workplace to garner appreciation by rewarding and manipulating others into supporting them, or punishing and eliminating those who do not support their fantasy life. This compensatory response to feeling unworthy, deficient, not respected, and unable to achieve sufficient control of what others think, feel, and do is aimed at feeling good about one's self. In this regard it resembles an expansive solution to anxiety (Horney 1950) where the individual is largely consumed by self-centered pursuits and exaggerated self-importance (Rycroft 1973). Within the workplace, with its ascending hierarchy of role-based power, authority, and status, individuals who seek to compensate for low self-worth and an inner sense of emptiness often seek higher positions that command respect, thereby compensating for this distressing inner experience.

The second response is one of acceptance of the experience of being devalued, discounted, and worthless. Inner feelings of worthlessness yield an individual who identifies with this experience, thereby making little or no effort to achieve anything at work. Karen Horney (1950) describes this kind of response as the self-effacing solution to anxiety. These individuals are willing to support others, who are then expected to take care of them. In this regard, these traits are much less likely to be an adaptive recourse for executives or those seeking executive roles.

Anxiety

Anxiety is self-experience that serves to orient us to a sense of threat. We become anxious about what is going on when we perceive a threat to our self or sense of self. The perception of a problem may signal a loss of control that makes the individual feel unable to cope and unworthy of respect. In the workplace, leaders are confronted with a vast array of possibilities, many of which may evoke a sense of threat. Anxiety exists along a continuum ranging from an experience that motivates the individual to rise to the occasion to, at the opposite end of the spectrum, crippling panic attacks. The threat can be experienced as so great that the ability to think it through is compromised by out-of-control emotions. Anxiety leads to defensive responses and reliance upon familiar coping mechanisms (regression).

Psychological Defensive Splitting and Projection

Psychologically defensive splitting and projection is a more complicated aspect of the psychological nature of leadership. This dynamic involves coping with a sense of anxiety or distress about current self-experience by first denying it, then splitting it off from the self, and finally, projecting it onto another person. The other can be thought of as possessing projective "hooks" that make him vulnerable to this dynamic (Grotstein 1985). An example is helpful: A leader may be particularly invested in appearing to be powerful and in control. It is to be expected that this individual would feel challenged and anxious when confronted with a difficult-to-master set of workplace circumstances. However, to the extent that the circumstances contain a real sense of threat and the accompanying distressing experience of excessive anxiety, it becomes critical for this leader to reinforce her self-experience of acting powerfully and taking control. Those parts of the self that seem to be weak, ineffective, and threatened are denied and segregated off from self-experience. They are then spotted in others (subordinates) who are perceived by the leader to have this self-experience.

The leader must act to save these people from themselves. She now possesses self-experience that restores a sense of being powerful, in control, and up to the task. Just as important, others are now in need of her because they are known to feel weak and vulnerable and unable to master the problem at hand.

Psychological Withdrawal

Psychological withdrawal is a pathological quality that can be found in leaders who have made it to the top by *not* being offensive and threatening to others, nor taking unnecessary risks (Horney 1950). Such leaders are not infrequently hired to heal an organization by binding up its deeply felt wounds and drawing people together. However, a leader with these attributes deals with hard-to-manage and out-of-control self-experience by withdrawing and retreating. He is AWOL just when strong leadership is needed. Everyone may look to this leader for direction, and to everyone's horror, it is not provided. An experienced senior-level executive shared with me the following story: The leader of his organization was respected as a humanist, but not for his strong leadership abilities. This was not a major problem until the organization encountered some tough times where an effectively led response was essential. However, none was provided. The organization's long-term well-being was threatened, and others in senior management had stepped up to the plate to provide leadership. Their leadership was, however, only welcomed by the leader up to a point. If their efforts were seen to be usurping the leader's power and authority, or casting him in a negative light, he stepped in to suppress their efforts, sometimes with public humiliations that were uncharacteristic of him. This had clearly been a painful and frustrating experience for all involved.

Individual and Group Pathology

Leaders must have followers who are supportive. Group process relative to leaders has been alluded to. Group members may be thought of as team members, "associates," and even members of a special order or elite group. And it is clear that leaders can be expected to be all too human and bring to their roles of leadership personal needs and foibles that may at certain times dominate their leadership style, and at others permit them to rise above their personal limitations. Groups, however, also have their own agenda when it comes to the leader. In a sense, the leader can be thought of as partly the creation of the group process, where group members are supportive of some behaviors but not of others. The leader and her behavior are, therefore, shaped by rewards and punishments imposed by followers. (Behavior modification was discussed in Chapter 5.)

Many researchers (Allcorn and Diamond 1997; Levinson 1981; Kets de Vries 1984, and Kernberg 1979) have scrutinized the dynamic relationship between leaders and followers. This vast body of examination and theorizing yields a few fundamental understandings of the impact of group dynamics upon leaders.

First, much of this dynamic takes place out of immediate awareness and is most of the time not discussable if observed to be taking place. Leaders very often examine groups and their members for their responsiveness to new ideas and the issuance of instructions. A good leader is, in many ways, intuitive and willing to modify her thoughts, feelings, and behavior to maintain sufficient group support so as to remain the leader.

Second, these dynamics, while most often not observable, are very powerful. An example of powerful and observable group dynamics is illustrated by the fragging of gung-ho officers in Vietnam. New lieutenants who were eager to attack the enemy were a threat to personal survival in an otherwise purposeless war. The political arena presents a less violent but equally visible group dynamic in which the leader may be removed and replaced. The failure of the leader to protect his flock (base) introduces an almost undiscussable collapse in the group's fantasy life that dramatically and adversely affects the psychic well-being of his followers. Czander (1993, 154) notes, "Discovering that the leader is not omnipotent undermines his or her perceived capacity to protect the subordinates and to stand up for them. The leader's weakness makes the follower feel vulnerable and exposed, undermining the leader's legitimacy. More importantly, it makes them feel betrayed, as if the messiah has turned out to be an imposter."

Third, the psychodynamic process of denial, splitting, and projection already discussed serves to create leaders who unconsciously introject the projections onto them made by group members. This process is often referred to as projective identification; in it, the leader comes to unconsciously identify with the projected images and their content. Employees may feel that an executive who is effective at working with budgets and financial statements is not a people person. By being constantly treated in this way the executive may well come to experience himself as not a people person. Czander (1993, 250) also discusses the fragility of maintaining the fantasy creation of an all-knowing, all-powerful, and nurturing leader: "The once loved leader is now hated because during the group's struggles with ambivalent representations of the leader as ideal and nurturing, they also experienced him as persecuting and frustrating." The idealized leader may be destroyed for having feet of clay that evoke a sense of paranoia and threat about his abilities to fulfill follower idealization in the face of a not always supportive workplace reality.

Fourth, group dynamics can also be viewed as enabling the leader to advocate points of view that are not always ethical, moral, or good for the organization. Much like the alcoholic parent whose addiction is explained away and ignored by family members, the executive, drunk on power and focused on achieving personal wealth, may be enabled in much the same way. Those closest to the executive can be thought of as codependent and willing to change themselves to help the executive control his self-experience and support toward them in order for them to control their own self-experience such as being valued by the leader.

In sum, leader/follower dynamics are omnipresent and complex. Leaders who are pathological are most often enabled to remain so, and leaders who do not start out as pathological may become so as a result of a constant press of projections.

In Final Analysis

Leaders have a powerful influence over the organizations that they control. Sadly, it is all too often the case that leaders possess personal and character qualities that introduce considerable organizational and interpersonal dysfunction into the workplace. The range of possibilities is limitless, and it is not uncommon upon entering an organization as a researcher, consultant, or new hire to be surprised as to how the organization actually operates. It is also important to remember that leaders are not alone in acting out their dysfunctional behavior. They may not only be supported or enabled in remaining dysfunctional, they may be actively encouraged by some to become more dysfunctional. There is, therefore, a complex blending of individual leadership propensities and group dynamics that presents the consultant with the ultimate challenge in identifying and changing core problems.

The next chapter incorporates leadership pathology into a rather more systemic inspection of workplaces as cultures that contain many violent aspects. It is critical to appreciate that leaders must have followers, many of whom seek to serve their leader and her foibles to the disadvantage of the organization. Organizations can come to have as a whole a culture that contains a pervasive sense of violence and threat driven by leaders and supported by some or many employees.

7

Cultures of
Organizational Violence

> In the mature organization—if it has developed a strong
> unifying culture—culture now defines what is to be thought
> of as "leadership," what is heroic or sinful behavior, and how
> authority and power are to be allocated and managed. Thus, what
> leadership has created now either blindly perpetuates itself or
> creates new definitions of leadership, which may not even
> include the kinds of entrepreneurial assumptions that started the
> organization in the first place.
>
> —Edgar Schein, *Organizational Culture and Leadership* (1985)

The contemporary workplace is, unfortunately, filled with many aversive influences, such as excessive interpersonal competitiveness, discrimination of many types, and various forms of institutionalized and ritualized aggression. There are also more sweeping forms of organizational violence, such as downsizing and postmerger restructuring. Many of these aspects of work life, while common, are also frequently disposed of via denial, rationalization, and intellectualization, and not open discussion. At the same time, their frequency makes them a dominant factor in how we experience each other, our organizations, and ourselves. In particular, employees may be readily made to feel marginalized, disposable, replaceable, and, in general, as though they are a human resource to be numbered and managed.

The ebb and flow of waves of mergers and acquisitions introduce yet another consideration when it comes to understanding this darker side of organizational life. A prominent merger such as America On Line (AOL)/Time Warner illustrates just how violent corporate life on the fast track can really be. We won. You lost. We have it right.

You have it wrong. Of course AOL, now dropped from the name, did not have it right after all. These and many other assertions that arise from a chauvinistic cultural attitude, create a sense of violence and threat that is palpable. The merger of two organizational cultures, histories, and loyal groups of employees is much more complex than play time with metaphoric corporate building blocks (Allcorn et al. 1996).

Much like the corporate world, the public sector is often combined, recombined, cut down, eliminated, and outsourced. The for-profit corporate world does not hold a monopoly on these many violent, destructive, and ultimately dispiriting aspects of the workplace (Allcorn 2002). Public employees are whipped in many different directions as the winds of political change blow over their agencies. Implementing a political mandate to expand, limit, or eliminate an agency within the time boundaries that exist between election cycles creates heavy-handed and usually less than informed organizational interventions by political appointees. These appointees often threaten career employees as well as those who are to be served. Much the same can be said for charitable and religious organizations that harbor many forms of organizational violence, such as the sexual abuse in the Catholic Church and the gross mismanagement of charitable resources that has led to excessive salaries and expenses inconsistent with the mission (the United Way for example).

This chapter is devoted to understanding these caustic organizational dynamics. Avoiding their creation and finding ways to address them are both critically important. To begin with, we will examine the violent nature of organizational culture. During the last decade of the twentieth century there emerged management fads driven by a legion of consultants who espoused the theory that in order to save the organization you first had to destroy it (Micklethwait and Woolridge 1998). The nature of this and other forms of organizational violence can be further understood from the perspective of four cultural quadrants—narcissism, arrogance, dependence, and avoidance.

Organizational Downsizing, Restructuring, and Reengineering

There are a great many ideas on how to improve the profitability of organizations. Possibly some of the most destructive arise out of Hammer and Champy's book, *Reengineering the Corporation* (1993). This thinking, when combined with a driving need to earn income on the part of consultants, created a toxic stew of management fads. Notions such as downsizing and its more euphemistic companion, rightsizing, when combined with organizational restructuring, reengineering, and redesign, have been criticized for not achieving useful results, as indicated by the fact that these changes are usually followed by additional rounds of change. Much like a magician directing our attention away from the underlying manipulation, the executives who created the problem are left in place to further direct the gradual destruction of their organizations. These organizational dynamics are so destructive that it is often hard to tell who the victims really are—those who stay or those who have been "outplaced." Based on research into a major hospital downsizing and restructuring, both those employees who left and those who stayed experienced considerable stress and emotional discomfort (Allcorn et al. 1996; Stein 1998). It was also the case that the numbers-driven rationality of the downsizing process concealed instances of personal and intra-organizational vendettas. Those who had offended the people in charge at one time or another were not infrequently among the employees escorted out the door carrying their box of personal items.

Implicit in these images is a sense of unpredictable and possibly out of control organizational violence driven by consulting companies that are incentivized by how much they can cut (see Chapter 5). Downsizing and reengineering are not often explicitly described as acts of organizational violence. Nonetheless, a close inspection of these ideas and how they are imposed by top management unavoidably yields the realization that they contain a nihilism that is exceptionally destructive of operations and, more importantly, employee loyalty, trust, and morale. More broadly speaking, there emerges a sense of individual and organizational spiritual destruction (Allcorn 2002). A former senior executive of a large utility who spoke to me about organizational downsizing described waves of downsizing that had occurred during the past few years in her organization. She said these management actions had cut the heart out of her organization.

Since organizational downsizing, restructuring, and reengineering are but one route to organizational change, one might wonder why they have been seized upon as an ongoing management tool, especially when Michael Hammer points out in his book *Beyond Reengineering* (1997) that he did not get it right when he advocated reengineering. An explanation drawn from experience suggests that these harsh, threatening, top-down, and many times consultant-driven processes seem to fit the world view and personality of the leaders who seize upon them as the answer. When provided an opportunity to ramble on about their use of these methods, these leaders get around to talking about excising useless organizational fat and transforming the organization overnight into something that is lean and mean. Not infrequently they speak of sending a message about performance to employees (threatening the stick). The coded message is "Shape up or you too may ship out," "My way or the highway." All of these images evoke the feeling of being powerful, in control, and seen as an instrumental mover and shaker. Downsizing tends to be announced toward the end of a quarter, thereby driving up stock values. I am also confident that at some level these chief executive officers (CEOs) are communicating to the board and stockholders, "I am in control here and acting powerfully to reduce costs and increase profits." It is, therefore, reasonable to conclude that executives who rely upon these methods do so for multiple reinforcing reasons that focus on feeling powerful, in control, and admired, or, failing that, feared by others. Also to be considered is that they, as leaders, have not been very effective and are using these methods to cover up their failings. In this regard, there exist deeply held underlying unconscious fears and anxieties associated with self-experience that contain a sense of helplessness and out-of-control experience accompanied by feelings of low self-worth. Discussed below are cultures of narcissism and arrogance, which further explain the complex interrelationships between this unconscious self-experience and the use of one's position to exercise power and control in the service of being admired and feared.

Mergers and Acquisitions

Mergers and acquisitions are a second type of common event in our work lives that often create hard to anticipate and control outcomes, as underscored by chaos theorists. Any time two organizations are merged, system, method, process, and cultural conflicts must be adeptly managed. Of utmost importance is the question of who will be in control. Leaders who act as though they must win at any cost and seek to dominate and control, while most certainly introducing exceptional drive dynamics into acquiring or merging with other organizations, also leave little room for compromise. The only real question for these leaders is whether they will remain the top dog (the alpha male or female). An issue such as dominance and submission revisits earlier life experience. Submission and subservience to not always adequate parental figures can become the unmentionable quality to subsequent interpersonal relations in which similar distressing experiences are avoided at all costs. Submission, or anything like it—even collaboration and the sharing of power and authority—is not an option. An ancillary to this consideration is the seeming inevitability of the acquiring organization's executives feeling as if they have defeated or caused to submit the executives and employees of the acquired organization: we won and you lost. The problems of merging information systems, production methods, marketing plans, and the like often pale in comparison to the vast nuanced swamp of cultural chauvinism and interpersonal competitiveness and their accompanying arrogance and interpersonal aggression. As mentioned, the AOL/Time Warner combination is representative of these types of extraordinarily bad outcomes.

The Quadrants of Organizational Violence—Leaders Who Destroy Organizations

Leadership, as discussed in Chapter 6, is often far from a positive influence. Bear in mind as well that leaders are not able to accomplish threatening and morally violent outcomes by themselves. There is a complex interactive and reinforcing quality to the relationship between leaders, loyal followers, other organization members, and those they presume to serve. The leadership pathology discussed in Chapter 6 should be familiar to most readers. Since the leader is so often the driving force, I provide the following four-part schema as a way to understand the nature of violent organizational cultures and their blend of leadership and followership pathology. It is important to recognize that there is a complex interdependency that goes on between leaders who act out pathological tendencies and employees who rely upon coping strategies that may magnify the leader's effect upon the organization. Leaders are most often enabled by others to fulfill the greatest destructive potential of their personal pathologies. Also to be appreciated is that a leader may actually be made sick by those who follow, to the point where they may demand behavior that is foreign to him. In sum, by focusing on leadership pathology and how it permeates organizational life, I do not want to ignore the much greater complexity of leader/follower interactions. These interactions serve to create a cultural context for organizational life that circumscribes how employees understand what is going on and why, and how they are to work together. The following four types of commonly found organizational cultures contain different forms of organizational violence. Employees may find themselves constantly manipulated, dominated, or put into decision-making roles that they are not paid for, or simply abandoned by their leader and management when the going gets tough.

Provisos and a Time-Out for Theory

Before proceeding, a proviso is in order regarding the use of a typology. The characterizations in the quadrants I use below are informed by Karen Horney's work on human growth as she applied it to the workplace (1950); they are described as pure types. It is important, however, to appreciate that they are parts of the self and represent a greater whole in which each part may be realized at different times. This appreciation is informed by the following theoretical discussion and the possibility that, for example, the narcissist, who wants to be admired, may, upon not achieving this goal, feel that he has little to lose by becoming arrogant and vindictive. In the event that the self-construct of arrogant pride is toppled, he might then eventually give up and assume a role of dependency or withdrawal, thereby avoiding dealing with others altogether. This proviso leads to exploring the theoretical underpinnings of the four quadrants.

Karen Horney's theoretical categories make intuitive sense despite more contemporary theorizing. The approach here is to split apart her expansive solution to anxiety into two parts in order to describe two organizational cultures—pathological narcissism and pathological arrogance accompanied by vindictive violence. This adaptation can be briefly explained as follows: The infant and child is confronted with, first, a loss of fantasized control of caretakers, who are experienced largely as mental representations and not as separate individuals. When control is lost, the "other" is experienced along a range from good to bad and nurturing to not nurturing. Good enough parenting introduces optimal frustration of the infant's and child's self-directed and self-centered behavior. Others come to be respected as autonomous individuals. However, consistent parental failures may not provide the child with sufficient security and self-validation. As an outcome, the infant retreats to a fantasy world where control is regained. Others are experienced once again as mental representations that can be manipulated at will in fantasy. The infant and child may then experience self as all good and the other as all bad, thereby needing to be dominated and controlled. Conversely, the self may be experienced as primarily bad, where others are created as all-good images. The infant must in this case be controlled by others to contain his badness. This internal good/bad world is primarily black and white with limited shades of gray where object splitting (self and other) is not entirely maintained.

This discussion can be recast as the infant and child responding to sufficient and continuous lapses in caretaking by either fighting back or submitting. The submission contains elements of self-perception such as unworthy, unloved, uncared for, and unadmired. This self-experience is accompanied by deeply held anxieties, and fears and paranoia may arise from the out-of-control elements associated with the experience of the other (the caretakers). Parents who are self-absorbed or addicted to drugs or alcohol fit into the example of a childhood setting in which the caretakers are not predictably available emotionally or in terms of their caretaking behavior. They may come home drunk and violent or in need of caretaking themselves. These two outcomes create very different adults in the workplace—executives and employees who may either fight back or submit.

Fighting Back

The infant and child, who resists by every means available this distressing experience, may be thought of as striving for love and admiration by endearing himself to these parental figures. The striving results in self-change, thereby creating a false self that compromises or extinguishes elements of the true self (Masterson 1988).

The adult responds to this depleted inner self-experience, where good self-experience is not available from within (a narcissistic deficit), by seeking the love and admiration of others. This pursuit becomes a not-so-hidden interpersonal agenda in which manipulation of others is authorized as a necessity for acquiring external narcissistic supplies—good self-experience. Others, it is hoped and expected, will approve of, love, admire, and respect this individual, who is willing to do whatever is necessary to evoke these thoughts, feelings, and actions on the part of others. "He therefore depends on others for constant infusions of approval and admiration. He 'must attach [himself] to someone, living an almost parasitic' existence" (Lasch 1979, 85).

This parasitism is recast here as pathological narcissism, where others may be thought of as being sucked dry of their milk of human kindness. The parasite is incessantly demanding and compromises the host's own self-experience. The host may feel as though meeting the omnipresent needs of the "other" is sucking him dry. The interpersonal transaction is largely unidirectional. Bi-directionality may arise only when the host threatens to withdraw from the relationship, thereby evoking an energetic response on the part of this interpersonal parasite to sustain the relationship.

A second form of the fighting back reaction is to concede to one's unlovable and even despised status. Being loved and admired is not really an option. This response, it must be noted, does not constitute submission (discussed below). It contains a highly liberating interpersonal quality: "Since I do not care what others think of me, I can use and bully others any way that I see fit to meet my needs of the moment as well as fend off their aggression and their working of their hidden interpersonal agendas against me." Additionally, a grandiose self-construct emerges that necessitates a vigorous defense during reality testing. This grandiosity may take many forms. Common ones are superiority, a high degree of competitiveness (winning is all-important), and a preoccupation with controlling and dominating others who are feared to be out to get him.

This individual takes great pride in himself (stronger, better, more attractive). However, this pride is constantly threatened by reality testing. The notion of pride going before a fall applies here. Pride and grandiosity are frequently threatened by others, or in fantasy, where paranoia may reign supreme. This prideful self-concept must be defended at all costs, leading to highly energized interpersonal competitiveness and a willingness to escalate interpersonal violence until the opponent is driven off, humiliated in defeat, or annihilated. Virtually any organizational behavior is authorized in pursuit of this goal, including misusing organizational resources and disrupting productive work. This pride and expansive grandiosity are most often described as arrogance. Arrogant leaders tend to create arrogant organizational cultures.

In contrast to these fighting back reactions, we turn now to those who accept their inferior status and submit to the opinion and will of others.

Submitting

This response to the collapse of parental caretaking results in the infant and child internalizing the absence of good self-experience and the presence of an out-of-control interpersonal world by abandoning self-efficacy (assuming a role of pathetic dependency) or withdrawing as much as possible from the coercive and controlling nature of the relationship. The former response leads to adults and leaders who just do not seem to have the "right stuff." Even when in roles of leadership, they continually look to others to take care of problems and provide leadership. These passive and laissez-faire leaders are consistently unavailable to provide leadership when needed.

The infant and child who responded by retreating and withdrawing as an adult prefers to be left alone to do her work. Instructions, supervision, and working in teams are experienced as containing coercive elements of interpersonal control. This experience is to be avoided. Those who end up in roles of leadership will likewise experience the expectations of others and the demands of decision making and problem solving as coercive, stressful, and important to avoid. This response, if widespread, creates an organizational culture of avoidance. No one seems to want to deal with problems. A subset of this response is that this individual is highly resistant to authority figures who provide direction and supervision, but is effective at providing direction to and supervising others, thereby fulfilling half of the role of a manager in a hierarchy. Also to be noted is that Horney (1950) concludes that individuals who can strive neither for love and admiration nor mastery, control, and dominance, nor become submissive and dependent, are likely to give up and withdraw (the resigned solution to anxiety). This psychic dilemma results in the individual "taking her ball and going home."

This review of theory provides the basis for the following discussion of the four quadrants, where additional content is added to illuminate their nature.

Quadrant 1—Cultures of Pathological Narcissism

Narcissism, as a concept, can be defined and used in many different ways. In general, all of these uses focus on the self as the center of attention and love. The narcissist can be thought of as self-absorbed and only interested in himself (Rycroft 1973). This individual can be said to have an egocentric view of the world. What others think, feel, and do is invariably interpreted vis-à-vis its effects upon this self-centered individual. Everything is personalized. In a sense, this individual's world revolves around his creating for others the perception of himself as the focus of everything. It can also be said that this egocentric world view reveals the individual as lacking a sufficient sense of self and self-esteem. Inner experience that is not soothing and self-sustaining leads this individual to focus on the external world to provide narcissistic supplies in the form of love, support, and admiration. This helps to account for the egocentric world view in which events and the actions of others are often taken as personal affronts that do not provide this individual with sought-after narcissistic supplies. In the end, there is never enough approval and love to satiate this individual's empty inner core. Close observation of the relationship between the leader and follower may reveal that "ties are not in reality those between two separate individuals who cooperate in a rational and purposive endeavor, but instead, that the individuals who position themselves around the leader are to him only as reflected images of himself taken from his infantile past. These executive structures then become dramatic reenactments of fantasies that existed to restore the self-esteem of the individual during his early experiences with disappointment" (Kets de Vries 1984, 236).

In the workplace, the narcissist creates a variety of settings in which she is the agenda and in which being admiring, loving, and supportive are important responsibilities assumed by those around her. In particular, this leader may espouse to grand visions for the future that are engaging, and encourage others to see her as a visionary. Failure to be admiring leads to rejection and ejection. However, being powerful and in control contains a paradox. It is more important to be liked, and the use of brute force threatens that. On the other hand, having a powerful position with these attributes fulfills the need to be admired. In a way, the narcissist wants to be the alpha female (or male) without being dominating. Most often, this individual is caring and sensitive toward others up to a point, thus encouraging others to respond with love and admiration. However, failure of others to do so can lead to gradually increasing forms of aggression by the leader, culminating in termination. There is, therefore, an inauthentic hidden agenda to much of the narcissist's interpersonal behavior. Those who do not provide consistent and sufficient narcissistic supplies are not rewarded and may be threatened or eliminated if they do not get the message. In fact, the notion of narcissistic rage has its place here. Those who threaten and diminish the socially constructed network that provides this individual with the sought-after narcissistic supplies may evoke a real sense of existential threat and anxiety, accompanied by rage that is acted upon to decimate or eliminate any other who is "not a team player."

This interpersonal world creates an organizational culture dominated by narcissistic pathology. In much the same way that the leader may be observed to have a narcissistic deficit that he seeks to compensate for by receiving (demanding) the love and admiration of others, those around a narcissistic leader may feel sucked dry of good self-experience. They may then turn around and seek narcissistic supplies from those who work with them. In a sense, the narcissistic deficit that lies within the leader creates a cascade of narcissistically depleting self-experience that descends the organizational hierarchy.

This culture of narcissism or, more accurately, depletion of healthy narcissism produces some recognizable outcomes. In particular, the leader may consistently not use the power and authority of his position to create change that is beneficial for the organization. The desire to be loved, liked, and admired may be so strong as to preclude using power to redress serious performance problems, with the exception of instances in which rage arises. The leader is infuriated by having to deal with major problems that others should have avoided or taken care of. In these instances, there will be a history of instances where the leader suddenly blew up and took someone out. Many of those who surround the leader may be observed to be highly attentive to the leader's every need to ensure that his self-experience is favorable. Thus, a hidden and undiscussable codependent agenda dominates the organization and how it works (Allcorn 1992). This group also serves to filter or eliminate adverse news, events, and the actions of others—they become the loyal in-group. Yet employees at all levels will speak of the leader in admiring and loving terms, and the organization as a whole might be thought of as having a high social focus that is preoccupied with maintaining employee contentment. In this regard, there is a low-task quality to daily work and tough decisions are often put off, sometimes indefinitely. The pursuit of good feelings leads to a partial leadership void that spans all levels of the organization. In particular, decisions and actions that threaten the narcissistic supply chain are avoided.

In sum, narcissism exists along a continuum from healthy narcissism, where most of one's good self-experience is derived from within, to pathological narcissism, where others are depended upon to provide comforting self-experience. In practice, it is the range that is important and not the poles. The world is not black and white. Leaders may seek external narcissistic supplies intermittently, frequently, or much of the time; their behavior will inevitably co-vary with how much stress they are experiencing, where more stress yields greater anxiety and hunger for soothing self-experience that is not available from within. The notion of the continuum applies equally well to the remaining three quadrants.

Quadrant 2—Cultures of Arrogance

In contrast to the vulnerable self-centeredness of the narcissist, the arrogant individual is excessively self-assured, opinionated, self-righteous, presumptuous, and indifferent to what others think, feel, and do: "I am right. You are wrong." The world contains a quality of being black and white. There is little room for doubt. Decisions are informed by these features of the self, and once made, usually not revisited. This individual is, at times, frustratingly disengaged, disinterested, and unwilling to consider all sides to an issue or operating problem. She wants to be powerful and in control, and expects others to be loyal and submit. This is not necessarily going to lead to being loved and admired. Loyalty, if not volunteered, is acquired via fear, threat, and intimidation that encourage identification with the aggressor and pathological submission. This leader holds all of the vision and direction. She may be described as prickly, insensitive, demanding, unlovable, remote, and in absolute control. This individual gets rid of others who are in the way. Her appointees are expected to be admiring and servile. The notion of the iron fist within the velvet glove applies here. The world is seen as so threatening that it requires strength, power, and control as a response.

In general, this arrogant individual presumes to dominate everybody and everything and is usually known to be someone who is dangerous to cross (Horney 1950). In particular, those carrying adverse messages may be dramatically laid waste to. This leader's rage is not driven so much by narcissistic deficits as by a defense against feeling worthless and helpless. The world is a hard place to live in and has many hard edges. The response is to create a self that is all-powerful, all-knowing, and in control—a construct that reality testing constantly challenges. False pride, arrogance, and the need for vindication can be thought of as a reaction formation to poor childhood treatment that encouraged the child to feel powerless and dominated by others. In response, this individual adopted a world view and self-image that expresses "I am great and powerful even if I do not merit being loved and taken care of." Horney (1950,

198) writes of the compulsive need to defend this false sense of pride: "As a matter of fact [the arrogant individual] cannot tolerate anybody who knows or achieves more than he does, wields more power, or in any way questions his superiority. Compulsively he has to drag his rival down or defeat him. Even if he subordinates himself for the sake of his career, he is scheming for ultimate triumph. Not being tied by feelings of loyalty, he easily can become treacherous."

The downward transmission of a culture of arrogance can be thought of as propagating authoritarianism. Kernberg (1979, 46–47) writes:

> Adorno and his co-workers (1950) have described the "authoritarian personality" as tending to be over conventional, rigidly adhering to middle-class values, and oversensitive to external social pressures; he is inappropriately submissive to conventional authority, and at the same time, extremely punitive to those who oppose such authority and to those under him; he is generally opposed to feelings, fantasies, and introspection, and tends to shift responsibility from the individual into outside forces; his thinking is stereotyped, rigid, and simplistic; he tends to exercise power for its own sake and admires power in others; he is destructive and cynical, rationalizing his aggression toward others; he tends to project onto others—particularly "out groups"—his own unacceptable impulses; and finally, he is rigid with regard to sexual morality.

Although this notion of sucking up to powerful figures while dominating subordinates may seem dated, you may, nonetheless, see situations like this in the workplace. While the arrogant-vindictive individual is out to dominate others (including the boss), an appreciation of the authoritarian character adds additional nuance. The willingness to submit unquestioningly to the power and authority of a superior while conversely dominating subordinates contains an inner consistency. This individual may identify with the aggressor while also waiting for an opportunity to replace him. It is most certainly true that early life experience and the psychological coping mechanisms of the child relative to its parents dominate the relationship with authority figures.

In sum, when an individual feels he must be in control and dominate others, our natural response is to label the behavior as arrogant, self-serving, and indifferent to others. Also to be observed is that a short fuse can lead to rapid escalation of interpersonal hostilities to the point where the pervasive sense of threat encourages others to back down. It is truly a case of "My way or the highway."

Quadrant 3—Cultures of Dependence

An organization may come to have a leader who has not been selected for his strong leadership qualities (Bion 1961). There are a number of common routes by which such a leader reaches his position. He may be a member of the immediate family. Professional organizations have a tendency to acknowledge the technical success of a member via promotion. Another common promotional route is to find someone who is a healer and will accept direction from others so that they may dominate the organization through the leader. This individual is often sought out to repair the organization and its members by reconstituting the sheltering, inclusive, and supportive image of the happy family. It is not uncommon to find organization members who seek out a leader with this focus after a particularly demanding leader has damaged the organization with poorly conceived and implemented change. Or perhaps a particular group has enough power to influence the selection of a person believed to be a "good leader" who will leave them alone.

An organizational culture of dependence arises when a leader does not see herself as an authoritative, dynamic visionary who can provide clear direction, deal effectively with threats, and seize the moment when opportunities to compete more effectively arise. Fearfulness that takes the form of risk aversion is a dominant theme (Bion 1961). This pervasive sense of a lack of self-efficacy encourages this leader to look to others to provide direction and, perhaps more importantly, assume the risks associated with leadership. Dependent leaders may constantly delegate, form committees, and focus on data collection and analysis in the belief that if enough information is collected, the answer will become clear. In this regard, this leader's lack of leadership may actually provide many personal growth opportunities for those around her so long as she does not begin to feel threatened (Horney 1950). If her dependency needs are consistently met, she may assume a role in which, at times, even humiliating submission is preferable to having to step up to the plate and provide leadership. This leader may be seen by some (perhaps those who are arrogant) as needing to be displaced by none other than the adversaries themselves. They may constantly strive to humiliate this leader, who consistently accepts this behavior.

An organizational culture of dependency can readily arise from this leadership dynamic. From the perspective of individuals in the organization, the experience of this culture is one of waiting for someone to make a decision (Bion 1961). Doing nothing is an option, although some individuals may be constantly pointing out the need to do something. These individuals may be marginalized within this culture as Chicken Little, doomsday advocates, grinding their own ax and the like. The organization may also have a long history of complacency that has threatened its current and long-term survival. Shapiro and Carr (1991, 68) note, "There are few people who on reflection cannot identify dependence—rational or irrational—as having been discernable and problematic in their experience in organizations."

There is a second route to achieving this pervasive sense of dependence. CEOs who possess narcissistic preoccupations and/or arrogance that must be vindictively defended may encourage alienation "where staff respond to the CEO's personality by withdrawing into passivity" (Czander 1993, 289). Striving for ever-better control of staff may evoke anger and aggression. In describing a case example, Czander (1993) notes that the CEO in question appointed a second individual (Mr. O.) to take charge of the organization and overcome the passivity, thereby redirecting employee rage onto this new manager. The CEO then assumed an enfeebled role that distanced him from responsibility and employee rage. "By placing Mr. O. in his position, the CEO ensured his return to his former position as the admired, benevolent leader over a dependent, guilt-ridden staff" (289). Mr. O. thereafter became the surrogate victim of employee rage over their unfulfilled dependency needs.

In sum, organizational cultures of dependency are not particularly threatening unless one is concerned about long-term organizational survival or perhaps chronic interpersonal and intergroup conflict that is seldom acknowledged or resolved. This culture may be comforting for some and frustrating for others who prefer strong leaders who act decisively and authoritatively. Cultures of dependency share some of the attributes of cultures of avoidance, although the underlying individual, interpersonal, and organizational dynamics differ qualitatively based on the underlying basic assumptions.

Quadrant 4—Cultures of Avoidance

Leaders and employees who prefer to be left alone to do their work can be thought of as avoiding a sense of being coerced by the expectations of others (Horney 1950). They prefer to avoid being directly supervised and having performance targets or incentives set for them. All forms of interpersonal manipulation are avoided: "Just leave me alone to do my work." To quote Baum (1987, 73), "In short, in order for someone to feel prepared to take initiative in acting powerfully toward others, this person must feel confident that he or she can act autonomously without encountering shame or self-doubt." These individuals may, however, still have leadership roles thrust upon them.

Family businesses may draft the least threatening family member. An organization may reach a point of disparateness and seek out someone with long tenure or someone who has accomplished a lot professionally but has done so in a lab or office, closed off from the rest of the organization. These individuals, once placed in leadership roles, may try to rise to the occasion, and some may shed their propensity to shy away from the spotlight. Some who have retreated from a threatening, punishing, and in general unrewarding and unfulfilling world may be flattered by all the attention and feel empowered to take as near as possible absolute control. However, in those cases where avoidance is a characterological quality, a role of leadership may simply reinforce the experience of coercive expectations and withdrawal. These leaders are more interested in protecting their career, not taking risks, and not being seen as the "go to" person. They do not want to be in control or the center of attention. They delegate a lot and let others take risks. Such leaders are seldom seen or heard. Employees may likewise strive to reduce their own perceived responsibilities to avoid recognition. Baum (1987, 54) describes this culture of "responsibility without responsibility" in which organization members "attempt to control definitions of responsibility so that they may withdraw from responsibility under cover of tactful obfuscation." This tactic is implicit within the notion of "plausible deniability."

Decisions are made and things happen, but no one is very sure how. The executive suite may take on an atmosphere of subordinates working hard to shelter the leader from bad news and leadership expectations. Leadership opportunities may be discussed in theoretical and abstract terms that reveal some of what this individual believes. Those who maintain contact with the leader are, therefore, in a position to interpret and recast whatever the leader has to say into operating terms that are perhaps more consistent with their own point of view or possibly even what is good for the organization. It is, however, critical to keep the leader from feeling too anxious. Decisions cannot stray too far from this leader's system of beliefs, and all information reaching the leader is first carefully evaluated with the aim of reducing the leader's anxiety.

Avoidance dynamics may become a substantial aspect of organizational culture. As mentioned, decisions are made and actions are taken, yet many times it is almost as though they arise in a mystical manner. Since no one is sure exactly what was taken into consideration by whom to arrive at the decisions, they have a disconnected quality. Employees are, however, expected to carry out directives without questioning why. Since the fundamental decisions about organizational direction contain these mystical qualities, it is not uncommon to see leaders throughout the organization operate in much the same way. Employees do not see their leaders or understand who exactly is in charge. Ambiguity may abound. Employees are expected to submit and be loyal to their invisible leader.

In sum, cultures of avoidance contain an underlying quality in which members are much more focused on their experience, their work, and what is good for them. At an extreme, this creates excessive organizational fragmentation whereby individuals, teams, departments, and divisions are resistant to notions of coordination and collaboration. Organizational silos are constructed and rigorously defended, as are rules and regulations (Diamond, Stein, and Allcorn 2002). They block coercive interventions from without. In a sense, the Weberian notion of bureaucratic organizations fulfills its fullest dysfunctional potential in a culture of avoidance.

In Final Analysis

This chapter has been devoted to exploring the proposition that our organizations are filled with many forms of potentially devastating violence. Some forms of organizational violence can be viewed to be institutionalized in the form of cultures of violence within the organization. These cultures are most often driven by pathological leadership styles that contain inherent forms of interpersonal and group violence that are transmitted downward within the organization to encompass all levels and employees. This chapter has also suggested that many aspects of organizational life may contain violence, and that spotting its presence is not always easy to do. The fusion of leadership pathology with organizational culture, therefore, creates toxic and hard-to-change patterns of behavior in which those advocating change can expect to be killed off. As a result, organization members resign themselves to accepting the pathology and violence, thereby abandoning hope that things will change for the better. There ensues a dreadful embrace of despair. Life at work is only bearable when submerged in a larger fantasy life.

A colleague shared with me a story about a senior executive who, when asked about his work life, reflected a moment and pointed to a picture of himself and his family on a sailboat. His retreat from worklife and into the picture of his life outside of work, permitted him to work without becoming completely burned out. Michael Eigen (1996, 3) characterizes this sort of experience as psychic death. He writes, "One adapts to being less than one might be, to feeling less than one must feel. One talks oneself into imagining one is about as happy as one *can* be, as happy as one is *going* to be. One more or less succeeds in believing oneself, since one fears (rightly) that things could be worse." Cultures of organizational violence create the experiential context for this alienating self-experience, which must be compartmentalized in order for organizational members to have a psychic life.

The next chapter takes up the task of further exploring the relationship between self and the other (the organization). Psychic life is juxtaposed with organizational life to examine the interplay of the psyche and the workplace.

8

The Human Psyche in the Workplace

psyche: 1. The soul or spirit, as distinguished from the body. 2. The mind functioning as the center of thought, feeling, and behavior, and consciously or unconsciously adjusting and relating the body to it social and physical environment.

—*The American Heritage Dictionary* (1975)

How we experience ourselves in the workplace contains a subtle inter-active psychological complexity that must be understood if executives, employees, and consultants are to be effective (Czander 1993; Gabriel 1999). The encounter of the objective workplace with the unconscious and irrational elements of the subjective workplace introduces two different lines of inquiry that must be acknowledged and examined in order to avoid compromising the workplace and ourselves. First, the workplace, with all of its more concrete aspects, influences who we are and how we experience ourselves. It can be said to contribute to creating our psychic structure (soul or spirit). Conversely, our human nature leads us to create the workplace in our own image. The juxtaposition of these two perspectives raises some thorny questions. Can the workplace or human nature be thought of as one being the product of the other? Do we create organizations in our own likeness, or does the organization create us in its likeness? This line of inquiry seeks the origins of structure by looking within and without.

There is also a second and equally valid way to think about the juxtaposition of human nature and the workplace. This point of view examines the need for change after creation. Organizational membership is experienced with some anxiety (loss of autonomy). This anxiety leads to psychological defensiveness and the restructuring of either the workplace or ourselves to alleviate the anxiety. There are admittedly at first glance only shades of difference between these two additional perspectives. Nonetheless, these lines of inquiry direct our attention to the initial creative act involved in forming an organization and a self, and the subsequent change of the organization and the self as a response to what has been created. In particular, these four perspectives introduce a four-quadrant matrix that encourages in-depth inspection and appreciation of the true complexity of the workplace. Much like the matrix discussed in Chapter 7, this approach encourages a reflective approach to understanding the workplace. This chapter begins the inspection of creation and change with an overview of the confrontation of scientific rationality and the subjective irrationality of human nature within the workplace. There then follows an inspection of how self and the workplace interact to create each other as well as subsequently change each other.

Rationality Versus Irrationality in the Workplace

The idea of organizational rationality dates back to Max Weber's early formulation of bureaucracy (Gerth and Mills 1946). Our organizations are today turned every which way in order to achieve better designs and improved performance and profitability (Hammer and Champy 1993; Hammer 1997). Organizational attributes are quantified, engineered, and reengineered to yield just the right empirical rendering. Efforts such as these determine the exact number of employees for "right-sizing," the optimal organizational structure to balance centralized control and decentralized work, and the right mix of production and service variables to create organizational success.

A vast array of organizational attributes is amendable to quantification and systems analysis. They are the substance of the expression, "If you can't measure it, you can't manage it." It often seems that no aspect of an organization is immune to the application of scientific management methodologies that continuously improve, restructure, redesign, and right-size organizations. Employees magically become quantifiable human resources, operations are optimized, and the economic man is manipulated by carefully designed incentive systems. Soiling one's hands by having to manage people is no longer necessary inside of this quantified and overengineered organizational existence (see Chapter 5).

The closing decades of the twentieth century, however, have produced a considerable amount of critical inspection of these rational and quantified methods. Engineering and reengineering of the workplace is not

so effective or rational (Allcorn et al. 1996). A great many psychologically informed perspectives, such as ego psychology and object relations, have been used to inspect the workplace for the effects of
not-so-rational human nature (Diamond 1993; Levinson 1976; Zaleznik
and Kets de Vries 1975). Organizational leaders now have their character, psychological defensive tendencies, and all-too-human needs analyzed in order to to stave off performance anxiety and bolster self-esteem
and narcissism analyzed (Kets de Vries 1991; Zaleznik 1966). "Psychoanalytic organization theorists want to know the significance of, and the
reasons for, the private images people hold of organizational life—the
participant's psychic reality. That includes unconscious fantasies, expectations, attributions, assumptions, fears, and anxieties about themselves and others in their mutual organizational roles," writes Diamond
(1993, 37). Organization members have also been examined from a psychosocial perspective (Allcorn and Diamond 1997; Bion 1961; Diamond
1993; Hirschhorn 1988; Kets de Vries 1984; Levinson 1972).

These insights into the workplace set forth a paradox. If human nature introduces hard-to-understand psychosocial dynamics into the workplace, how then are we to understand the use of scientific principles to
manage organizations? This paradox underlies the following discussion
of organizational structuring and restructuring, the creation of psychic
structures, and the organization's restructuring when faced with distressing anxiety that introduces psychological regression and defenses. What
is the transactional nature of organizational and psychic structure?

Organizational Structure Versus Psychic Structure

The juxtaposition of human nature and the organization introduces a
hard-to-dismiss tension between self and other. Czander (1993, 105)
notes, "Given the lack of malleability of intrapsychic structure, the goals
facing employees are twofold: (1) to adapt to the organization and (2) to
alter the organization to meet the requirements of the employee's own
psychic structure or as Kets de Vries would suggest, 'to suit his/her personality.'" At the extreme, this amounts to a zero-sum game of sorts
in which one or the other must be adapted. I would assert here that there
is a greater sense of malleability than Czander suggests. In this regard,
the unconscious encounter with the organization may change one's
psyche or personality just as the organization may also be reshaped on a
level out of immediate awareness.

This discussion begins by making clear one assumption. Understanding organizational structure can be approached in a manner that does *not* include psychological defensiveness and change as a response to membership anxiety. This is the subject of the next section, that seeks to answer two questions: In what ways are the structures of our minds (or brains) externalized to create organizational structure? How does the workplace with its many attributes serve to structure our minds and self-experience?

Organization Structure and the Creation of Self-Image

What we see and hear directly affects what we think and feel. A movie may be moving. A fiery speech can be motivating. And we may pale to insignificance when standing at the Grand Canyon. Our confrontation with organization similarly affects us. Organization, according to Gabriel (1999), contains the following attributes: impersonality, hierarchy, size, power, wealth, duration, goals, efficiency, boundaries, control, and work. Our encounter with organization, regardless of how it is defined, unavoidably creates an imprint upon our consciousness and unconscious that structures experience and creates meaning, thereby imposing structure upon the self. Schein (1985) points out that the workplace provides us with taken-for-granted basic assumptions about how things work of which we gradually lose awareness. This eventuality can be described psychologically as fused object relations, lack of self/other differentiation and boundaries, normal autism and symbiosis, and primary narcissism (Greenberg and Mitchell 1983). Ogden (1989, 51) suggests, "The object (as sensory impression) is attributed meaning and responded to in an organized and organizing way, and in a way that involves a mutually transforming interplay of (nascent) self and object." Klein (1976, 292) writes, "Experientially, when identification is successful, there is no separation between 'where I got this particular role from' and the role as distinctly 'mine.'" Rycroft (1973, 67) notes, "Primary identification is the state of affairs presumed to exist in infancy when the individual has yet to distinguish his identity from that of his objects, when the distinction between, 'I' and 'you' is meaningless."

The unconscious creation of organizational self is analogous to superego formation. According to Rycroft's *A Critical Dictionary of Psychoanalysis* (1973) the superego contains unconscious elements arising from parental introjects (internal objects) where introjection is a process whereby the functions of an external object are taken over by its mental representation. Parental rules are thereafter followed as if punishment may occur in the absence of the parent. Organization introjects may likewise be hypothesized to exist as internal objects that unconsciously interact with other internal objects and self, thereby creating psychic conflict that becomes the basis of the restructuring of organization and self discussed below. This *organizational self-image* becomes one of a number of possible self-images that may be simultaneously held and integrated by the real self. Masterson (1988, 24) writes, "The real self consists of all of our self-images plus the ability to relate them to each other and recognize them as forming a single, unique individual." This is to say we may be different people in different settings (work, home, a patient in the hospital).

Our encounter with organization can be thought of as containing many infantlike experiences in which the self is confronted with the "other" and its many attributes that serve to unconsciously structure thoughts, feelings, and actions. We are changed in ways we are not aware of and not particularly anxious about. Organizational hierarchy is merely accepted along with role-based power and control. Quantitative methods are embraced as taught in schools of business and not subsequently questioned as anything other than a logical necessity of the organizational setting. Our unconscious mental representations of organization serve to unwittingly orient us to life within the organization, creating our organizational self-image.

The Self and the Creation of Organization

Our innate cognitive and psychological processes inevitably leak out to create and influence the world around us. How we see and know the world, and by extension manipulate and control it, are outcomes not so much of who we are but what we are. Organization, therefore, contains elements derived from our genetic endowments and innate predispositions.

Building upon Noam Chomsky's notion of linguistic deep structure, Ogden (1990, 15) writes, "The infant is not born with the knowledge of, or phantasy about, tearing at the breast, but has a powerful predisposition to organize and make sense of experience along specific lines." This biological code or deep psychological structure creates genetically based out-of-awareness psychic processes that organize experience within fantasy or based on sensate experience. The innate ability to understand language is an example. Ogden (1990, 32–33) writes, "But even more basic than the notion of projection is the idea that the infant is incapable of doing anything but attributing meaning to experience on the basis of his inborn codes, the life and death instincts." Stern (1985, 6) writes, "It is [my] basic assumption . . . that some senses of the self do exist long prior to self-awareness and language. These include the senses of agency, of physical cohesion, of continuity of time, of having intentions in mind, and other such experiences." These perspectives direct our attention to the notion that how we structure the external world, and by extension our organizations, is a product of these types of innate, genetic, instinctual, albeit not necessarily knowable, dynamics.

Ego psychology offers additional insight. Simply put, id, ego, and superego have their counterparts in organizations. Superego-like functions are implicit within the voluminous rules and regulations, policies and procedures that may be thought of as countervailing the baser tendencies of employees to simply do what they want (id-like properties). Management can be thought of as serving an ego function, balancing id and superego and sustaining reality testing—an executive function. Organizations might also be thought of as cultures that contain object relations–based developmental issues (no, part, and full object relations) (Allcorn 1995). Individual, interpersonal, group, and organizational experience have been studied by many from an object relations perspective (Czander 1993; Greenberg and Mitchell 1983). It is, therefore, reasonable to accept that we unconsciously create organizations in our own image, the result being organizations that are much more alike than different.

In sum, two theoretical perspectives have been discussed. It is reasonable to assume that experience (nurture) plays an important part in formulating the self. At the same time, the self (nature) cannot be denied as an active contributor to the formulation of reality and organization. Also to be again noted, this discussion focused on theoretical perspectives to suggest that each of the points of view can be articulated without introducing the notion of psychological defensiveness. However, the encounter of organization and self unavoidably contains anxiety and concomitant psychological regression and defensiveness that drive the process of changing one's self-image as well as the organization.

Organizational Restructuring Versus Psychic Restructuring

The workplace possesses the quality of preexistence. We are hired into the workplace where we are expected to conform to its rules. This confrontation between "us" and "it" can be stressful. Czander (1993, 7) suggests "that working in a formal organization will precipitate psychic conflict." The workplace frequently falls short of providing a welcoming, fun, and supportive context in which to live our lives. The rational workplace, filled with controlling rules, regulations, and policies, encourages not-so-rational responses to cope with losses of individuality, autonomy, and personal integrity.

Employees, starting with the chief executive officer (CEO), introduce psychodynamics that are hard to account for and manage, in an all-out effort to defend themselves from the occasionally hostile, threatening, and inappropriate thoughts, feelings, and actions of their superiors and colleagues (Allcorn and Diamond 1997; Czander 1993; Levinson 1972). As a result, employees end up defending themselves by relying upon psychological defenses (change themselves). The second avenue of defense involves employees trying to control what they can of their work and their interactions with others, including superiors. Job descriptions may be informally rewritten to include desired activities, while less desirable ones are minimized or eliminated. As a result, one's work and, by extension, organizational performance are affected, sometimes favorably and sometimes not so favorably.

This complexity is further increased by the notion that the two types of individual defenses described above are combined with those of others to create a shared social defense (Bion 1961; Menzies 1960; Kets de Vries and Miller 1984). That which is anxiety-provoking to one individual is often an adverse experience for others, who come to rely upon similar defensive approaches. Everyone is in the same experiential boat. Employees may respond by creating a constant press upon superiors who, encouraged to conform to employee wishes, many times respond by unconsciously introjecting employee projections (Grotstein 1985). A chief financial officer may be consistently treated as though he has no interpersonal skills or a chief information officer as a geek with no personality. Each may grow to be like they are treated. The workplace may then be understood to be composed of "stuff" that evokes anxiety and psychological defensiveness that, when acted upon, creates a rich milieu where organization members transform themselves and the organization in the pursuit of psychic safety.

Workplace Restructuring of the Self

The workplace contains many elements that encourage employees to change themselves in order to better fit organizational and group purposes and work methods. The coercive nature of this context has been described by Schwartz (1990) as the displacement of one's ego with that of the organizational ideal. Confrontation of the individual with the workplace results in psychological collapse of self-efficacy (submission) and a repudiation of one's spontaneous true self in favor of securing adequate attachment to the workplace (Masterson 1988). The loss of the true self results in the assumption of a false self aimed at securing organizational nurturing and protection (Winnicott 1965). This anxiety-ridden encounter can be thought of as a baptism by anxiety that transforms the unruly new hire into a loyal convert who, in return for being provided a job, acquiesces to external authority and control (Czander 1993). Employees come to unwittingly embrace a fantasy organization containing hoped-for perfect nurturance where everyone knows what he is doing. Conflict and coercion are absent, communication is open and direct, and everyone works diligently on organizational tasks (Baum 1987).

The embrace of the organizational ideal may allay membership anxiety, personal vulnerability, and one's sense of loss of self. Czander (1993, 12) underscores this outcome by noting, "The structure assumes regulatory authority over the subordinate only when the subordinate assumes a submissive position. The regulator's authority takes over the superego functions, such as conscious ideals, morality, equality, self-observation, and the reality testing ego. The regulatory authority is external; it is embedded in the structure and is, under certain conditions, incorporated by employees over time through participation in organizational activities, rituals, myths, ceremonies and tasks." The significance of the perspective bears some additional elaboration.

The point being made is that in the workplace, the spontaneous self is supplanted by the organizational self (Maccoby 1976; Schwartz 1990). The new employee possesses, at least to some extent, a malleable self-identity that, when confronted with the stressful nature of the workplace, seeks conformity and acceptance. The image of the self as a valued employee willing to accept instructions displaces the true self.

Baum (1987) also offers insight into this self-displacement. Bureaucratic organizations contain rational designs for work that evoke specific feelings, some conscious and some unconscious. We may feel small, powerless, helpless, infantile, and dependent upon the approval of supervisors for self-validation. These feelings, which exist to some extent out of immediate awareness, continually evoke anxiety. The distressing experience of this signal anxiety is then minimized by perfecting one's false self by becoming the ever-more-perfect worker. True self is compromised, restructured, and as a result, partially lost to the employee. He is changed. LaBier (1986, 4) writes, "While adaptation to the organization allows us to get ahead and develop our intellectual abilities with enjoyable material reward, it also has a downside. It can bring out the negative side of normalcy, like feelings of guilt over self-betrayal or of trading off too much. These feelings underlie the rage, depression, anxiety, and escapism found among many otherwise successful careerists." Attachment needs take precedence over sustaining the authentic self (Masterson 1988).

Schein (1985) argues that organizational culture constitutes a pattern of basic assumptions about one's work, others, and the workplace that allays anxiety. Employees are oriented in the correct way to perceive, think, and feel. The process of embracing organizational cultural reality creates a filter that strains out thoughts, feelings, and self-experience that are inconsistent with how one should be at work. We are changed. Whatever we thought we knew is displaced by enculturation that sustains membership. Employee perceptions, thoughts, and feelings converge to achieve comforting organizational uniformity. One's world view is altered, thereby perhaps permitting employees to act out immoral, unethical, and anti-social behavior, as illustrated by Enron and WorldCom.

Morgan (1986, 12) believes that "our theories and explanation of organizational life are based on metaphors that lead us to see and understand organizations in distinctive yet partial ways." Metaphors such as the organization running like a machine and developing like an organism subtly limit our experience of ourselves. In our minds we may become cogs in a machine, members of a team, co-equal associates, or possibly comrades.

The workplace, in final analysis, is neither a benign presence nor a good enough mother. It is an overarching context filled with anxiety-inducing conflict, hidden interpersonal agendas, overt demands for conformity, and behavior modifying systems of rewards and punishments. It is only natural that we respond by changing ourselves to "fit in" so as to allay anxiety or otherwise learn to cope with it by employing an array of psychological defenses such as denial, rationalization, fantasy, reaction formation, acting out, and splitting and projection. It is also important to note that psychologically defensive adaptiveness is but one way to understand the confrontation of human nature with the workplace (Gabriel 1999). In fact, we also inevitably try to restructure our work, relations with others, and the organization to defend against the disturbing and stressful features of the workplace.

Workplace Restructuring by the Self

Our organizations are adaptive, evolving, and frequently chaotic by nature. They must adjust to competitors, technology, economics, and social change. Executive leadership styles and methods must also change. Unquestioning submission to authority is more fantasy than reality. Sadistic and ineffective supervisors, managers, and executives are often dealt with. Change is, therefore, an organizational necessity.

Organizational change is also driven by human needs, irrationalities, desires, and fantasies, and the unrelenting drive on the part of many to maintain personal integrity and self-esteem. This occurs despite rational organizational prerequisites that seek conformity and submission in the service of perfecting ever-greater control to fulfill the not-so-humanistic profit motive (Allcorn and Diamond 1997; Amado 1995; Jaques 1995a, 1995b). Diamond (1993, 39) writes, "In these bureaucratic institutions, information and feedback that run contrary to the status quo of norms, policies and procedures and data that contradict planned schedules and routines are typically censored by collective individual and organizational defenses—what I call externalized self-systems." The workplace changes in many ways and at all levels to better fulfill the needs of those who staff it. Some duties may be attended to while others are not. New preferred duties may also be added. Kets de Vries (1984, xvi) notes, "On the contrary, organizations are made up of individuals each of whom brings his own unique personality to bear on decision-making processes. Inevitably, the framing of decisions by individuals, given the complexities of individual personalities and the intricacies of group interaction, causes distortions."

The cumulative effects of these distortions driven by deeply embedded psychological defensive tendencies encourage us to appreciate that organizational life and decision making is not always so rational and economic minded. Levinson (1968, 24) reminds us that, "These assumptions [about personality as genetic and as a dynamic phenomenon] underlie two propositions. First, people bring to their job attitudes, expectations, and modes of behavior that have evolved from their life experiences. Second, as they work, they are continually trying to maintain their personality equilibrium." Organization members create and re-create the organization every day that they come to work in order to make a better life for themselves.

This section has underscored the bi-directional nature of change within the workplace. In practice, our organizations change how employees experience themselves, each other, and their organization. Employees continually strive to make sense of their workplace and to change it, not only to be more efficient and effective, but also to better fulfill their conscious and unconscious needs. This underscores the fact that the workplace is a conflict-ridden context in which organizational and human needs collide to create unpredictable outcomes.

Implications for Theory Building, Consulting, and Managing

It might seem that this chapter is too theoretical to provide any useful guidance to executives, employees, and consultants. There are, however, practical lessons and implications that can be drawn from this theoretical discussion. The balance of this chapter is devoted to exploring the implications of the psyche at work for management, consultants, and organizational researchers.

The Implications of the Organizational Self-Image

Our experience of the workplace unavoidably influences (bounds) what we think, feel, and do. Much of what we end up doing in the workplace—our behavior—is shaped by organizational artifacts such as work design, hierarchical structure, rules, positions, ideals, values, and culture that irresistibly shape member experience (Schein 1985). Corporate values may be reduced to creating stockholder value. Leaders may be fantastic mythical figures that appear on the covers of popular business magazines. Recent stories revealing anti-social and unethical behavior (Enron, Tyco, WorldCom) can be understood to have been shaped by organizational realities. Changing these organizational dynamics is, at the minimum, a challenge. Management and consultants must be sensitive and insightful and avoid evoking distressing feelings of shame and guilt that lead to additional psychologically defensive responses (Baum 1987). Calling the above artifacts into question can be depended upon to be greeted with disbelief and resistance. "This is how we have always done it." And more importantly, "This is how I prefer to do it."

No one might believe that an open, participative decision-making process will work when the internalized organizational image is one of rigidly enforced top-down management (Czander 1993). Organizational members can be expected to have difficulty finding other ways to work or redesigning operations and organizational structure. Changing these familiar and comfortable organizational dynamics is always challenging. The internalized organizational self-image will, however, change as a response to changes in workplace experience. Education, the promotion of reflection, and the sponsoring of efforts to create embraceable, incremental organizational change can yield results. A constant and uniform press for change that fundamentally alters organizational experience sets the stage for changes in the organizational self-image (Masterson 1988). It may gradually become acceptable to think that change is possible and that one can change as well. Organizational self-images may therefore gradually be displaced by new self-images that better fit the now modified experience of work.

The Implications of Creating Organizational Structure

Fundamental aspects of work contain unknowable influences that arise from our deeply embedded cognitive and affective predispositions and contribute to resistance to seeing other ways to design an organization. How we process information and deal with dominance and submission issues, self-experience, relations with co-workers of the same or opposite sex, competitiveness, and aggression and fear (fight/flight) contain deeply embedded genetic and biological elements. Change efforts must avoid directly challenging these autistic workplace qualities and the possibility of accentuating them (Ogden 1989, 1990). These primitive aspects of knowing, thinking, feeling, and acting require the utmost respect for their contribution to organizational structure and dynamics.

Accepting this encourages the careful selection of those elements of organizational life to call into question.

Consultants and executives who are involved on the front end of creating a new department, division, or organization are confronted with the problem that much of what is considered in this process possesses these genetic and biological elements. Certain aspects of the organization are just simply never held up for questioning. The leader, group, or organization has always done things this way. In this regard, there is a quality to the work of containing a compulsive repetition. These deeply embedded and hard-to-question elements of design must, nonetheless, be called into question in order create organizations designed to fulfill the potential of the organizational vision and mission rather than re-create something that is familiar.

Implications of the Restructuring of the Self

Work life contains many conflictual experiences. The desire to verbally or physically attack an insensitive manager must be contained. Organizational landscapes are filled with unconscious psychological defenses that change how organization members experience themselves, each other, and the organization. It may be critically important to believe that one is merely following orders to optimize stockholder value when blatantly anti-social, immoral, and illegal behavior arises (Adams and Balfour 1998; Stein 1998). Managers and consultants who challenge these reinforcing individual and collective social defenses can readily create greater anxiety and psychological defensiveness (Allcorn and Diamond 1997; Jaques 1971; Menzies 1960). Hard-won individual and social defenses are not readily abandoned. Denial, rationalization, and intellectualization may abound. These defenses create a reality-altering context that makes it hard for those pointing out problems and new directions to be heard. Czander (1993, 369) writes, "By suggesting change without careful analysis of internal dynamics, they [referring to authors who advocate "quick fix" solutions] are creating the same problems that typically plague managers. Internal dynamics require careful analysis because not only do they contribute to dysfunction, they ultimately add to or detract from efforts to change the organization." It is, therefore, critical to be patient and persistent when reality-tested organizational data is fed back, in order to encourage its acceptance. Organizational research and interventions must, in particular, not threaten leaders who can readily experience improved reality testing as threatening (Kets de Vries 1984; Kets de Vries and Miller 1984). In sum, careful data collection and analysis must be combined with an understanding of psychological defensiveness in order to create individual and group change (Levinson 1972).

The Implications of Organizational Restructuring

Changing organizational structure and how work is performed is a second line of defense. Employees invariably change their work and how they relate to peers and superiors to better suit them. The workplace is first defensively modified and the change then rigidly clung to so as to avoid the distressing experience of loss of control. Cooperation and information sharing, even when ordered by the highest of authorities, may only be minimally complied with. Executives, managers, and organizational consultants must fully appreciate this defensive drive on the part of employees to control their work. They may resist the most highly energized, risk-taking, and unilateral of mandates. Pressing through the resistance to create change can also lead to unintended consequences that further degrade organizational performance. The finest of consultant insights and management decisions may go unheeded. Challenging these externalized defensive systems can result in the paradoxical outcome of reinforcing them. It may be thought that all that has to be done is tune up the current organization. Some may recall that the proposed change has been tried in the past without success. It is therefore critical to appreciate the impact of externalized individual and social defenses when it comes to changing our organizations. Inevitably, changing roles, working relationships, and organizational structure is energetically defended against. It is essential, then, before plunging into organizational change, that attention be given to understanding the defensive nature of the current organization design and its operation.

Organizational hierarchy and use of power and control may be gradually called into question despite their deeply entrenched content (Argyris 1983; Argyris and Schon 1982). A gradual process of change is essential when changes to the organizational self-image are the hoped-for outcome.

This offers insight into why highly energized resistance to change that is not overcome often results from the harshest of unilaterally imposed change methodologies. Organizational attributes invested with "genetic material" can be expected to be exceptionally resilient. In sum, successful organizational change must acknowledge that organizational life contains primitive, regressive qualities that are hard to know and manage and require the utmost of patience and perseverance to change. No amount of brute force may suffice. In particular, this characterization very often fits leaders who have developed rigid styles that do not yield to coaching. The narcissistic and arrogant leaders discussed in Chapter 6 can be exceptionally resistant to change when the proposed change directly or indirectly affects their power and authority as well as their carefully developed group of supporters who provide much valued but seldom acknowledged narcissistic supplies. It is also the case that leaders who are dependent or avoidant are resistant to the kind of organizational change that challenges them to take charge and show leadership. In sum, leaders as well as other individuals and groups that are influential have worked hard to create an organizational context to their liking, and it can be challenging to pry their hands off the control. These difficulties in changing the organization, its structure, and how it works lead directly to trying to change the leader and his followers first, so as to permit change to occur.

In Final Analysis

Consideration of the psyche at work raises four important elements of organizational life that must be attended to in order to fully appreciate the true complexity of organizational change. A response to one perspective must necessarily take into account the other three. The psychodynamically informed context explored in this chapter encourages reflection upon the many psychosocial-technical forces present in the workplace. One or two of the four perspectives may be observed to have much greater significance in terms of understanding organizational dynamics. Perhaps some of the perspectives may be observed to be interactive and reinforcing. Placing what one learns about organizational life into what amounts to a four-quadrant matrix permits a more informed understanding of the complex whole, helping to create an insightful organizational diagnosis. In particular, organizing the information acquired during the organizational diagnosis in a manner that fits the matrix promotes learning and organizational reflection of the kind that enables organizational change.

Finding solutions to problems and putting them into operation is no easy matter. Each idea should be assessed for relevance and evaluated relative to the quadrants. A process such as this contains the artful nature of psychologically informed consulting. Is an ineffective CEO the product of his life experience or the carefully constructed puppet of subordinates? Is organizational fragmentation the product of separate sites or the outcome of silo-like, psychologically defensive "us versus them" organizational thinking? These questions hint at the challenge of creating successful organization change. Finally, knowing the "lay of the land" as revealed by the organizational diagnosis (see Chapter 13) helps managers and consultants to improve not only their performance but also their personal survival in terms of maintaining self/other boundaries, personal integrity, and self-integration.

The understanding developed here for the initial structuring of self and organization and the restructuring of both creates both change and resistance to change (Chapter 2). These dynamics may occur in a great many ways. Chapter 9 directs attention to one fundamental way in which changes and resistance occur: some employees stay and others leave, creating an ever-more-homogenous workplace.

9

Selecting In and Out: Creating Organizational Homogeneity

> When one large group interacts with another, "we-ness,"
> whether it is described with reference to religious, ethnic,
> national, or racial affiliation, acts as an invisible force in the
> unfolding drama. . . . [I]ndividuals are not usually preoccupied
> with their large-group identity until it is threatened. When a
> group is in continuing conflict or even at war with a neighbor
> group, members become acutely aware of their large-group
> identity to the point where it may far outweigh any concern
> for individual needs, even survival.
>
> —Vamik Volkan, *Blood Lines* (1997)

There are often forces embedded in organizational dynamics that, if pointed out, create one of those illuminating moments. Much of what takes place in organizations is taken for granted, and some organizational dynamics are spread out over time and have a gradualism that makes them hard to spot. One of these is the process of selecting in or out—members deciding to stay or to leave. In and of itself, employee turnover is to be expected. People come and go all the time. Some who leave express a discontent with their work, their supervisor, the work of the organization, and more generally, its culture. Not as noticeable but just as important are those who do not leave or move on to new jobs in different sections of the same organization, some staying for decades. However, those who stay and those who leave are not merely benign manifestations of organizational turnover. The process of selecting in and out contains a subtext, one that creates a more homogeneous work force within sections, departments, divisions, and the organization as a whole. In the military there are the "lifers." They have pursued a military career and embraced the mission, methods, and the command-and-control hierarchy without a pressing sense of discomfort. Conversely, there are those who have simply wanted out after enlisting or, in the past, being drafted.

The process of selecting in and out can be recast in a more scholarly fashion as the creation of organizational homogeneity. Those who stay most often become more alike. They may share a common religion and sense of good and bad and right and wrong, and they may identify with the organizational mission, whatever that may be. Homogeneity can also support the development of a group of sycophants who love their powerful leader. More perversely, some may unconsciously enjoy being controlled and dominated or feel more secure and even morbidly dependent upon a leader who provides clear direction. In other situations, the leader may be more of a humanist and embrace notions such as developing others, discouraging dependency, and creating opportunities for self-realization. Those who prefer a powerful, unilateral, dominating leader will feel anxious in a setting such as this. Programs such as mentoring and personnel policies that include psychological screening and selective promotional opportunities may further accentuate the subtext of homogeneity. There may, in the end, be no difference at the top (Allcorn 1990). All of top and upper management may live in the same area, dress the same, and espouse the same view, and their management styles may be similar.

This chapter is devoted to the proposition that organizational homogeneity is a frequently overlooked organizational dynamic that is steadfastly pursued by those in charge who prefer a loyal and dependable workforce that supports their management style and world view. This makes it important to better understand it. There are a number of ways to examine the development and maintenance of organizational sameness. Discussed here are in- and out-groups, organization fragmentation, sentience groups, and attacking and defending against others. All of these organizational dynamics create and reinforce homogeneity. To these must be added the constant press of selecting in and out of organizational life and the underlying psychological nature of creating and sustaining organizational homogeneity.

In-Groups and Out-Groups

In most instances, there are groups of people who are much more attached to, dependent upon, and supportive of a leader with a particular ideological point of view than others within the same organization.

Chapter 3 discussed some of the organizational dynamics. Those who are members of the in-group consciously and unconsciously tend gradually to see themselves as alike. At the same time they also see themselves as differentiated from others who, while usually representing many different groups and segments of the organization, may be described as the out-group. A good example at the national level is the membership of the far right and far left, who have arrived at a polarized view of what each group stands for. Deviations are not welcome, and when they occur, the individual may be disciplined or even banished from the group. In this regard, unconscious denial, splitting, and projection serve to create black-and-white, readily comprehensible and threatening images of out-groups.

Organizational Fragmentation Revisited

Chapter 3 described the many sides to the psychological processes of denial, splitting, and projection. The significance of unconscious individual and group dynamics is that they serve to create a soothing sense experience of self and of others who come to embrace these dynamics. This creates a powerful synergistic group dynamic that accentuates the creation of splits. These synergistic outcomes create a world unto itself that becomes more extreme, more black-and-white. It directs attention to maintaining group consistency, cohesion, and sameness while simultaneously creating a hated and feared external group or object that is manipulated to reinforce the need for group defenses. This is stated in extreme terms to underscore what might actually exist or come into existence given the right leader and a suitably threatening context. One could say that union leaders need an enemy to justify their existence. Invading a foreign country necessitates the creation of a murderous enemy with weapons of mass destruction and evil intent relative to the benevolent liberating invader.

The psychodynamic nature of these processes is reasonably clear. Leaders and supportive group members focus on believing in certain points of view that make intuitive sense, feel right, contain utility, and are readily known and understood. Add to this the emergence of a system of beliefs or dogma, and the leader and his group of supporters establish the prerequisites for membership. A clear boundary around the group is created that requires conceptual crossing to achieve membership. There are numerous examples. Religious denominations, athletic

teams, alumni groups, residents of towns, cities and countries, and ethnic and tribal groups contain these elements. Within the workplace, divisions based on specialties and location create a sense of sameness and
homogeneity based on profession, special languages and skills, or geographic location within tall buildings or at distant sites.

Psychologically the organizational splitting that facilitates the creation
of polarized in- and out-groups involves denying certain aspects of self
and self-experience, splitting them off from one's self, and projecting them
onto and preferably into others. *Into* implies the other is unconsciously
influenced by the projections and changes her behavior and self-experience
to conform with the projections (Tansey and Burke 1989). This is referred
to as introjection. For example, an individual who is feeling angry may
pick a fight with another individual not specifically connected to the origins of the anger. The feelings of anger are not acknowledged to exist.
Nonetheless, the observed behavior contains aggression that is motivated
by anger. Any suggestion that the person is angry is denied. The fight-
picking process continues in any way that seems to work to irritate the
other person, who may initially not be responsive. However, with persistence most of us are not immune to criticism, unfounded assertions, and
the like. We may begin to feel angry and set upon. Once this anger emerges,
the fight picker may suddenly not feel angry but rather ask, "Why are you
so angry?" This is something that might have been frequently alleged to
be the case along the way. The first person is now temporarily free of
deeply felt anger and feels relieved. The other person, who was initially
having a nice day, now feels angry and distressed, having introjected the
projected anger (projective identification). It is easy to see this same type
of behavior between competing groups who may attack each other to evoke
a response, thereby creating a drain on organizational resources. Thus,
this dynamic draws much of its energetic nature from commonly shared
feeling states.

Sentience Groups

Implicit within this discussion of sameness is the notion of sentience
groups. Sentience, as used here, is defined as emphasizing feeling over
thinking and perception. The development of groups based on sentience
emphasizes a shared identifying with a particular feeling state associated with a particular point of view. A good example is the strong identification some people have with pets. These individuals discover others

who have the same sentiments. A group may then form around the need to take care of animals, which are felt to have an innocence that should be protected from commercial exploitation. It can also be argued that these strong feelings amount to a form of identification with animals in which we project some of our inner qualities and self-experience onto the animals, thereby introducing reification. By protecting animals we protect ourselves. Most groups we have occasion to encounter and perhaps join include some sentience-based identification with the group. Citizens of a country identify with their country and flag and are willing to sacrifice themselves for its defense. A group that feels that it has been discriminated against shares many feelings associated with being excluded, limited, maligned, and victimized. Self-help groups may form around many powerful emotions such as those associated with surviving or dying from a dreaded disease.

The point being made is that groups contain more than a declared purpose, agenda, and leaders. The most highly motivated groups contain a shared set of feelings that may not be directly accessible or discussible. The feelings and self and group experience merely *are*. As a group member, I do not have to think about this quality of the group or myself. Sentience groups, therefore, provide a subtle and often unappreciated underlying dynamic that serves to create and reinforce the homogeneity of not only thinking and doing but also feeling. Patriotism, as mentioned, is a good example. Anyone in the United States who questions capitalism, nationalism, and democratic values may be readily identified as "not one of us." Much the same can be said of members of other nation-states and ethnic and religious groups. Deviance from the group's norms, ideologies, and systems of thinking, feeling, and doing are not tolerated (or only minimally so). This compromises the possibility of adaptive change that may arise from differences. This defensive, closed-off posture leads not only to the creation of strong perimeter defenses, but also to efforts to change or eliminate opposing groups.

Reinforcing Homogeneity—Attacks Across Boundaries

The elimination or conquest of others who are different is as old as recorded history, starting with family groups and tribes to the more contemporary notion of nation-states. "They" are regarded with suspicion and must be constantly watched and guarded against, as discussed in the next section. "They" may also pose more than a passive problem or threat, and this may lead to a proactive intervention. Among nations this amounts to armed conflict. Within organizations it translates into a wide assortment of strategies and behavior aimed at neutralizing the "other" by taking away their work and resources or, from a political perspective, maligning and stabbing them in the back. Regardless of exactly how the aggression is acted out, it is experienced as a threat by the other, who will feel set upon and perhaps fight back. Organizations are filled with this incessant and ritualized mortal combat that consumes organizational resources, usually compromising the achievement of both the mission and organizational survival.

An example of an "us versus them" situation that led to the departure of the offending person is illuminating. A small group of loyal favorites of the chief executive officer (CEO) played an active roll in creating a moderate to serious failure that compromised organizational performance. In particular, an information system designed by one of the favorites was pressed into operation with few of its elements functioning. Management and operating reports were also not available. The outcome was predictable. In one instance it was documented that more than thirty employees spent two-thirds of their time on unproductive work trying to find someone to call from a huge database. The system did not generate a call list. In a second instance, mailings to customers were compromised by a large number of deficiencies that led to the mailing of confidential information to the wrong customers. During a meeting to discuss the problems, a new executive opened by saying that most of the operating problems were the result of system problems. He only got "sys-" out of his mouth before the CEO cut him off by saying loudly, "There are no system problems!" The executives at the table closed their notebooks and pushed back from the table. This same CEO, at the urging of his inside group of loyal followers, had already terminated a number of senior-level executives. The message was clear: if you wanted to work for this organization, a prerequisite was not criticizing, even indirectly, the CEO, the systems, and the members of the loyal group of insiders who created the systems.

Ideally, others and groups that are seen as a threat for deviating from the norm (above or below it) are eventually eliminated or "put in a box," thereby reestablishing organizational homeostasis and homogeneity. This outcome signals to others that they could also become disposable, thereby inhibiting the creativity and experimentation that support the survival of the organization.

Reinforcing Sameness—Defending the Boundary

Large twenty-first-century organizations are segmented hierarchies based on work specialization and professionalization (see Chapter 3). Organization charts are filled with departments and divisions such as finance, accounting, human resources, legal, marketing, operations, and research. These divisions include subdivisions with large numbers of employees who inhabit columns within the chart that are often referred to as organizational silos or smokestacks (Diamond, Stein, and Allcorn 2002). Yet rigid boundaries are not created by the organizational chart and its divisions based on specialization and professionalization. They are created by the people who staff these specialized divisions whose shared world view leads to an "us versus them" experience across the organization. Marketing staff may view the production people as bunglers who cannot get anything right while marketing continually innovates change to sell products. Accounting may feel obliged to rigidly enforce travel and entertainment guidelines for the sales and marketing divisions to keep them in line. Human resources must defend its schema of positions and payroll in the face of constant demands by other divisions to hire better employees and pay them more. All of this and much more is part of the workplace experience. It is also how the boundaries in mind, the silos, are defended. "No, you don't." "Not in my backyard!" Walking through the door of the travel-expense accounting section can be an intimidating experience for the salesperson trying to get reimbursed. The production or operations division may try to ban sales and marketing staff from showing up to speak directly with employees, foremen, supervisors, and managers about product problems and delivery deadlines.

Once again, these experiences reinforce homogeneity by defending internal organizational boundaries that serve to fragment the horizontal nature of the workplace. Much the same can be said for the boundary layers that make up the organizational hierarchy. Middle management may view top management with suspicion, encouraging paranoia among top management that drives them to overcontrol and dominate middle management. The inevitable outcome is for each sector to defend against outside influences that call its decisions into question; this is done by blocking access to people and information. The often-heard refrain is, "These are my data, my report, and my department."

The Process of Selecting In and Out

Organizational splitting and sentience groups are two major contributors to the homogenizing process of selecting in and out. This process takes many forms within all types of organizations. The following snippet illustrates the process occurring within the federal government. It is a synthesis of an article by Katrina vanden Heuvel that brings to our attention a process of selecting out from the George W. Bush administration that will presumably leave remaining those most supportive of the neoconservative agenda. In her article "The Coalition of the Rational," vanden Heuvel (2003) discusses a number of people who left the Bush administration. Some of those listed were not supportive of what she asserts is the use of manipulated intelligence, a preemptive war policy, and arrogant unilateralism.

- Rand Beers, a National Security Council adviser to five administrations, recently resigned saying that the administration's handling of the war on terror was "making us less secure, not more secure."
- Joseph Wilson, the highest-ranking American diplomat in Baghdad immediately before the Gulf War, argues that the war in Iraq imposes a Pax Americana that breeds resistance in the Arab world that will sorely test our staying power as an occupying force.
- James W. Ziglar, Sr., Bush's former immigration commissioner and a Barry Goldwater conservative, warns that the administration's aggressive anti-terrorism tactics may violate our constitutional rights.
- Greg Thielmann, the former head of the State Department's Office of Strategic Proliferation and Military Affairs and a career foreign service officer who served under three Republican and two Democratic presidents, went public with his anger and disgust about the misrepresentations of Iraq as an imminent threat to U.S. security. He asserts that intelligence information has been systematically manipulated to support a neoconservative agenda, referring to the process as "faith-based intelligence."
- John Brady Kiesling, a career diplomat for nearly twenty years, warned in his letter of resignation that the pursuit of war with Iraq would squander America's international legitimacy, a fear he believes is shared by most of his colleagues, some of whom resigned shortly after his resignation.

- Ray McGovern, who worked for the Central Intelligence Agency at high levels for twenty-seven years and regularly briefed Bush's father in the 1980s, resigned to protest the Bush administration's misuse of intelligence briefings.

It is not my purpose here to advocate one political view over another. However, the example of the Bush administration, as evidenced by this partial listing of names of people leaving the administration and their reasons for doing so, serves to illustrate the process of selecting in and out and how greater uniformity and homogeneity emerges. Implicit within this politically based context is the element of sentience in aspects such as patriotism, a preference for a black-and-white world, and unquestioning support of the leader. It is not difficult to observe these same organizational dynamics in universities, state government, corporations, and not-for-profit organizations.

In sum, it is not uncommon to find organizations driven by a leader who splits the organization into those who are supportive and those who are not. This dynamic is accompanied by a world view, agenda, and administrative process that leave little room for discussion. Sentience groups emerge quickly. All too often there are those seeking a strong, authoritative leader who provides an unquestionable sense of direction and is willing to get rid of those who question her direction, tactics, and methods (see Chapter 7).

A localized example within a small research division was a leader who, by constantly criticizing and verbally abusing employees, created an unusual outcome. His behavior was described as making the women cry and the men mad. They felt abused, coerced, and cornered. Gradually, many left, as did a number of rounds of replacements. This individual's administrative assistant represented those that ended up staying. She frequently complained of feeling disrespected, constantly watched and micromanaged, and verbally abused. She had, nonetheless, stayed in her position for a number of years. It was also common knowledge that she was married to a physically and emotionally abusive alcoholic and that she had a history of these types of relationships in life (Allcorn 1992). It was also the case that others in the division had sought out counseling and therapy and a few were known to be taking mood-altering pharmaceuticals. The story of this division is painful to hear. The process of selecting in and out over time yielded a relatively homogeneous group that, for various reasons, was not opposed to, and indeed found familiar, this leader's dominating, controlling, and abusive behavior. Those who did not want to put up with his behavior left. These psychodynamically oriented considerations encourage a further inspection of organizational homogeneity through the lens of psychoanalytic theory.

The Psychodynamics of Homogeneity

We unconsciously adapt to the presence of organizational power, authority, and rules and regulations throughout our lives. We learn to adjust in order to survive in the workplace. We unconsciously take in the organization's unique attributes. We also try to shape and modify the organization, its attributes, and how it works to better fit our needs and those of our group. This bi-directional dynamic is fueled by many unconscious individual and group dynamics that need not be further examined here. Chapter 8 has this covered. There is, however, something more to be said for homogeneity and homeostasis. In particular, homogeneity and homeostasis hold the promise of stress reduction and anxiety abatement, but also paradoxically may promote anxiety by requiring conformity.

Anxiety Reduction

The workplace is filled with a substantial potential to make employees feel anxious. The insides of our organizations are not safe havens. Employees are often faced with unrealistic productivity demands, interpersonal aggression of all kinds, and the ever-present threats of downsizing, restructuring, and reengineering that can turn a loyal employee into organizational fat. We may have occasion to ask ourselves implicitly anxiety-provoking questions: Will we make the quarterly numbers? Will we get the project done on time and within budget? Will I be able to master new skill sets as a result of changes being made to my work? Will I get a raise, receive a promotion, and keep my job? Will others outperform me or stab me in the back? Why is he so angry with me? The list of anxiety-generating workplace experiences is limitless. As individuals and as members of groups and organizations, we may also be threatened by competitors within the global economy, changes in technology, and governmental interventions. Therefore, individual and group processes that limit and control these occurrences are usually welcomed, although there are always those who enjoy challenges and taking risks. To this anxiety-ridden experience may be added the unintended outcomes of trying to control our surroundings so as to avoid anxiety.

Psychologically, the experience of anxiety is a signal that a threat exists. A threat may arise from within or from outside of us. If not resolved, it may "eat us up." We are nervous and may feel threatened or angry either with others or ourselves. Our expectations for our own performance may not measure up to what we are actually accomplishing (a dissonance gap). Similarly, we may not measure up in the eyes of others. Regardless of the source of the anxiety, we respond by changing ourselves and trying to change others, the organization, and the situation. In this regard, a group of individuals all of whom encounter anxiety end up sharing the same or similar experiences, feelings, and individual psychologically defensive responses that, in turn, result in a convergence toward shared group processes. We may have all shared high expectations for our own and the group's performance that we did not achieve. We then feel anxious and disconcerted and work toward rationalizing, denying, and intellectualizing what has happened. We may also create a scapegoat who can be safely sacrificed. There is then some comfort to be had by the sameness of these shared individual and group dynamics. We are all in the same experiential boat.

Avoiding excessive anxiety is desirable. Getting control of the workplace is essential if distressing experiences are to be avoided. Although there is never enough control, we can admit that its pursuit leads to the development of rule-bound and rigid bureaucratic outcomes in which change is strictly metered out. Also to be appreciated is that control is most easily accomplished if nothing much has to change. Employees are theoretically all treated the same way in a bureaucratic organization. Promotions and raises are carefully controlled. Power and authority are routinized. Supervisors, managers, and executives are expected to do their work by the book. Above-average performance and innovative ideas are discouraged or, if offered, carefully scrutinized and delimited. In the end, one individual's contributions may be attributed to others.

In sum, everyone is preferably the same (homogenous) and change is controlled, thereby maintaining stable predictability (homeostasis). We are relieved of anxiety-inducing workplace experiences so long as the sameness and control and predictability are maintained. However, control requires conformity. The presence of chaotic workplace and task environment elements assures that there will never be enough control to lock everything down safely.

The Double Bind—Control Creates Anxiety

The person/organization encounter, in addition to containing the anxieties mentioned, is also filled with many deeply experienced forms of anxiety that are attached to the pursuit of control. The pursuit of anxiety-allaying control implies submission to the power and authority of remote authority figures and to supervisors who may abuse their power and authority. It also implies loss of personal autonomy, pressures to conform, and compromising one's values and personal integrity. An executive may be expected to go along with the presentation of misleading financial reports or have her career progression threatened, possibly followed by termination. An accountant may be asked to tweak the numbers by reallocating expenses or revenue among quarters. Loss of authority and personal integrity are part of the fabric of organizational life.

However, the reduction of anxiety by controlling the workplace contains a larger problem. Attempting to control what people think, feel, and do can lead to ever-more-bureaucratic measures that introduce organizational rigidity, which is most often associated with losses of adaptiveness (resistance to change, see Chapter 2) and compromised organizational survival. And no amount of control will eliminate organizational stressors and anxiety. Inevitably, control must be considered a strategy doomed to failure. It consumes organizational members and resources at an ever-increasing "burn rate" as they seek to overcome the self-defeating nature of control.

In sum, controlling the workplace frequently makes it more stressful. If the response to this stress is the same old answer—more control—then there develops a self-fulfilling prophecy in the form of an overcontrol feedback loop. The problem is defined as too little control where more control creates more, not less, stress. This type of experience can be traced back to how the infant coped with these same issues where trying to control parental figures met with resistance.

Psychological coping mechanisms are invoked when power, authority, demands for conformity and submission, and personal compromises are encountered, whether it be as a child or as an adult, at home or at work. Chapter 2 addressed the origins of resistance to change. It is equally true that there is psychological resistance to authority, being dominated, and being expected to conform. A broad range of psychological defense mechanisms may be employed to change or defend against the encounter that is also filled with transference. What one thinks and feels in the moment is brought forward from the past. What one has historically thought, felt, and done in response to the same or a similar cue is unwittingly acted out. Transference is the introduction of familiar coping mechanisms that may or may not be adaptive to the current situation. Becoming enraged at being ordered about is not uncommon as a child, but the same response as an adult in the workplace is not adaptive. This response is, however, indicative of a psychologically regressive process in which an earlier coping mechanism is brought forward—a temper tantrum. The order may also be accepted but not embraced, thereby introducing safer passive aggression into the workplace. Having received and apparently accepted the order, the individual may move slowly to act on it, change it, or not act on it at all. In these cases denial, rationalization, and intellectualization are psychological defense mechanisms that can be observed. It is also possible that an all-or-nothing, black-and-white outcome may emerge, fueled by psychological splitting and projection. The authority figure is seen to be malevolent, controlling, and evil, thereby warranting resistance and fighting back.

In sum, the experience of anxiety and the response to it are a part of one's past that influences one's encounters in the present. Many individuals in the workplace will share the same responses and defenses, thereby creating the emergence of shared thoughts and feelings, which creates sentience groups that have a lot in common. It is, therefore, not over-reaching to acknowledge that homogeneity is part of the psychologically defensive response to membership.

In Final Analysis

This chapter has examined why organizations are so much more alike than different, not only in terms of how they are organized and function, but also in terms of how their members think, feel, and behave. Within an organization there exists a strong tendency to create homogeneity, where the employees and their thoughts, feelings, and behaviors are much more alike than different even if these shared attributes have many unique qualities. Football teams, for example, are all organized and function in much the same way. However, a close inspection of each team reveals that there are many unique aspects to each team that are shared in common by most of the members. Changing teams entails reconfiguring one's thoughts, feelings, and actions to fit the new team. It may become immediately clear that "We don't do that here." Homogeneity is a well-spring of organizational resistance to change in which the familiar and the impulse to keep things as they are sustain the sameness that, while seldom acknowledged as a basic assumption (Bion 1961), is most often a dominant aspect of organizational life.

It is also important to underscore that these hard-to-resist organizational trends can build into the organization and its culture not just a resistance to change but also the loss of the ability to envision and implement change. Not unlike a monoculture in agriculture, the sameness introduces a very real sense of inability to adapt. A single pest or disease may ravage a vast crop of genetically engineered corn or rice. The sameness not only introduces the threat of failure but also does not enable adaptation. There is no biodiversity to build upon. Much the same can be said for organizations that have not only achieved homogeneity but also, within the homogeneity, have created a context in which creativity, originality, play, risk taking, and innovation have been designed out. It is, therefore, not uncommon to find in the workplace individuals and groups that simply cannot think of anything that they would do differently. This context is a fertile opportunity for trainers, who provide a few hours of entertainment to promote thinking outside the box. Taking this notion back into the workplace can, however, be a career-limiting decision that evokes the near futility of promoting divergent thinking within a larger organizational and cultural context where one is expected not to think but merely follow orders.

Like Chapter 3, this chapter has explored a quality of organizational life that has a very real presence in the conscious and unconscious experiences that drive us. We not only see differences, which create safety and threat, we also sense them to be there even though they are not a concrete presence. This chapter has addressed the very real experience of boundaries that create inclusion or exclusion. Organizational boundaries contain a rich complexity more befitting the notion of an experiential surface. The next chapter brings forward the experience of this complexity for further inspection. Boundaries may be conceptually explored as surfaces, much like a fence is a surface that demarcates a property boundary.

10

The Surface of
Organizational Experience

> The characteristic of specialized areas of decision following the functional division of labor is common to all organizations. It represents a feature of bureaucracy in which the job-holder succeeds in making his job self-contained and as independent as possible of all other jobs. . . . The officials responsible for accounting or production or personnel come to think in terms of their professional specialization within a framework peculiar to their own line of work. As the ideas unique to a specialty become more specialized, associates in other departments of the firm are more inclined to stay out of the area of the specialist, partly because they are no longer familiar with his frame of reference or comfortable with his jargon.
>
> —Robert Merton et al., *Reader in Bureaucracy* (1952)

Human experience embraces a wide assortment of sensory and self-experience. We see, hear, smell, taste, and touch, and self-awareness introduces experiences such as love and hate and fear and anger. Our ability to sense and make sense of our experience is not left behind at the portal to the workplace. This chapter is devoted to the proposition that our sensate experience in the workplace can be better understood. The stuff of organization and work is sensed and experienced in a great many ways. Understanding the full spectrum of this sensing, experiencing, perceiving, interpreting, and knowing is challenging if one steps back from what seems to be commonplace. One way to think of the workplace is that it contains surfaces that, while not available to touch, nonetheless, have a very real presence in our minds. The use of language and words many times implicitly incorporates these sensate surfaces that exist in our consciousness. We may speak of fear or aggression as being palpable. Women report encountering glass ceilings; Churchill conjured the iron curtain. We may speak of walling off a portion of an organization to encourage innovation within a skunk works (Peters and Waterman 1982). We may also speak of communication barriers when none are noticeable to the touch. Ogden (1989, 1990) explores these organizational surfaces by theorizing that organizational experience contains a rhythm, shape, and feel that we are for the most part unconsciously aware of, and, while unique to every individual, these experiences are largely shared by all those in the workplace.

Ogden's theoretical perspective embraces the psychologically primitive, preverbal, presymbolic, and presubjective characteristics of work experience. Organizations, despite their concrete properties, are also created by executives, workers, clients, and customers when they unconsciously project individual and collective unconscious fantasies onto them. We create and share the organization as an object in our minds that we can then change and manipulate in practice and in fantasy. In this regard, the juxtaposition of these unconscious individual and shared dynamics creates a homeland worthy of the ultimate sacrifice, an athletic team that merits our support and workplaces filled with attributes that we as individuals and members of a group are a part of because we put them there. In each instance there may be understood to exist an object that is unconsciously manipulated to meet our individual or group needs. It is, therefore, important to look beyond traditional behavioristic empirical and positivistic methods that are anchored in the notion, "If you can't measure it, you can't study it" (Diamond, Stein, and Allcorn 2002; Diamond and Allcorn 2004). The balance of this chapter explores this aspect of organizational experience, beginning with further grounding of this theoretical perspective in daily experience.

The Surface of Organizational Experience

In their book *The Culture of Oklahoma*, Stein and Hill (1992, xxii) write in the introduction:

> The nature of cultural boundaries is far more problematic than many social scientists and native peoples everywhere contend. What is a cultural boundary? To begin with, although cultural boundaries might be demarcated by political borders, they are not limited to these. It might be better asked: Where is something located in existential space? We take bound-

aries, "there-ness," for granted yet they first and foremost exist in the imagination, built from our sensation of our own bodies and those of our early caretakers. Projected outward and subsequently reincorporated, boundaries come to "exist" in reality by the strength of group consensus (literally "sensing together") on what a group is and where it is located "out there"—where it begins, where it ends, how to recognize it.

Organizational turf is divided up much the same way. Organizational boundaries may be understood not to have many of the concrete qualities that executives who presume to control and manipulate them believe they have. Much of their significance exists in the hearts and minds of organization members. The point being made is that shared psychic artifacts and taboos contribute to the creation of the organizational attributes such as boundaries that are just as clear and inviolate as a stone wall. Organizational experience is filled with these fantastic constructions that create meaning. They likewise create many of the familiar organizational attributes that dominate work experience and organizational performance.

Organizational Silos as a Case in Point

The notion of organizational silos or smokestacks is a familiar one, implicit in the organizational charts of our hierarchical organizations (see Chapter 3). Divisions, departments, and sections are arrayed on vertical and horizontal axes based on some type of work specialization that divides workers one from the other. Different locations, language, methods, philosophies, professional identities, and value systems reinforce this. It would be fair to say that tax accountants, marketing executives, electrical engineers, and truck drivers see things differently from each other. A new middle manager may well experience an increase in heart rate when stepping off the elevator into the executive suite or the loading dock.

Organization members who are interviewed as part of a consultation frequently volunteer silo-like images. They may move their hands up and down to form a cylinder in the air. These hand gestures represent an attempt to articulate what has become an inaccessible and autistic experience. These silos can be thought of as a point of contact or surface that contains experience, not unlike a glass cylinder. One cannot see the cylinder, but it is there. It restricts us but may also protect us. It is this sensation of being confined, closed off, and protected that conjures the existence of organizational surfaces. They signify an experience of isolation and powerlessness, of being confined or stuck within a three dimensional silo. Also to be considered is that the silos evoke a sense of safety, blocking out threatening people, events, and influences. Language use pertaining to these experiences is revealing. Expressions such as "the left hand not knowing what the right hand is doing" or "we are not all on the same page" reflect a sense of organizational separateness and fragmentation. Phrases such as "following the chain of command," "organizational turf," and "us versus them" point to the presence of this experience in the workplace. Losses of collaboration, collegiality, mutual respect, and trust between organization members and the divisions, departments, and sections within which they work are implicitly a part of this experience.

The metaphor of silos speaks to organizational fragmentation that exists not only within horizontal relationships but also vertical relationships in which hierarchical layers do not function well relative to each other. These problems are represented by distorted and lapsed communication up and down the management hierarchy. It is not uncommon to hear complaints that management does not have a clue as to what is really going on. The presence of interpersonal rivalries, organizational politics, and competition for organizational resources and promotions further increases interlayer disarticulation and organizational fragmentation.

It is also important to appreciate that workers tend to experience the organization as a whole and do not necessarily differentiate between vertical and horizontal fragmentation. Employees may simply report that things are not working as well as they should. This fusion adds to the difficulty of locating and describing the problem. In addition, fragmentation on one axis is reinforced by fragmentation on the other. In this regard, organizational change must be evaluated for its systemic implications.

In sum, the metaphor of organizational silos symbolizes a primitive workplace experience. Silos divide the organization into parts, divide their members from one another, and fragment self-experience, fostering a sense of personal isolation dominated in part by split object relations (Greenberg and Mitchell 1983). Other employees, divisions, and departments are then assigned attributes as part of an unconscious process driven by denial, splitting, and projection. This experience of organizational silos as containing and restricting is referred to by Ogden (1989) as one of autistic objects that have hard surfaces and the qualities of being an individual and social defense. Ogden writes, "An autistic object is a safety-generating sensory impression of edginess that defines, delineates, and protects one's otherwise exposed and vulnerable surface" (1989, 56). This protective surface is associated with words consistent with silo experience such as armor, shell, crust, danger, attack, separateness, otherness, invasion, rigidity, impenetrability, and repulsion. These words suggest that the silo metaphor represents individual and group psychological defenses against anxiety. It is also the case that these silos in mind, while serving as a defense, paradoxically promote anxiety by creating uncertainty as to their protective functions and by fostering organizational dysfunction that makes the organization vulnerable to being penetrated, dominated, taken over, or destroyed in the marketplace. These considerations make it essential to further explore the psychodynamic theory that helps to explain this autistic experience.

Ogden's Extension of Kleinian Object Relations Theory and Its Significance for Understanding the Workplace

Thomas Ogden (1989) identifies three modes of organizing experience that create meaning (depressive, paranoid-schizoid, and autistic-contiguous), rather than the two identified by Klein (depressive and paranoid-schizoid). These three modes of experience provide insights into the nature of the surface of organizational experience.

The Depressive Mode of Workplace Experience

In the depressive mode, individuals know that the symbol (person in mind) and that which it represents (the person who has independent thoughts and feelings) are different. This mode of experience provides for a stable awareness of self and the autonomy of others who have a diversity of attributes—some good, some bad. It is also an acknowledgment that one no longer possesses omnipotent control of the object as person in mind. The depressive position also provides for historicity where time exists along with the present, past, and future.

Awareness of self and other opens the door to reflection, empathy, and the assumption of personal responsibility and organizational learning. Organization members are able to nondefensively embrace divergent thoughts, feelings, and actions in the workplace as well as larger external events. Psychological regression is, for the most part, avoided or limited, and reliance upon psychological defenses is minimized. As a result, individual, group, and organizational intentionality is maintained. Accurate reality testing is sustained. The ability to reflect upon and learn from experience is present and valued. Organization members feel up to the task and ready to respond as individuals as well as together to internal and external challenges and opportunities. Diamond (1993, 111) provides a concrete example of this dynamic:

> After a lengthy and painful exploration into how the group reacted to environmental circumstances, such as expanded work roles, the group members improved their ability to process the emotional nature of their work relationships so they could avoid counterproductive behavior. This involved clarifying and then redefining the interdependent nature of their roles required to complete shared tasks. Once the unit members associated their thoughts and feelings with group tendencies under stress, they realized the need to explore their reactions to constant change in the environment regularly. That realization altered their work group culture and facilitated the emergence of a more reflective and consciously aware group process.

This example points to the possibility of striving for intentionality, learning, reflection, and creative play in the workplace. However, the dysfunction of the two more primitive modes of experience is not so much extinguished as it is temporarily avoided. The primitive modes (autistic-contiguous and paranoid-schizoid) remain as a latent group potential that may be realized at any time and especially during periods of high stress.

The Paranoid-Schizoid Mode of Workplace Experience

The paranoid-schizoid mode of experience is based in part on object relations. Others are experienced as nurturing or not nurturing, loved or hated. This black-and-white, either/or treatment of the object (person) differs from the depressive position in which the object is understood to be both good and bad. This split creates anxiety related to loving and hating the same object. As adults, we might think a person is so good that he could not have done anything bad. This intrapsychic process, while allaying anxiety, also introduces anxiety in that effort must be expended to keep the good and bad parts apart when reality testing indicates otherwise. The paranoid-schizoid dimension directs our attention to reliance upon denial, splitting, projection, and projective identification to cope with an anxiety filled with fragmented self-experience (Kernberg 1979; Kets de Vries and Miller 1984; Diamond 1993; Allcorn and Diamond 1997; Stein 1994). A detailed inspection of this theoretical perspective is informative and serves to further anchor the following discussion in object relations theory.

This position is characterized by paranoid persecutory anxiety. Self-experience includes an awareness of internal images filled with a foreboding sense of threat. The response to the distress is to split it off from one's self. Grotstein (1985, 11) writes, "a part of one's being has undergone alienation, mystification, mythification, and re-personification—in effect, has become someone else, an alien presence within." Experience of one's self as incompetent, not valued, and unworthy may be split off and projected on a supervisor who, as a mental object, is now experienced as possessing these qualities. Magically, the anxious and distressed individual, having disposed of this negative self-awareness, is comforted by the remainder—the creation of a self as mental object who is competent, valued, and worthy. Additionally, in this individual's mind it is now the incompetent supervisor who is the source of the bad self-experience. According to Grotstein (1985, 11), "This 'layering' phenomenon, according to Klein (1946), is the epitome of the schizoid state." This outcome creates a surreal quality to self-experience where reality seems to be on two tracks and overall self-awareness contains a vague sense of dullness, numbing, and disjointedness. The internalized objects (idealized self and despised other), Grotstein (1985) notes, seem to exist separately. The supervisor in mind may be experienced as so separate as to have his own personality, will, and agenda. It is also important to note that the supervisor may, in fact, value the projecting individual, although imperfectly, thereby creating a projective hook. The supervisor in mind, however, most closely resembles the hook rather than an individual with many attributes. Similar experience of self also takes on a surreal quality in which self is good and effective, and any reality to the contrary is temporarily overcome. There is then a loss of self-and-other integration. Self-and-other experience is fragmented.

Within the workplace this defensive mode of experience is encouraged by the presence of discrete divisions, departments, sections, groups, skill sets, knowledge bases, and professions. The successful integration of these organizational parts into a whole conception of the organization can be elusive. A division such as human resources can frustrate line managers who need to discipline or remove workers. A finance department may be reluctant to publicly support the admission of a consumer problem with a product, whereas the legal and marketing departments may express grave concern about using cost-effectiveness as the rule for measuring corporate responsibility. It is, therefore, common to find conflicting points of view within organizations that promote distrust and paranoia, which in turn evoke denial, splitting, and projection, summed up in the attitude, "We are right and you are wrong."

The Autistic-Contiguous Mode of Workplace Experience

Human beings most fundamentally experience the world through surface-to-surface contact. Touch reveals the many qualities of a surface, such as hardness or softness, warmth or cold, pattern and shape, and, at the point of surface-to-surface contact, a sense of containment that confirms my surface as well as the nature of the opposing surface. This self-affirming sensation of surfaces can be contrasted with the losses of spatial and temporal boundaries and instances of sensory deprivation in which timelessness and boundlessness expose the person to a formless sense of dread. A more detailed exploration of the theory is in order.

This mode of experience, Ogden suggests, is the most elemental form of experience. It is presymbolic and dominated by sensate experience of rhythm and surface contiguity. Our sense of touch is fundamentally limited to the sensation of two surfaces coming together. This represents a different form of experience and relatedness from the subject-to-subject relatedness of the depressive and the object-to-object relatedness of the paranoid-schizoid (Ogden 1989). In this case, the dominant experience is "pattern, boundedness, shape, rhythm, texture, hardness, softness, warmth, coldness, and so on" (Ogden 1989, 33). The infant lacking a sense of self (I) or other (it) is largely only reaffirmed in terms of experience by surface-to-surface contact. This contact creates a boundary (my skin) relative to (the skin of) the other. This affirmation is soothing and creates a stabilizing orientation for experience without "I" or "it." It is also the case that, if this sensate affirmation is not available, the primary anxiety of this mode of experience arises in the form of terror—what Ogden (1989) refers to as "formless dread." In sum, the autistic-contiguous position offers a sense of groundedness and integrity of experience through sensory enclosure, or as Ogden (1989) refers to it, a sensory floor. This characterization, while abstract, speaks of concrete daily experience that we are most often not aware of and take for granted. If I take a moment to close my eyes and clear my mind, what is my experience? With concentration, I feel the surface of this book in my hand. My hand does not fuse with it or pass through it. This surface-to-surface contact is, therefore, affirming of my separateness from the book. My experience is within my skin.

The workplace is composed of many physical surfaces such as that of a chair, a door, or a wall. Yet the door to a senior manager's office is also a conceptual surface that contains unconscious meaning. The substance of the door symbolizes the *surface* of organizational experience. One touches more than a mere door. Its psychic surface may be forbidding, threatening, mysterious, and may evoke a formless dread filled with existential anxiety. What will happen beyond the door? Conversely, this surface may be confirming and supportive of self-integration much like the mother's touch upon the baby's cheek, where formlessness is replaced by the life-giving reassurance of sensate surface-to-surface contact. Perhaps a promotion, a raise, or a new rewarding opportunity lies beyond. Organizational silos are not unlike the door. They possess an experiential surface that offers to those within the promise of safety and comfort and the experience of a soothing surface. Yet they may also be experienced as limiting, and tending to fragment horizontal and vertical relationships between workers (Diamond, Stein, and Allcorn 2002). In sum, psychic surfaces can provide life-giving containment that affirms mind and body, or a loss of containment (dissolution into a liquid pool).

A Word on the Dialectic

Ogden (1989) locates the above three experiential modes within a larger dialectic where each defines the other. They simultaneously create, negate, and preserve each other. Psychological health is then understood to arise from the flexible interplay within the dialectic of the three modes of experience. Each serves to contribute to our experience of self and other. If this dialectic tension is compromised, psychological regression arises. According to Ogden (1989, 46):

> Collapse toward the autistic-contiguous pole generates imprisonment in the machine-like tyranny of attempted sensory-based escape from the

terror of the formless dread, by means of reliance on rigid autistic defenses. Collapse into the paranoid-schizoid pole is characterized by imprisonment in a non-subjective world of thoughts and feelings experienced in terms of frightening and protective things that simply happen, and that cannot be thought about or interpreted. Collapse in the direction of the depressive pole involves a form of isolation of oneself from one's bodily sensations, and from the immediacy of one's lived experience, leaving one devoid of spontaneity and aliveness.

The loss of the dialectic can therefore be understood to produce relatively predicable outcomes that result in personal disintegration, rigid reliance upon psychological defenses, and a loss of connection to others. These outcomes may be dominated by one of the three experiences or switch between them. We may feel isolated or experience things as just happening to us. At the extreme, the absence of life-confirming boundaries may create existential anxiety, dread of loss, and a melting away or dissolution of the self that compromises authenticity, responsibility, and competent performance.

Conversely, the dialectic that binds together the modes may create a rich texture to life, experience, and the creation of meaning. These are the ingredients that must be present to create a whole, such as rock, cement, and water combined to create concrete. The dialectic permits locating experience and meaning by one's ability to access and merge unconscious knowledge into a life-sustaining whole, thereby creating a balance between the forces of personal disintegration and integration that promotes adaptive responses.

In sum, the surface-to-surface sensate nature of work life directs our attention to the presence of primitive, preverbal, presymbolic, and presubjective experience that influences our thoughts, feelings, and actions, and, by extension, organizational performance. Primarily autistic experience must be made available to examination, inspection, and mutual validation as a first step toward recovering the sense of balance implicit within the dialectic. This is challenging because this experience must be carefully and sensitively explored to avoid creating anxiety and further regression from the dialectic.

Surface Discovery and Transformation at Work

Organizational experience has thus far been discussed as possessing a multidimensional complexity that contains sensate surfaces. This characterization blends unconscious individual and group dynamics to make sense of such things as organizational silos and layers, which function as protective restricting cocoons and filters. We most often sense that they are there.

In practice, the questions are: How do we identify these surfaces? How can we understand how they affect the workplace? How might they be modified or overcome to avoid the organizational dysfunctions that they create? Our fragmented experience of organizational surfaces is very often the origin of organizational dysfunction. Let us now address the questions one by one.

How do we identify these surfaces? This is not a challenge, in that they are everywhere all of the time. However, this taken-for-granted omnipresence contributes to their virtual disappearance from organizational dialogue. They are part of the way things have been, are, and ought to be. Raising them to consciousness signifies calling them into question—something that will make members of the organization anxious and resistant. It often falls to new leaders and consultants not only to see these surfaces for what they are, but also to call them into question. If this work is done within a larger context of interpersonal engagement, openness, and inquiry conducted within a safe enough holding environment, the existence of surfaces and the obvious problems they create is more likely to be acknowledged.

Identifying them is not so much a process of developing a careful analysis that reveals them. Rather, we find them by sensing or being aware of them. An employee may tell a story about a problem that developed when several divisions or departments failed to coordinate their work. Resources, it may be observed, do not seem to be being rationally allocated. There may be excessive levels of finger pointing and references made to no one's being in charge. Information flows, both horizontally and vertically, may be described as simply not happening in a complete and timely manner. All of these common workplace experiences, as well as many others, speak not only to organizational fragmentation but also to the experience of employees of being walled off from each other. Ideas and communications can be spoken of as being piped in or lofted over a wall. When executives, managers, and employees are asked to explain how these problems have come into existence, they often speak of being cut off from each other. This experience is concrete to them, as evidenced by the at times considerable emotion attached to recognizing and discussing it. Their experience can also be observed to have unconscious and autistic qualities that make it difficult for them to recognize the origins of the experience. Rather, they may simply convey the experience by holding their hands in the air to form a cylinder, or pressing them in the air against an invisible barrier. If the consultant mentions the image of a silo, the employee often validates it. "How did you know that?" might be the response. In sum, locating these surfaces of organizational experience is enabled by dialogue and historical narrative (Chapter 13).

How can we understand how they affect the workplace? The surfaces that compose organizational fragmentation create substantial organizational dysfunction as well as confusing and hard-to-grasp individual and group experience. Why is it that we keep on making the same mistakes? Why can't we work together more effectively? Beyond losses of productivity and organizational adaptability lies an arena of self and other experience that contains frustration, threat, safety issues, and, by extension, stress and anxiety attached to compromised organizational performance. More profoundly, these surfaces that contain unconscious and primitive qualities of experience are most often autistic in nature and not available for identification and dialogue. There is, then, a quality of an elephant being in the room that everyone may sense but no one can exactly identify (autistic experience). Why is it so dangerous to move between these surfaces? Why does if feel safer inside one's division or department? Herein lies the ultimate source and meaning of the surfaces, as well as their effect upon the workplace. They are not really open to discussion, and as a result, the problems are persistent. No one seems to learn from mistakes that are made again and again. Organizational learning is foreclosed.

How might the surfaces be modified or overcome to avoid the organizational dysfunctions that they create? Beyond identifying the surfaces and the dysfunctions that they introduce into the workplace, it is essential to find ways to communicate their presence in ways that are heard, thus opening them up to inspection that leads to change and avoidance of future pitfulls. However, their hard-to-recognize autistic nature makes raising them to consciousness challenging. Organization members experience them daily, but they are so commonplace as to be accepted as part of the fabric of the workplace. Also, these surfaces may be said to "serve and protect," and if they are called into question, the questioning can introduce a sense of immediate threat. If not silos then what? Their confining, restricting, regimenting, and dominating aspects are also distressing to discuss. No one wants to speak of a senior executive's behavior that serves to create the organizational fragmentation out of fear of being disciplined. Thus, beyond the problem of recognizing the surfaces, there is an implicit double bind in bringing them forward for exploration and change. Herein lies the need for a safe enough holding context that has sufficiently playful aspects within it to constitute a transitional space and time. The basic steps to creating this context are fairly straightforward:

A new executive or manager, or an external consultant, encounters organizational dysfunction created by these offensive, defensive, and restricting surfaces. To start, care should be taken to document the dysfunctions and identify the surfaces. The citing of specific operating problems is usually not threatening, as most employees know of them. Resolving them is also to everyone's advantage. If possible, the problems should be quantified and concrete examples provided. It is important to be aware that executives, managers, and employees, if pressed for an explanation as to why the problems exist, may be evasive and fearful of speaking out. Others may, however, be bolder and readily point out what or who they think is the cause. In these cases, references to culpable individuals have to be clarified. Asking employees to specify a name or names can make even the bold employees anxious, although they know exactly whom they have in mind. Making it clear that the discussion is confidential may not overcome the perceived threat. A few brave souls will most often provide this information. Those who are uncomfortable with being more explicit should not be pressed. In sum, this process of data collection and documentation reveals a picture of organizational surfaces and the operating problems that they create.

Contemplation of an intervention must also include an acknowledgment that the interviewing and data collection process creates a listening context in which executives, managers, and employees are being actively heard. This might be considered to be the start of an intervention process that creates trust and respect for all employees (Stein 1994). The actual process of intervention must be designed to fit the organization and findings. However, there are a few overarching considerations that are common to all interventions.

A safe enough holding environment can be created by calling together a cross-section of the organization, ranging from the chief executive office to the supervisors over the lowest positions. In large organizations this diagonal slice through the organization need not include representatives from every area, although areas known to be especially encumbered by surface-generated operating problems should be included. The goal here is to not create a working group so large as to be unmanageable, but one large enough to be representative. Once the group is assembled, the consultant or executive has to work toward creating a context that focuses on trust and respect and nondefensive listening to various points of view. It is critical to police these criteria to avoid the appearance of a hidden agenda in which management might, for example, be seen to be identifying scapegoats. Group process facilitation starts with presenting examples of problems and the supporting documentation. In each case, the group should be asked to locate the underlying causes. In the case of a group with more than ten to fifteen people, this might be best accomplished by breaking the group down into task groups that are then charged with an analysis. Bringing the groups back together to share their work introduces the necessity of blending the findings into a consensus document thorough open discussion. This process builds trust and respect, and the confidence that those present can work together on stressful issues without destroying each other. As this work proceeds, the organizing concept of organizational surfaces such as silos and layers provides an important cognitive and experiential anchor for placing all of the findings into a context that accounts for what is thought and what is experienced. In particular, the offensive, defensive, and confining aspects of the experience should be opened up for discussion. The final step is to have the group break down to determine solutions that also address the underlying contributors—the organizational surfaces.

In Final Analysis

This chapter has presented what may at first seem to be a theoretical and abstract discussion of one element of the workplace. However, the notion that our traditional hierarchical and specialized organizations have silos or smokestacks and layers of management is not new. These characteristics are present and consistently introduce organizational dysfunctions that compromise coordination, cooperation, and communication. What is new about this discussion is that it draws attention to the presence of the experiential surfaces of social constructs that are very real to organization members. A new idea for improving profitability may be contested by other departments and blocked and modified as it moves upward through the ladder of management, never to be heard of again. Recognizing the existence of the offensive and defensive surfaces permits them to be addressed and their contribution to operating problems minimized. This opens up the possibility of changing or removing them to improve organizational performance.

In sum, this chapter has explored an intangible but nonetheless very real aspect of the workplace. Things do not have to physically exist or be easily measured to have a major influence upon work and the people who perform it. The next chapter continues this discussion by examining additional workplace elements that lack concreteness but also impact work experience and the organization as a whole. It explores what seem at times the almost magical properties of how things get done at work.

11

Mysticism in the Workplace

> *mysticism.* Any belief in the existence of realities beyond
> perceptual or intellectual apprehension but central to being and
> directly accessible by intuition.
> *mystification.* The act or an instance of making something
> obscure or mysterious.
> *mystify.* To awe or perplex; bewilder.
> *mystique.* An attitude of mystical veneration conferring upon an
> occupation, a person, or a thing an awesome and mythical
> status; the special cult of anything. A mystical or philosophical
> conception used as a guide, especially for political action.
> *myth.* Any real or fictional story, recurring theme, or character
> type that appeals to the consciousness of a people by
> embodying its cultural ideals or by giving expression to deep,
> commonly felt emotions.
>
> —Excerpted from *The American Heritage Dictionary* (1975)

The idea that the concrete world of corporate management, production, and numbers contains some and possibly a great deal of mysticism, mystification, mystique, and mythology has been hinted at in earlier chapters. Notions such as goals and incentives are many times relied upon to magically direct and limit human behavior in the workplace. Profit as a goal, incentive, or motive may not be the final arbiter of rational business practice. The same holds true for the many presumably noble goals of national, state, and local governments and the not-for-profit sector. This irrational faith in goals and incentives is, however, so omnipresent, so persistent, and so unquestioned that it amounts to a belief in the existence of realities beyond perceptual or intellectual apprehension but central to being, and accessible by intuition. This directs our attention away from the value-added realm of rational planning, goal setting, measurement, and mid-course corrections in pursuit of a clearly defined objective and toward fuzzy systems of beliefs, intuitive process, and gut feelings. Also to be incorporated are the mostly unconscious dynamics individuals and groups bring to the table.

Mystifying executive behavior, managerial mystique, and organizational myths are each explored for their presence within the workplace and their contributions to workplace experience. These insights lead to consideration of what is really involved in creating organizational change. They add new dimensions to the notion of resistance to change.

Mysticism and Its Companions

The above definitions direct our attention to everyday aspects of the workplace. The workplace is filled with events that contain many aspects of mystical experience. One need not be particularly openminded to grasp the significance of the argument presented here. In this chapter, mysticism and its derivatives are first linked to the workplace, followed by an examination of the significance of mysticism in understanding common workplace attributes and dynamics.

Mysticism

The existence of workplaces filled with executives who grasp at management fads in the hope of magically repairing their organizations is all too common (Micklethwait and Woolridge 1998). A great deal of what we call management today has little or no scientific justification or rationale drawn from rigorous reality testing (Allcorn et al. 1996). Rather, many executives rely on management methods that make intuitive sense to them, such as setting grand goals (Chapter 4) and creating performance incentives (Chapter 5) that are almost magically expected to direct employee effort. In fact, it often appears that the embrace of one management fad after another amounts to a collective self-delusional state shared by executives in many organizations. A close inspection of public and private organizations reveals additional examples of mysticism in the workplace. The following brief examples point to mysticism in the management suite, where executives rely upon intuitive versus intellectual apprehension and self-delusional versus accurate reality testing.

At the risk of appearing to introduce a political agenda into this work,

I direct the reader's attention to what have been referred to as "faith-based" rationales for decisions made by high-level government officials in the early twenty-first century. The use of religion, and more specifically God, in informing public policy directly introduces intuitive processes (knowing God and God's message or will) and unknowable organizational realities into consideration. A leader who reports that he is informed or directed by God to do something sets forth a context in which further inquiry and analysis of an intellectual sort is not necessary or stifled. Once the decision is made, there is no need to look back upon it or question it. Equally clear, regardless of the outcome, it is going to be God's will, or to add a slightly different spin, Allah's will. In a world of incomplete and imperfect information, decisions are nonetheless made.

When it comes to self-delusion, one has to wonder, "What were they thinking at Enron and WorldCom?" to list but two examples from recent events in which organizational reality turns out to have been stranger than fiction. Can these otherwise intelligent and well-educated executives really believe that they could indefinitely falsify, pyramid, and conceal poor operating results via acquisition and an obfuscating paper trail? Will the outrageous spending of chief executive officers on themselves, compensation packages, and golden parachutes, forever go unnoticed? Perhaps not, based on the recent departures of the CEOs of American Airlines, FreddieMac, and the New York Stock Exchange, to list but three.

Little more need be said. Intuitive management decision making and self-delusion are not uncommon and are most often supported by other processes such as mystification. Before proceeding to an inspection of mystification in the workplace, a time-out is needed to review both sides of the argument associated with mysticism. Mysticism, as defined, embraces the unmeasurable, nonscientific side of life that is frequently filled with spiritual, religious, and intuitive experience that is part of life, including the workplace. Since rational values and processes do not govern the workplace, understanding workplace mysticism in greater depth is important.

A Time-Out to Inspect Both Sides of the Coin

It is not difficult to find negative organizational qualities and outcomes when mysticism is involved. Intuitive decisions and gut reactions are not always right, and the development of a homogeneous group of believers by a leader (Chapter 9) can lead to disastrous self-sealing and self-fulfilling outcomes. Extreme examples are religious cults that lead their members into mass suicide. However, it is also important to not throw the baby out with the bath water. Mitroff and Denton (1999, xiv) write,

> We believe that organizational science can no longer avoid analyzing, understanding, and treating organizations as spiritual entities. We not only believe that organizations must become more spiritual if they are to serve the ethical needs of their stakeholders, but we also have important evidence to support our beliefs. Indeed, our data contain some of the strongest statistical findings we have ever witnessed. At the same time, we are the first to acknowledge that our data are far from conclusive given the limited samples in our study. Nonetheless, the data suggest strongly that those organizations that identify more strongly with spirituality or that have a greater sense of spirituality have employees who (1) are less fearful of their organizations, (2) are far less likely to compromise their basic beliefs and values in the workplace, (3) perceive their organizations as significantly more profitable, and (4) report that they can bring significantly more of their complete selves to work, specifically their creativity and intelligence—two qualities that are especially needed if organizations are to succeed in today's hyper-competitive environment.

Mitroff and Denton conclude that management of spirituality in the workplace has always been, should be, and will become a fundamental management task. And to the extent that, as the twenty-first century begins, religion, faith, and New Age spirituality are pressing their way to the forefront in politics, society, and the workplace, mysticism will become an ever-increasing part of work life.

William Guillory (2000, 25) directly links organizational success to adaptiveness that is supported by spirituality. He writes,

> [S]piritual values are often the source of an organization's ability to adapt effectively to change, particularly during difficulty or crisis. Unfortunately, adaptation is too often motivated by survival; and a survival mentality promotes short-term, adversarial behavior. On the other hand, adaptation based upon enduring spiritual values promotes behavior that is truly beneficial to customers, the organization, and the business system.

In this regard, spirituality is defined in a secular sense as inner consciousness and the source of inspiration, creativity, and wisdom. It encompasses a way of being that guides our lives and that need not be linked to religion and religious systems of beliefs, which Guillory (2000) believes are merely one form that spirituality can take.

It is also my belief that there is a spiritual and mystical presence in the workplace that must be considered alongside rationality and irrationality. Howard Stein, in his foreword to my book *Death of the Spirit in the American Workplace*, notes, "Much that has been written about organizations is a gloss on the surface of workplace life. It is not so much wrong as superficial and thereby incomplete. It attends to what we have come to agree is important and neglects what lies beyond the horizon or consensus" (Stein 2002, viii). In an effort to close this section with balance, it is important to note that there is a profoundly darker side to this consideration as well. Stein (2002, vii) cites the following sobering example from history:

> Clearly, workplace "spirit" and "soul" can signify many things. To the Nazi SS, it was bound up with an elaborate unconscious fantasy and conscious ideology of fatherland, motherland, nation, menacing Jews, and a radical split between "us" and "them," "good" and "evil" (Koenigsberg 1975). The "defensive" spirit of "good" was predicated and dependent upon a concomitant malevolent group spirit, that of the Jews. The SS were specially "called upon" to help eliminate—exterminate—that evil. Himmler's use of "spirit" is now better understood to be constitutive of a defensive, rigidly closed system of thought, feeling, and action that occupies the core of all "totalitarian spirit."

This grim reminder of the darker potential in organizational spirituality underscores a sense of social responsibility that must accompany any discussion of mysticism and spirituality in a workplace where believing is more important than knowing. This once again returns us to examples of early-twenty-first-century corporate corruption, where glorified corporate leaders led their flocks astray by relying upon mystification in financial information and reports.

Mystification

When it comes to mystification, the old phrase "If you can't convince them, confuse them" comes to mind. In particular, managers and executives throughout an organizational hierarchy often expend a considerable amount of time and effort obscuring what is actually happening.

They do not want to be held accountable for adverse operating outcomes that will, they hope, not be discovered on their watch (Baum 1987). It is also not uncommon for organization members to have no idea how a particular decision was made. It may have been conceived and handed down by the CEO who, it could be said, believes, feels, and intuits that the industry will be moving in a certain direction or that a particular product or strategy will be successful. Concrete information and first-hand knowledge of operations can, in those instances, take a backseat to intuitive and possibly delusional organizational dynamics (wishful thinking). It would not be unfair to say that many things that happen in our organizations are shrouded in mystery, as revealed by subsequent investigations of organizational failures and analyses of major public policy legislation.

A brief vignette is informative. The former CEO of a large corporation once a year closed the door to his office and stayed in there for days. He slept there. Food was ordered in. His office had its own bath. Prior to assuming this isolated hibernative state, he collected up immense computerized reports to digest behind his closed door. Days later he emerged with the new marketing plan in hand. No one knew how he created it, and it was not open to question. The organization suddenly had a new direction (right or wrong) that everyone was expected to follow. Questioning its validity was not permitted nor indeed possible, as no rationale was ever provided.

Examples of mystification in the workplace are so abundant as to resemble background radiation or organizational wallpaper. Among the most common aspects of organizations where mystification is found is how the vast array of "numbers" found in the information system are managed. Numbers, however, need not necessarily mean anything at all, and they are frequently "massaged" to provide support for one view over another. In Vietnam, the numbers did not lie. We were winning the war right up to the point we lost it. In this case, not only were the numbers of enemy dead, missions flown, and tonnage of bombs dropped distorted as they flowed up the chain of command, they were the wrong numbers to measure results. The numbers selected by management (George McNamara) to evaluate operations did not ultimately mean anything, and, worse, their use in some instances detracted from the possibility of achieving success. Much the same can be said for private entities such as large corporations that often have good numbers right up to the point of bankruptcy, as evidenced by the growing frequency of stockholder lawsuits. As we will see below, mystification is also often accompanied by awe-inspiring images generated by CEOs and executives.

Mystify

Part of the management repertoire of many senior-level executives is a tendency to try to awe others with their power and authority while, at the same time, being hard to hold accountable. Efforts to hold them accountable lead to a perplexing array of bewildering responses and assertions. In some ways, this effort to mystify follows the old adage, "The best defense is a good offense."

The first response might be to retreat behind one's power and authority, implying that bullying, threatening, and intimidating others is the likely next step. "How dare you question my decision?" "Any problems with its implementation are the result of incompetent others and not following directions." The "shock and awe" strategy can work very well in the practiced hands of a senior-level executive or CEO. Any further questioning can become a career-limiting proposition.

The ability to mystify on the part of senior-level executives all the way down to supervisors is a common element of our daily work lives. Many times the possible emergence of "shock and awe" is enough to cause everyone to keep their heads down and seek shelter in their organizational foxholes. The fact that it is often too dangerous to speak out is underscored by the notion of having to protect whistleblowers. The messenger is often dependably maimed, discredited, and even summarily disposed of via termination. A dictator or cult figure may have more permanent measures in mind. No one wants to make such a career-limiting decision.

It is also clear that the ability to mystify directly acts to support mystification and organizational mysticism. This ability to "shock and awe" is also reinforced by the mystique of the all-powerful CEO who can become much more like a cult figure that we often like to admit.

Mystique

Mystique figures heavily in both the workplace and the political realm. The covers of *Fortune* magazine serve to elevate CEOs to a hard-to-touch venerated status, and some of these leaders come to have a presence that is larger than life. Highly visible cultlike figures such as former

Chrysler CEO Lee Iacoca, former GE CEO "Neutron" Jack Welch, former New York mayor Rudy Giuliani and, of course, none other than "Chain Saw" Al Dunlap (who single-handedly decimated Sunbeam, leaving behind a trail of mystifying, misleading, and false numbers) are examples. Public figures like these have achieved royal and even godlike status within their organizations and the business community. Questioning them somehow does not seem prudent or even survivable. Their skills, abilities, and results are described in such a way as to elevate them to an awesome and mythical status that encourages a cultlike following both within and outside their organization. They may also articulate leadership and management philosophies that are not always easy to pin down in practice. These leaders' larger-than-life status makes them imposing and not readily questioned, which serves to support intuitive decision-making on their part. It also protects them from reality testing that may shatter self-delusion as to their inherent greatness and the righteousness of their vision and direction. The CEO as mythic character is discussed further below. Their presence and exploits are also often writ large in organizational mythology.

Myth

Organizations are filled with rich mythologies of what it is like to work within the organization and who the leader is. Myths include symbols that are incorporated in shared beliefs and emotional themes (Diamond 1993; Schwartz 1990). In practice, interviewing organization members often brings to the surface stories about great successes and humiliating defeats, as well as those that tell of noble deeds and destructive interpersonal behavior.

Workplace myths are created by the gradual subjection of events to revisionism. Some aspects of the event are forgotten, others are accentuated, new elements are added, and it is eventually recast in the best of traditions of narrative history and storytelling. Not only is it interesting to hear the myth, it is important to appreciate that it conveys information about what it is like to work within the organization. Examples of organizational myths are abundant.

One good example is a story that is told about the new chancellor of a small liberal arts college. The college has, as a part of its culture and heritage, a focus on being student friendly and supportive. The chancellor, so the story is told, was in the student cafeteria one day and asked a student if there was anything he could do for him. The student did not recognize the chancellor and, thinking that he was a member of the cafeteria's staff, requested a soft drink. The chancellor dutifully went to fetch the drink while the student's friends informed him just who was fetching his drink. A story such as this stresses the importance of valuing students and their development and well-being, and the value of humility on the part of faculty and administrators in the service of this goal. Yet the story is more important than what actually happened.

At the other end of the spectrum, myth can be used to transform an event into something more acceptable for organization members. A university course in public administration included a learning opportunity that was intended to be stressful so that students might observe group dynamics and themselves when operating under stress. Two group process consultants entered a classroom full of students who had taken it upon themselves to rearrange their chairs from concentric circles set up by the facilitators into a giant circle. Two chairs had been left in the middle facing each other for the consultants to sit in. Clearly, the class members were anxious about the learning experience and responded by displaying a considerable amount of aggression toward the not-yet-present process consultants. The facilitators occupied the chairs and the group unavoidably focused on their presence in the center. Why were they there? What were they doing or not doing? Eventually a student acting alone dragged the facilitators sitting in their chairs out of the center and into the large circle. This represented a physical assault of sorts and the second consultant, before being dragged out of the center, expressly requested not to be. This event occurred at the start of the semester, and two subsequent experiential learning opportunities were provided, with the last ending in an opportunity to discuss the overall experience of these students. The discussion proceeded as though this event had never happened. When brought up, it was initially ignored. After several efforts to get the group to discuss what had happened, one student said something along the following lines: What he could recall was that the group was trying to be friendly and helpful to the facilitators. They were all alone in the center. By dragging them out they were taking care of them. Others spoke up to agree. This is an extreme, but not entirely uncommon, example of how organizational events such as mass layoffs, a particularly vicious dressing down or termination, or a major accident (the *Challenger* disaster) are often transformed in myth to be more digestible.

At this point its should be reasonably clear that mysticism and its companions are a common feature of the workplace, although we may not often realize it. Our discussion thus far has focused on illuminating the nature of workplace experiences to anchor them in the reader's first-hand experience of the workplace. The profound impact of the leader merits some additional elaboration.

CEO as Mythic Figure

Very often organizations are dominated by their leaders, among whom there is a wide range of interpersonal and leadership styles. These styles can range from caring and nurturing to combative, threatening, and bordering on dangerous and anti-social. This range of behavior must be blended with issues of technical competence and insight and the ability to effectively envision and direct work in the pursuit of profit and mission fulfillment in the public sector. Many combinations of leadership style elements are possible, making the variety of CEO leadership styles limitless. These styles can also change over time and may vary based on the leadership context.

The idea of the CEO as a mythic figure in organizational life adds a somewhat different dimension to the mix of considerations. This mythic presence will have some of its origins in the CEO's style. His performance may additionally contain stories with mythic properties that take on a timeless nature. The CEO is also the "leader in mind," meaning that he is partially a mental creation of employees, who develop their own idea of who the leader is and then act as though this is true. The leader may then be treated in a manner consistent with these mental representations. As a result, the leader may begin to see himself to be like these representations—after all, everyone seems to think so.

A convergence of the leader's personal desires to be admired and feared with his ability to perform well in a role of leadership and his leadership style (nurturing, intimidating, laissez-faire, micromanaging) gradually develops. This convergence must also include the response of followers, who may gradually have become more homogeneous as a result of selecting in and out. The notion of the mythic figure also contains qualities of a historical and cultural nature that inform how leaders should lead and how they have been seen over the ages. In particular, literature, theater, and movies are filled with mythical images of grand leaders that predispose us to respond to corporate and institutional leaders by attributing to them superhuman qualities that place them above the masses. Soldiers on a battlefield, for instance, must believe that their leaders are omniscient and all-powerful and will not err and lead them to their death. To a lesser extent, much the same can be said for employees' beliefs that the CEO will keep the organization functioning well to maintain their employment.

The Managerial Mystique

Abraham Zaleznik, in his book *The Managerial Mystique* (1989), suggests that one reason why American firms experience difficulty in being competitive nationally and internationally is a lack of effective leadership. The managerial mystique is described as a process in which form wins out over substance. Managers are perhaps trained, as well as encouraged, to focus on controlling processes and people in roles by relying upon primarily technical means, such as careful monitoring and incentive systems. This strategy revisits Taylorism and its reliance upon science and engineering principles to determine the best possible way to design, organize, and control work. The larger implication is that employees are like circuit boards in a computer. This dehumanizing perspective assumes that employees will accept and follow instructions, whatever they may be. Terms like *managerialism* and *administrationism* have been coined to describe this approach that routinizes leadership in the workplace. The negative potential of bureaucracy is fulfilled where hierarchical relationships and control mechanisms, resistance to change, risk aversion, turf protection, lack of creativity, and rule-mindedness abound. Krantz and Gilmore (1989) define managerialism as a technocratic ideology that views analytical tools, developed to help managers make decisions, as ends in themselves. They write, "when a tool or technique of management is treated as a magical solution, . . . members (of an organization) invest their hope in the technique or approach as if it, by itself, will help resolve complex, conflictual situations" (1989, 14). Doing it by the numbers to meet the numbers is not a particularly reflective approach. It does not encourage double-loop learning that calls into question what we are doing (Argyris 1983; Argyris and Schon 1982).

In sum, managerialism represents a form of ideology founded on the assumption that the pursuit of efficiency by scientific means is an invisible guiding hand that directs managers in optimally achieving organizational goals. Like all ideologies, it does not encourage reflection and critical thinking but rather uncritical acceptance. In effect, faith is placed in its efficacy being self-evident. Herein we once again return to a quality of mysticism where one *knows* that "managerialism" is the proper course despite perhaps considerable evidence to the contrary (Blau and Meyer 1971; Downs 1967).

The Challenge of Organizational Change

Mysticism, myth, mystification, mystique, and mystifying others have all been described as existing within the workplace. Like a magician's performance, they all serve to misdirect attention from what is really going on and why. Anyone endeavoring to understand or lead organization change must appreciate this. The balance of this chapter links these organizational properties to the possibility of creating change.

Understanding the Organizational Subtext

Myths, mythical figures, and organizational mysticism serve to create a sense of shared culture that unconsciously directs thinking, feeling, and doing (Schein 1985). In particular, mythology, while presenting a story and message, contains a subtext that contributes to the creation of organizational culture. The imagery of the chancellor who fetched a soft drink speaks volumes about being humble, caring, nurturing, kind, self-effacing, giving, and charitable, and about self-esteem and self-worth disassociated from powerful positions. The story encourages us to get in touch with these human qualities. Similarly, collective amnesia about a threatening, frightening, and negative experience indicates not so much the omnipresent potential for group violence, but rather human vulnerability and fragility and the need to defend oneself and the group from threat. Acknowledging the history can be too painful. Organizational myth, therefore, while containing mysticism and mythical figures, most importantly contains a powerful influential subtext.

Consultants, newcomers, and reflective practitioners are often presented with stories. These have mythical qualities that provide implicit guidance to employees and point out how outsiders should see the leader, the leadership group, employees, and the organization. However, reality frequently fails to support the mythical imagery and the leader is found to have feet of clay. The organization may also be observed to have many deficiencies. Nonetheless, the myths are clung to, which raises for consideration exactly what purpose they serve. A common feature of myths is that they are relied upon to cover up, deny, and change realities that are disconcerting and threatening. Past glories may be reflected in myths that fill the organization with nostalgia and recollections of a past not necessarily supported by hard evidence (Gabriel 1999). Nonetheless, successes may be magically transformed into "who we are." They are captured in the myth and carried forward with a sense of reverence. Myths about leaders may also be perpetuated for utilitarian reasons, such as presenting the public and competitors with what amounts to an organizational surface or front. This person, while not reflective of the organization's true characteristics and abilities, may be awe-inspiring, thereby serving as a perimeter defense.

These are a few examples of the underlying meaning of the myths that reveal important insights into organizational life—insights that are essential to understand when contemplating organizational change. If not open to examination, the underlying nature of the subtext can yield many hard-to-discuss and highly energized resistances to organizational change.

Organizational Change in the Face of Performance Mystification

Most people with work experience have observed some extraordinary instances of organizational mystification. One does not have to look any further than egregious public examples: Enron, WorldCom, brokerage houses, mutual fund trading, and, in particular, the political realm, where the notion of "spin" is almost solely based on the utilitarian use of numbers and information to change reality to one's liking. In fact, the most depended upon and presumably concrete aspect of the workplace—financial management and reporting—often contains mystification in one form or another. Numbers and information may be omitted or selectively used. Analyses may contain unrevealed assumptions, or if they are revealed, mystification occurs in detailed footnotes that are almost unintelligible. There are also many opportunities to recast numbers by using graphs that mix in historical numbers that may not be comparable. Explanations may be immersed in excessive detail, which discourages insight by burying what may be learned in vast, complex, and hard-to-read reports. Mystification can also be extended to include interpretations of the data in which what one observes is not really true or there.

There is, then, little question as to whether mystification is present. Finding it is often as simple as having an awareness of a perceived gap between what is being said and reported and what one observes to be the case. Herein lies the significance of mystification when it comes to planning and implementing change. Much like the magician's performance, having one's attention focused on the numbers to the exclusion of knowing the organization serves to validate the mystification. This removes the important opportunity to call into question what is being said and reported. Concrete examples, in which what is reported does not appear to fit the operating realities, should be developed for discussion with the top management and organization members. In particular, it is important to not let the focus devolve into only examining the examples. It is essential to keep the focus on the examples as representative of a larger picture in which data collection, analysis, and reports can obfuscate reality and protect those responsible for the operating problems.

Mysticism and Workplace Irrationality

The presence of mysticism in the workplace is not hard to find. But there are limits to how much information can be collected and analyzed, and these limits are often compounded by time constraints. Executives are often called upon to make decisions and provide direction in situations where they depend upon their best judgment and practiced hand, both of which are linked to notions such as intuition and gut reactions. The executive chooses one decision over others and a specific direction from among many possible choices. If these actions are closely examined, there is many times limited evidence to support the choices being made. Nonetheless, "When in doubt, proceed." It is important to "not fiddle while the organization burns," or "sit on one's hands," or reach the point of "analysis paralysis." Many executives are of a mind to consistently do little investigation of a situation and the alternatives. It just does not suit them as individuals, and their style is a reflection of these personal propensities to avoid detailed data collection and analysis. After receiving a synopsis, they prefer most often to "shoot from the hip."

Many times there are no clear paths for decision making, and while some choices are better than others, almost any choice will do. How can this be in the rational workplace? The answer is, the organization, at least in the shorter run, may have achieved success in a niche where competitive threat is minimized and client or consumer loyalty somewhat assured. Decisions, and the giving of direction, may be "good enough." In these instances, executives and managers are not particularly encouraged to do their homework. However, the cumulative effect of "winging it" can eventually compromise organizational performance, or more commonly, compromise profitability. The CEO of a company in which there are many opportunities to reduce cost and improve operations may be of the firm opinion that she is doing just fine. The company is making a substantial profit, so "Why rock the boat?"

This discussion has made more concrete and accessible the notion that irrational processes, as well as mysticism and its companions, are common attributes of organizational life. Organization members do not consistently use their intellectual abilities to comprehend what is going on and why. Rather, there often emerges a process filled with hard-to-know and hard-to-explain dynamics driven by psychologically defensive leaders who have embraced leadership styles consistent with their unconscious propensities. The answer may be handed down from on high, not to be questioned. Work methods and organizational culture that contain many hard-to-grasp intuitive processes are often accompanied by an irrational context that taps the possibility that realities exist beyond perceptual or intellectual apprehension.

Organizational life, therefore, often depends upon maintaining some myths regarding the unquestioned efficacy of such things as rational organization design, perfectly engineered work processes, and the search for excellence and profit. Considerable faith is usually placed in the notion that organizations can be scientifically designed and engineered to be just the right size. In the 1990s, wave upon wave of organizational reengineering, redesign, and downsizing occurred. Consulting companies determined just the right size and organizational design and, although not supported in most instances by good operating outcomes, they continue to pursue their craft with a missionary zeal usually only associated with religious mysticism (Micklethwait and Woolridge 1998; Schwartz 1990).

Much the same can be said for the more mundane aspects of organizations that are supposed to run like a clock. Everyone and everything, it is hoped, is rationally coordinated, economized, and fine-tuned to produce continuous growth of sales and services that are demonstrably cost-effective. It is, however, often the case that organizations do not resemble a Swiss watch in operation. A brief inspection usually reveals unresolved conflict, interpersonal competition and aggression, wasted resources, inefficiencies, and missed opportunities to improve and innovate. Images of organizations as open systems and belief in organic growth are similarly relied upon to almost magically explain how they work (Morgan 1986).

Where unconscious individual and organizational dynamics are at work, many aspects of organizational life will contain mystical qualities accompanied by myth, mystique, mythology, and mystifying analyses and pronouncements. Unconscious and irrational organizational dynamics that, most often, may not be directly called into question leave in their wake hard-to-understand processes, direction, and outcomes. In this regard, organizational mysticism and its companions can be thought of as the long shadow cast by less-than-rational leaders and group dynamics.

In Final Analysis

This chapter has called into question the rationality of the workplace, where rational decision making is the key to achieving organizational success. Many organizations endeavor to capture information with their information systems and analyze it. However, in most organizations, all of the important data are not captured and the available data, if accurate, timely, and representative, are frequently not turned into knowledge. Thus, the workplace is filled with many intuitive and not-so-rational processes that, if explored, reveal an ultimate reliance upon workplace qualities and realities that are sensed rather than understood intellectually.

The next chapter continues the task of inspecting and reflecting upon the workplace and workplace experience. There are a number of workplace attributes that are found with enough frequency as to be considered common. These attributes contain or contribute to organizational dysfunction and are largely driven by irrationality and mysticism.

12

Uncommon Commonality

> The task is the study of human nature. At the moment of starting to write this book I am all too aware of the vastness of such an enterprise. Human nature is almost all we have.
>
> —Donald Winnicott, *Human Nature* (1988)

It is much easier to spot something that is moving against an unchanging background than to see prey or a predator that does not move. In the organizational world, twenty-five years of research, organizational analysis, and intervention have gradually led to the perception of a discomforting presence of hard-to-see commonalities in the workplace. While differing in their specifics, they are distressingly the same. If all organizations are different and all leaders are different, why do they so often seem to be the same in terms of how they operate? It is almost as though, like background radiation in the universe, organizational life and leaders possess an irresistible and universal tendency to re-create the commonalities.

This sense of commonality contains elements that are consistently found across a broad array of organizations. This commonality is also familiar to everyone who has work experience, although it is most often not observed because it blends into the background. The list of common elements described in this chapter is not intended to exhaust the possibilities. In fact, it is often hard to see what is right in front of you. The elements presented here are provided in the spirit of self-discovery on the reader's part. There are other elements that careful scrutiny and critical thinking will reveal.

The list of common elements leads to an obvious question: Why do these commonalities exist? The insights and theoretical perspectives presented by many authors have been mulled over and explored for their utility in answering this question. However, each perspective has fallen short of explaining the overreaching commonality encountered. There appears to be only one commonality that is everywhere within organizational life that, in its diversity, can account for the existence of commonality. This necessarily reductionist but intellectually sound explanation finds that human nature is the commonality that, despite is many faces, yields the commonalities discussed here.

The Elements of Commonality

There are some features one consistently finds in most organizations. The following categories are so frequently encountered as to permit the conclusion that organizations share them in common. These categories, while discussed separately, are interactive and cannot be easily separated one from the other. Depending on the organization and its leader, one or two may take precedent over the others. The linkages between these elements of commonality may also be seen not only to reinforce each other but also to be points on a circle. This emphasizes the systemic nature of the relationships among the elements that should be fairly obvious to those who have encountered them in the workplace. Yet they may be so common that they are merely accepted as part of organizational life. The goal here is to make the distinction.

Bad Management

Bad management, one might think, is not omnipresent in the workplace. It is to be avoided. However, one consulting company bet its bottom dollar on finding bad management. It used as its marketing and sales tool the offer of a free organizational assessment. This involved paying several consultants for usually a two-week interval to evaluate the operations of a company. This was not a small expense and on the surface might appear to be a problematic risk-taking approach. How often were significant enough operating problems going to be found to produce a large service contract to fix the problems, thereby paying back the cost of the consulting engagement and creating profit for the company? When asked, a seasoned executive with over thirty years of experience who worked for this consulting company reported a number of concrete examples of typical costly operating problems that had been found and led to contracts where many millions of dollars of savings could be had. Distressingly, the examples he provided made achieving easily obtainable cost savings and improved performance a "no brainer." In fact, he reported only a few instances in which a company was found that was really well run.

The unavoidable but distressing conclusion one has to draw is that most corporations and public organizations are not run very well. They are, in fact, often badly managed. Bad, poor, and marginal management is a pervasive commonality that is perhaps, upon reflection, no news to anyone. Things just do not run like they should.

These organizations usually make sufficient income to stay in business, which some might describe as "good enough management." The problem is, of course, things could be run better, yielding more profit, greater success, and creating sustainable growth and future organizational viability. Bad management can also be thought of as having many shared attributes. The list of possibilities spans from executives who just simply do not seem to have a clue how to operate a business to organizations dwarfed by their own history of exceptional dysfunctions, in-fighting, and failure to thrive. The number of possible examples is limitless. A few will have to suffice.

A large clinical department in an academic health sciences center requested help from another department in dealing with a professional fee billing problem. Staff trained in systems analysis, audit, and professional fee billing were volunteered to help out. A thorough analysis was completed and recommendations developed to repair the problem. However, during the review a number of additional problems were identified that were costing the department substantial lost revenue. A meeting was called with the department chairman and his administrator to discuss the findings and recommendations. Both were appreciative of the work and agreed that the changes would solve the problem. At the close of the meeting, it was suggested that other areas in the billing process could benefit from a similar review. The chairman and administrator looked at each other for a moment, and the chairman responded that they had everything else under control. A second effort that provided examples was equally unsuccessful. It was fairly clear that the chairman and the administrator lacked an in-depth understanding of billing processes and their department's deficiencies. In this case, ignorance resulted in costly bliss.

A large independent film-processing facility was experiencing a number of operating problems that compromised service. An experienced engineer was hired by the chief executive officer (CEO) to get things straightened out. The importance of this new role was highlighted by placing the engineer in a large office next door to the CEO. Expectations were high. He rapidly analyzed a number of major problems and developed ways to fix them. However, his work also revealed how ineffective the CEO had been in dealing with these problems in the past. The new role also implicitly limited the CEO's ability to make frequent but poorly informed changes to production processes. Gradually, many of the engineer's recommendations were rejected by the CEO, who also often countermanded changes he made to deal with production problems. The hoped-for improvements from the engineer did not materialize. There was also a growing tension between the CEO and the engineer. Consultants were eventually hired to take a look at operations. When they started, they found the engineer's office had been moved to a small office at the opposite end of the building from the CEO's. He complained he was not really allowed to do his job and had been ordered to work on buying used equipment (one source of the problems), which kept him on the road much of the time. His value added was minimized while the CEO continued to roam at will throughout the facility making misguided changes to operations. Not only were things not better, but the engineer's salary had increased payroll expenses.

These are but two examples of bad management. Many others could be cited. In this regard, the balance of the list of elements of commonality discussed here should be familiar.

Mediocrity

Mediocrity characterizes an individual or organization having neither a good nor a bad performance, but rather an average performance. Average is so common in organizational life that it must be a safe place to be. Those who are really bad employees are either brought up to speed or eliminated. Those who consistently exceed expectations (rate busters) threaten others by receiving rewards such as promotions and raises (Allcorn 1991). Those who achieve outstanding performance are most often systematically undermined, limited, maligned, bullied, shunned, and isolated until they either get the message, burn out, or leave. Mediocre organizations are often filled with stories about good ideas gone awry and instances where innovation was tried and failed. Those who led the efforts are no longer employed. An examination of organizational performance, including the performance of subdivisions, many times reveals that things have not changed much over time. The organization is, for the time being, holding its own relative to competitors and customer expectations. There is also often a track record of neither hiring the best individuals nor retaining those who distinguish themselves. Phrases like "the best need not apply" and "brain drain" seem to fit.

Mediocrity can be achieved by many means. A pervasive sense of mediocrity is often deeply embedded in an organization's culture. Employees come to understand that the leader and his or her management team are not really that interested or willing to assume the risk to move the organization to the next level of performance. A second common source of mediocrity is a CEO who micromanages just about everything. This individual's pursuit of control is threatened by new ideas, especially if they come from someone else. There may be few who are willing to follow the leader into the zone of risky business of innovation and change. The safety of keeping things as they are often seems to be the tacit assumption driving organizational behavior. Mediocrity is, therefore, a commonality familiar to most employees of large organizations as well as smaller ones.

Politics

Public and organizational politics are common features of work life. Government is infused with politics even though departments of state and their divisions and programs are supposedly organizations with clear missions, performance criteria, and public accountability. This is, of course, infrequently the case because of their underlying politicized basis for operation. Often, political struggles for control of the agenda lead to confusion, misalignment of budgets to operations, and, at times, rampant and poorly planned change that precludes the development of meaningful measures to promote accountability. The end result is that everyone loses, as is illustrated by the following example.

An inspection of a state division of family services revealed a staggering array of problems driven by the polarizing political ideologies of the left and the right. Social workers assigned to investigate and manage child abuse were not paid well and filling open positions was difficult. Many unfilled positions existed alongside a constant rate of departures. Social workers were assigned case loads that ranged from 300 to 500 and more. These numbers exceeded the time available to work the cases. The social workers, as a result, did little to no social work and were resigned to this situation. They were reduced to processing forms and dealing with critical incidents. They did not, in fact, even attempt to process all the paperwork that was required. There was too little time. One social worker, who had been on the job for more than a decade, reported how things had been done in the past: "We used to go out and see the families and children." The politics of the left had set the program up. The politics of the right had underfunded it. The social workers, parents, and children were caught in the middle.

This example is but one drawn from a vast reservoir of possibilities. Corporations are filled with "politics" as well. Interpersonal competition and rivalries, when combined with incessant jockeying for resources among divisions, frequently lead to destructive outcomes that unnecessarily consume time and resources, thereby compromising organizational performance. Once again, the possibilities are endless but also familiar.

Information Systems

The familiar management phrase, "If you can't measure it, you can't manage it," reflects the need for detailed operating information. Having said that, it is not hard to find organizations that (a) do not collect very much detailed information, (b) do a poor job of it if done, and (c) fail to use information to their best advantage if some or a lot of it is available. These situations have a number of companions, such as an unwillingness to invest in information technology and qualified information management professionals. Another frequent companion is the presence of a few executives who enjoy playing around with computers and information systems, including database software. At the other extreme, there are instances where significant investment has been made but yielded few results. It is not uncommon to find networking hardware and software that is not appropriately selected or developed. This leads to informational outcomes that no one is sure are accurate, complete, timely, or representative, and systems that are costly to operate and not user-friendly.

A case in point is that of a CEO who invariably responded to partial, inaccurate, and even meaningless management reports and analyses generated by a mostly out-of-control information system. He accepted the information at face value and proceeded to direct work to remediate the problems reflected in the information. His efforts usually resulted in a substantial redirection of time, effort, and resources to fix a nonexistent problem or perhaps worse, go about fixing a problem in a manner that was either not cost-effective, not going to work at all, or created a cascade of new operating problems. Once again, problems like these are why the consulting company mentioned above was so successful at making a profit. They could always find significant operating problems and easy-to-implement solutions.

Strategic Direction

Why are we doing this and where are we headed are good questions that deserve answers. Yet much of what passes for strategic planning does not entirely answer these questions. Once written, plans are often put on the shelf. Measures of variance from plan are not developed, and the plan is not kept current. Planning is ultimately more of a process than a one-time event. Often, the "great man," the leader of the organization, seems to hold a sense of strategic direction in his mind that remains forever undocumented. It is usually communicated in a fragmented manner that does not facilitate deducing the leader's vision. When plans are shared in small increments, the leader's personality features and character often drive the process. It is common to see organizations in which employees have no clear idea what the organization is striving to accomplish, where it is headed, and how it will get there. If such things as values and mission statements are available, they are not effectively communicated to employees nor followed by those in senior management. Management might say one thing and do another (Argyris and Schon 1982).

In sum, strategic direction creates a sense of unification as to purpose and the ability to evaluate organizational performance. This permits midcourse corrections and timely adaptive response to competitors. It also promotes organizational integration and accurate reality testing. Unfortunately, meaningful and operationalized strategic direction is very often missing from twenty-first-century organizations.

In Sum—The Elements of Commonality

These organizational problem areas are so frequently encountered that they can be thought of as being shared in common by all organizations, to some extent, most of the time. Anyone with work experience in a large organization will have encountered these commonalities and others not discussed. These elements of commonality can also be readily described, pointed out, analyzed, and changed by management and consultants in an endless, self-perpetuating cycle that reinforces their presence. It is rarely the case that the elements are fixed to the point that reemergence is not assured. We might then ponder why this is so. Is there an element of commonality that all of these share in common? I suggest that there is: human nature and the many complexities it introduces into the workplace dominate all aspects of organizations, the performance of work, and work life.

The Universality of Human Nature in the Workplace

Human nature as used here is an umbrella term for the many facets of personality, character, and psychology. Unfortunately, the darker side of human nature is so often a pervasive presence within the workplace as to constitute a fundamental underlying commonality. The difficulty of introducing human nature into this discussion is that it can be approached in diverse ways, such as exploring personality and character disorders or psychological defenses in the workplace (Allcorn and Diamond 1997). There can be no dispute that human beings and their psychological nature are the single most dominant influence in the workplace. What can then be said to illuminate this omnipresent complexity? The following conceptual organizers are drawn from the literature on psychoanalytic theory. Each makes a contribution to understanding human nature in the workplace. The different perspectives provided are intended to encourage critical thinking about human nature rather than provide a one-size-fits-all point of view.

Narcissism

If there is one thing about human nature in the workplace that introduces interpersonal and organizational dysfunction more than others it is likely captured under the heading of narcissism. Narcissism can be viewed as encompassing a range from pathologically excessive to pathologically absent with a mid-point of healthy narcissism (see Chapter 6). The narcissist thinks a lot of himself and wants to make sure others do as well. This individual has a big ego and takes up a lot of interpersonal and organizational space. He may be described as self-important, self-centered, and making egocentric self-attributions that do not readily match up to the self in reality, and this is a problem. The narcissist's self-inflated sense of his own capabilities and self-worth can be understood to be a reaction to deeply held but not acknowledged feelings of low self-worth. It is, therefore, critical that reality testing be strictly modulated and filtered to avoid the surfacing of this contrary self-experience. To this end, the narcissist in the workplace seeks the love and admiration of others by any means available. Others come to understand that failing to provide these external sources of narcissistic "feel-good" supplies will threaten this individual, who may respond with a temper tantrum and possibly aggression.

This discussion underscores the deeply psychological nature of narcissism. Narcissism is a means of coping with a distressing experience of anxiety about one's lovability, admirability, and efficacy. Many psychological defenses are employed to adjust for the reality that these self-conceptions are not entirely or even partially accurate. Psychological defenses such as selective attention, rationalization, denial, and intellectualization filter and transform reality. Instances in which others steadfastly challenge these perceptions may be met with psychological splitting and projection, where the other becomes all bad and must be annihilated to defend the all-good self.

At the opposite end of the continuum are those with pathologically diminished narcissism. These individuals see themselves as not meriting love and respect, and they respond by embracing this self-view, with the outcome that they may become self-effacing and dependent on others to take care of them (see Chapter 7 and the discussion of organizational culture). They essentially know themselves to be worthless and helpless. They will follow but not lead, and they will admire others who are not expected to be admiring in return.

In contrast to these pathologies, healthy narcissism permits the individual to perform accurate reality testing and accept the risks that come with innovation and change without feeling overly anxious and defensive. Others are experienced as supportive along a range, and others experience this individual as open to positive and negative feedback. There is, then, a sense a balance within the self and relative to others who are not dominated or submitted to.

We all have these tendencies from time to time. However, when they range toward the extreme and are constantly present, they may be observed to contain destructive qualities that harm individuals (loss of self), others, and the organization.

False Self

The notion of false self possesses explanatory power when it comes to understanding both self-experience and our experience of others in the workplace. Masterson (1988) suggests that we have many self-images. Who we are in a meeting with a superior may be at variance with who we are in a meeting with subordinates. Who we are at work (powerful or subordinate) may not be who we are outside of work. It is, therefore, obvious that these multiple and conflicting self-images can create a sense of being adrift in our own identity as well as experiencing ourselves as fragmented into various parts. What is important from Masterson's point of view is that these various self-images must be successfully integrated to create a unity of self that tolerates the different and compartmentalized self-images.

This discussion pertains to the workplace. A highly competent female executive may assume a role of submissive wife at home. An effective leader of a division, department, or group may be treated as incompetent and ineffective by a superior who aggresses against and denigrates the individual. This individual must submit to the abusive domination or fear losing her job. We may be admired for athletic, musical, or artistic prowess outside of work but relegated to menial and denigrating work in the workplace. More examples are not needed to underscore the presence of divergent self-images in our daily lives. They are there, and once again they are an outcome of human nature. We as individuals are not unidimensional, and it is this implicit complexity that drives the creation on our part of these self-images.

Masterson (1988) also notes that a failure to successfully integrate these aspects of the self can lead to the creation of a false self. One or both parents may consistently reprimand a child, who, by nature, enjoys loud and boisterous play. The child's basic tendency to enjoy this play thus takes on a new dimension. Children who are engulfed by an oppressive parenting process must gradually give up aspects of who they are and adopt a sense of self (false self) that is consistent with the parenting demands in order to retain life-giving attachment. Masterson suggests that Jean-Paul Sartre was such a child who retreated into a false self where "being and nothingness" were both present. It is, therefore, important to appreciate that the false self reflects existential anxiety in which the self is reduced, minimized, lost, or possibly annihilated, leaving only the experience of false self.

We are pulled in many directions throughout our lives. Within the workplace we might one day be rewarded for innovation and the next day punished for suggesting a new idea.

Ego Ideal

Howard Schwartz (1990) extends Masterson's reflections on the false self by using the notion of an ego ideal. He suggests, as mentioned in Chapter 8, that we tend to uncritically take in aspects of the workplace and that by doing so we displace our previously held ego ideal with an organizational ego ideal. This organizational ideal does not reflect what the organization is or how it operates in practice, but rather an image of how the ideal organization should operate. Schwartz writes that it must first be an image of ideal social interaction where employees relate "to each other in frictionless, mutually supportive, job-specific interactions" (1990, 36). Everyone is ideally the same and treated identically. If one person receives a reward, everyone receives a reward. Schwartz specifies two additional organizational ideal attributes: "Second, the ideal must be powerful—in the sense that the individuals, as organized, are rational, know what they are doing, and are competent to do what they are doing and in control of the situation. . . . And third, it must be free of anxiety at the level of identity" (1990, 36). Organization members avoid feeling obliged or compelled to conform to the workplace by identifying themselves with the organizational ideal, where they may experience their work and conformity as a desire on their part for free self-expression. The experience of internal and external is avoided. We become more than happy to do the bidding of the organization, as it is us.

The important critical aspect of this argument is that the organizational ideal, like its counterpart the ego ideal, is "formulated as a response to anxiety, and we are driven to pursue it by anxiety. It represents an end to the anxiety that drives us toward it" (Schwartz 1990, 9). Avoidance of the distressing experience of anxiety is, therefore, a critical component of our adjusting to life outside of the workplace as well as within it. Merely conforming and submitting is insufficient, as these acts are self-alienating and distressing. However, if we fully and uncritically embrace the fantastic creation of a perfectly nurturing and care-taking organizational ideal, we can then work within the organization without feelings of being dominated, controlled, vulnerable, and dependent. The self/other boundary can be thought of as collapsing in a fusion of self with the fantastic nature of the organizational idea.

This outcome results in a constant press to fulfill the fantasy while at the same time creating a context in which organization members may, without anxiety, shame, guilt, or conscience, seek to carry out the organization's will regardless of how socially pathological and morally corrupt these actions are. This assessment serves to inform our understanding of the "crooked E" (Enron) and WorldCom, as well as corruption in the financial markets. Good people did bad things that supported the unethical, illegal actions of others.

Basic Assumption Groups

Wilfred Bion (1961) conceived of the notion that groups that meet often seem to be working on things that are not on the agenda. His research and theorizing eventually revealed what he believed to be a number of underlying basic assumptions (pairing, dependency, fight/flight) about how group dynamics work. This perspective introduces the important notion that human nature is largely a part of and determined by the interpersonal world. In particular, the workplace is filled with group dynamics that are often hard to understand. Bion's notions can frequently be observed to be at work in all types of groups. Some may seem to be waiting to be saved by the emergence of several individuals who are willing to work together (pairing) or told what to do by anyone willing to offer direction (dependency). Similarly, some groups steadfastly avoid performing work that is assigned (flight from the primary task), or see fit to attack each other, formal and informal group leaders, and other groups beyond the boundary of their group (fight). These groups, as briefly described, can be readily identified in the workplace, especially when they do not seem to be making progress at performing assigned work or responding to the need for change. It may seem that almost anything would be better than doing the work, thereby creating the underlying basic assumption groups.

Basic assumption groups direct our attention to how human nature makes its presence felt in daily operations and group dynamics. Regardless of whether one embraces the notion of the basic assumption groups or other types of groups (Allcorn and Diamond 1997), it is important to appreciate that the individuals who make up groups and create the workplace when they come to work are not machines, systems, or organisms (Morgan 1986). Rather, their humanity shines through to create these and many other outcomes (Allcorn 2002). This will always be true, regardless of how leaders lead, how work is designed and managed, and what the task at hand is. Human nature is the dominant influence in these groups, and it is what makes them unpredictable.

The Psychologically Defensive Workplace

Psychological defensiveness is a part of who we are. Starting at birth, the infant must learn to cope with emerging self and other experience, some of which is rewarding and some of which is unrewarding, painful, and threatening. Throughout our lives we learn to cope with what we experience and what others say and do to us. Relationships with others and the workplace are not womb-like holding environments where every need is effortlessly anticipated and met. We all gradually create psychologically defensive strategies to cope with those aspects of self and life experience that evoke the distressing sense of anxiety that underlies painful, threatening, and otherwise unrewarding experience. Karen Horney (1950, 18) captures this reality:

> [T]hrough a variety of adverse influences, a child may not be permitted to grow according to his individual needs and possibilities. Such unfavorable conditions are too manifold to list here. But, when summarized, they all boil down to the fact that the people in the environment are too wrapped up in their own neuroses to be able to love the child, or even to conceive of him as the particular individual he is; their attitudes toward him are determined by their own neurotic needs and responses. In simple words, they may be dominating, overprotective, intimidating, irritable, overexacting, overindulgent, erratic, partial to other siblings, hypocritical, indifferent, etc. It is never a matter of just a single fact, but always the whole constellation that exerts the untoward influence on a child's growth.

The usually unavoidable outcome is alienation from self and other and a compromised sense of self. The child, and later the adult, becomes focused on personal survival, which depends upon fairly rigid dependence upon mutually reinforcing, well-established psychological defense mechanisms and a self-sealing sense of false self. Traditional psychological defenses that may be found to be employed are selective attention and denial, rationalization, intellectualization, psychic numbing often enhanced by self-medication in the form of illicit and prescription drugs and alcohol, and suppression and repression that do away with conscious awareness. These psychological defenses are an omnipresent aspect of the workplace, where human nature holds sway (Allcorn and Diamond 1997).

In Final Analysis

It is an understatement to say that the workplace is imperfect. Our organizations do not run like the fantasized perfect machine or the organizational ideal. Observers of organizations and how they perform consistently encounter the same types of experiences and organizational attributes. The examples of these commonalities provided here have not been intended to be an exhaustive list; rather, they point the way toward reflection.

The presence of these commonalities also raises a more profound question: Why are they there? This chapter opened with the observation that the one thing all organizations share in common is that they are created and operated by people who, in their humanity, can be said to introduce a pervasive influence into the workplace—their human nature. This obliges us to inspect others, our groups, and ourselves for how our encounter with an organization influences us and how we influence the organization (Chapter 8).

The organizational ideal is never achieved, but still held in fantasy as the ideal state. At the same time, our organizations are often blatantly unlike the organizational ideal in which the organization becomes a "good enough mother." Organizational life can be harsh, punishing, and unforgiving, as evidenced by top-down management demands for submission and destructive management fads such as organizational downsizing and reengineering. The end result is the psychologically defensive workplace where, if the idealized image of organizations is to be sustained in our fantasy life, our experience of ourselves, others, and events must be psychologically transformed.

The next chapter changes the focus from understanding workplace attributes and human nature to appreciating organizational life as a historical narrative. Organization members are in a very real sense part of an unfolding story that may have begun many years or decades before. Yet however true this observation may be, knowing the narrative and its meaning to organization members is not so easily accomplished.

13

The Narrative of Workplace Histories

History. A narrative of events; a story; chronicle.
Narrative. A story or description of actual or fictional
events; narrated account.

—Excerpted from *The American Heritage Dictionary* (1975)

This chapter is about constructing a narrative out of what might be considered to be a variety of data sets that are gathered from individuals who hold organizational memory. Most organizations have members who have been there a long time, if not from the very beginning. Interviewing these individuals, who are most likely scattered throughout the organization, often reveals a wide assortment of historical accounts and stories. An event known to everyone, such as a merger or the firing of a highly visible executive, can be expected to be described in different ways. What happened, what it meant or means, and how it affected everyone, influences the narrator. A secretary in a remote department may have merely heard of the event but have no other reaction. A middle manager may have been directly affected by a change in job duties and career progression. In particular, some of these middle managers may have been positively affected while others were negatively so. Much the same can be said of senior-level executives, who will often explain what happened from a perspective that maps their understanding of what happened to them.

In sum, organizational events are usually described in different ways, depending upon one's location within the organization and its hierarchy. Similarly, the meaning of the event and its effect upon the workplace also contains many unique but valid organizational interpretations. Organizational history is, therefore, not uniform and should not be expected to be uniform. The collection of organizational stories throughout an organization presents a consultant or researcher with the challenge of distilling an overarching theme within the disparate data sets (narratives). This careful collection, synthesis, and interpretation of the history leads to an understanding of the organization's story in all of its complexity. This understanding amounts to the development of a narrative of workplace histories that reflects an overarching consensus.

The development of an organizational story by consensus sets the conceptual stage for organizational intervention that avoids or works through resistance to change. Much of this chapter focuses on the transformative potential of a "negotiated reality" vis-à-vis organizational members and leaders. Attention is directed to making this process concrete and one that can be operationalized through a series of steps that build forward by inclusion to reach consensus. It is not my intention to exhaust all the possibilities or provide a rigid straitjacket for creativity but rather to point the way toward facilitating organizational change by using organizational history as a part of the process.

Organizational History in Practice

An organization's history is a window into how it functions, presenting a gateway to insight and intervention. The crush of doing daily business and making the quarterly numbers often produces highly focused work that can lead to not being able to see all of the possibilities. Finding out how we got into this mess can lead to a zealous pursuit of excuses, mystifying explanations, and very often a sacrificeable scapegoat. Organizational history, in this case, is ignored or used for political and survival purposes, thereby becoming selective and revisionist in the worst sense of the word. Mind-boggling disinformation and spin create a surreal organizational landscape where up is down and where the emperor does indeed have on his clothes. In sum, developing a shared experience of organizational life that creates meaning and culture is much like the blind men and the elephant. The elephant only appears when all of the stories are known.

Individuals and groups scattered throughout the organization each have a different piece of the organization's historical hide. This makes understanding organizational history a complex task. It is invariably a painstaking process to document organizational history. Most often, the subtext of the historical account is the critical determinant of what the history means.

The Subtext of History

The historical subtext adds to the complexity of understanding organizational history as well as locating it within the larger organizational context revealed by the recollected stories (oral histories) rather than "factual" accounts. In this regard, the historical narrative is discerned, discovered, and interpreted from the accounts offered. These stories, while perhaps differing substantially in content, may well share a common subtext. The stories may contain a theme such as excessively tight fiscal management, poor planning and implementation of change, or simply bad management.

It is also possible that past and recent history are so powerfully clear that there is little variation in what is heard and felt by organization members. In this case, an organization's history may contain one or more seminal events, not unlike an organizational 9/11, where a massive downsizing was abruptly announced or a merger of two divergent organizational cultures attempted (AOL/Time Warner), creating a caustic outcome that dissolved organizational identity and functionality. What happened, why, and how it affected everyone is not in doubt. Nor is the subtext of abandonment, fear, or oppression.

In sum, taking the time to find a sharable historical perspective, while challenging and potentially time-consuming, represents a critical first step toward what might be thought of as a new beginning that builds forward from the historical narrative and how it was experienced. The willingness of leaders and consultants to create a context where this history is heard is a start at truly listening to its subtext. Listening demonstrates a respect for and trust in those who step forward to report their piece of the organizational historical hide (Stein 1994). Indeed, a cathartic outcome may arise from the creation of a sharable historical perspective that reveals many of the organizational attributes described in this book, such as organizational splits, failures to create timely change that works, and problematic leadership styles and their effects upon the functionality of the workplace. Organization members scattered throughout the workplace may discover that they have always been in the same experiential boat—an outcome that draws people together.

Uncovering Organizational History

The problem of distilling the history of an organization can be approached in much the same way whether you are a new leader or a consultant. In either case, the naive newcomer can interview individuals throughout the organization in a manner that is objective and focuses on listening and learning. These interviews, if carefully distributed and conducted, yield, as noted, a wide variety of oral histories based on the person's length of employment and location within the hierarchy and larger organization. What is important to appreciate is that each story is equally valid as told from the person's unique perspective and recollection. Middle managers will report a different history than people in upper levels of management, as will also be the case for lower-level employees. Divisions within the organization will have their own unique history. This process of collecting historical perspectives most often yields an understanding that contains a great deal of diversity. There may also exist a formal written history that must itself be regarded as an interpretation, although many concrete organizational events are documented. It is not uncommon to have to return to a few individuals who have access to a lot of the organization's history to clarify critical incidents both in terms of how they came to pass and their effect upon individuals, groups, and the organization as a whole. Gradually, the larger historical context and its many parts emerge for further testing. This testing amounts to negotiating a historical consensus and its meaning for the organization in the moment.

Developing a Negotiated History

Anyone working to support organizational planning and change should, after initial interviews, ask for a meeting with most if not all up upper management to place the organization's history on a time line. This joining together to do the work permits testing out what has been learned during the interview process. It also allows the consultant or new executive to play the role of devil's advocate in the sense that, if some of the more important historical aspects of the organization are recast or omitted, the participants can be encouraged to inspect the recasting and omissions with an eye to inclusion. Two useful orienting concepts to this development of a negotiated organizational history are the creation of an organizational time line and the building of a consensus history. A brief word on group process is in order before proceeding.

The consultant, new executive, or group leader who facilitates these two steps must attend to every point of view and recollection expressed. In this regard, those participating must be continually encouraged to hear what is being said. This is important for several reasons. First, it is not unusual for one member of a group to say something important on behalf of the group. The actual content of what is said is less important than the fact it appears to have been offered on behalf of those present. This offering may be tacitly approved of by others not criticizing or attempting to explain it away, or by their building upon it by offering more information or insights. It is also not uncommon for this type of offering to fall upon deaf ears, thereby making it important for the facilitator to direct attention and reflection to the new content. Is there something about it that is important to ignore? In this regard, the facilitator may have come upon similar information during the interviewing process that permits the introduction of additional information and insights.

The second reason to address everything said is that the facilitation process must lead to the creation of a safe enough holding environment and transitional space and time to do the work. This is most often accomplished only by repetition. The facilitator must establish and maintain focus on the task as the group process strays into less desirable interpersonal and group dynamics where listening is not occurring and discrediting and intimidating of others emerges.

Developing a Historical Time Line

Working on a white board or large pad adds a liberating quality to accomplishing group work. The work is "out there" before the group and all of its members. This creates a group dynamic that promotes collaboration, a willingness to confront differences of opinion, and ownership by most group members. The outcome of accomplishing this is that the work becomes more open and fun. Those participating begin to hear what others have to say. There is something to be learned from everyone's contribution. The group begins to appreciate that organizational history is full of different experiences and recollections that, if successfully welded together, create a consensus.

As a technical matter, it should be noted that taping chart paper to the wall permits the adding of sheets until the work is finished. The starting point of the time line is flexible. There is seldom anyone present with more than thirty years of employment. Many organizations, divisions, and departments have not been in existence more than ten to twenty years. In general, the time line can begin as far

back as group members can recall, with greater attention being focused on the last decade.

The organizational history and time line should capture information
on a number of items. How the organization came into existence is important. Did a single individual found it? Was a division or department
created for some special purpose or in response to a threat or opportunity? Organizational size and growth is an important parameter. In particular, how fast did the organization grow? Explosive growth creates its
own problems. Slow and steady growth may have been achieved for
some underlying purpose not necessarily related to aggressively achieving profit and success. The growth of facilities and sites should be included. Reductions in size should also be considered. Who was the leader?
A ten- or twenty-year time line will usually include a number of leaders,
each of whom had his own unique style that made distinctive contributions to the history and culture. Changes in leadership may have been a
response to organizational problems and change. Each leadership style
should be briefly described. Last, an inquiry into what it was like to
work within the organization at different times is important. The
organization's culture will have changed over time. Employees will experience an organization that starts out small and grows rapidly to a
large size very differently at the start versus the present. Most organizations start small; those who can recall what it was like to work for the
organization during the start-up often speak nostalgically of feeling like
they were all in it together and that that everyone was a friend. This
sense of togetherness is often lost over time as organizations grow in
size. Leadership styles may also have changed along the way from op-
portunistic, entrepreneurial, and collaborative to styles that emphasize
getting control of all the work, often by a process of developing and
enforcing rules and regulations.

These basic parameters should be augmented as appropriate. Group
members might mention aspects of the organization that are not being
addressed. It is never too late to acknowledge this and go back and place
the information within the time line.

In sum, the construction of the time line is a creative process that is
facilitated at the start by capturing some specific information. However,
much can be learned by what is volunteered by group members that
does not neatly fit within the starting parameters. In the end, group members have to feel that they have been heard and that the time line is a
joint product, although everyone need not agree with every point or per-

spective. There must, however, be an overall "buy-in" that engages everyone in the group in terms of personal ownership. This is important for building consensus.

Building Consensus History—A Recapitulation

Any belief that the history of an organization is a reasonably concrete thing and therefore knowable with a little effort should have been debunked by now. Herein lies the difficulty. It is not uncommon to find that the simplest and most concrete aspects of organizational history are disputed. Building consensus is no easy matter. Large organizations often have a rich and diverse history that looks different depending upon where you are in the organization. On a larger scale, the history of an international conflict sounds different depending upon which side you are on and who won. Within an organization, interviewing those in management positions and those who have a long tenure regardless of position about the past often reveals a subjective complexity that is informative in terms not only of understanding the history but also understanding how the organization managed to get itself into its current situation.

Developing the historical time line permits the exploration of those parts of history that are recalled differently throughout the organization, and most certainly those instances where important history is omitted or has been subjected to revision in order to make it safe to talk about. The facilitation of the building of the time line, therefore, also permits the gradual exploration of different points of view.

The building of a consensus history is, therefore, a working through of many past and often painful and confusing organizational and interpersonal events in an effort to agree upon an overarching historical perspective. Implicit within this group dynamic is the discovery of new openness, trust, and respect that very often leads to some tension-reducing catharsis that gradually overcomes resistance to trusting and respecting others. A chief executive officer (CEO) may become better understood and accepted by upper and middle management. An organizational split within the management group may surface and be worked through.

The context of the safe enough holding environment created by the consultant or facilitator, combined with the group task of creating the time line, is a process filled with the potential for open confrontation of "the truth" that must occur in order for a true sense of consensus to emerge. In particular all points of view have to be heard. The facilitator must introduce other unmentioned points of view that were uncovered during the interviewing process. The facilitator must also continually strive for openness and the avoidance of the use of code words and phrases that imply an unwillingness to get the subtext out into the open.

In sum, the building of consensus is not an easy matter. However, as a first task for the management group to accomplish, it is an important one that sets the tone for planning and strategizing about the future. This consideration leads to the use of a traditional strategic planning tool—the SWOT analysis, an assessment of the strengths, weaknesses, opportunities, and threats an organization has or faces.

The SWOT Analysis as History

The traditional SWOT analysis is a useful way to understand organizational history and its implications for future organizational performance. One of the more interesting ways to do this work is to do it twice. The first round is the development of the analysis by a group of mid- to lower-level managers, supervisors, and employee representatives. This work occurs in a large group setting where it often feels safer for employees to articulate what exactly is on their minds. Upper management must be excluded from this work. The ability to allow this work to be done signals a readiness on the part of senior management to listen. The second round is the development of the analysis by the senior management group. The two analyses will differ, leading to an opportunity to reconcile the differences. How exactly this is done for any given organization will depend upon the many variables at hand. However, what is learned by exploring the perceptual gap is often important in terms of moving forward together.

The exploration of an organization's strengths and weaknesses in these two settings often reveals organizational splits and different views of operating problems. It might not be uncommon for upper management to view middle management and employees in a negative light. At the same time, the employees may believe that one of the organization's strengths is a loyal and hard-working work force. It is, of course, going to be the case that there is truth in both points of view.

The listing of threats and opportunities is also often informative. Employees and senior management may see things differently. Also, weaknesses become threats if not addressed. The inability to achieve meaningful and timely organizational change can also compromise the organization's ability to capitalize on opportunities. A good example is government bureaucracy that is big, cumbersome, slow to change, and not cost-effective. Employees may feel threatened with the outsourcing of their jobs or the elimination or trimming down of programs. Conversely, those in charge may see changes like these as being adaptive.

In sum, developing a SWOT analysis or something like it in this twofold manner offers facilitators many opportunities to reconcile differences and forge a consensus document. It may also be that participants agree to disagree over some of the content. In this case, both perspectives should be listed as a reminder to organization members of the true complexities involved in working together over time.

Divergence in Experience and History—What Was It Like to Work Here?

The development of an understanding of organizational history, while permitting an at times cathartic working through of what really happened when and to whom, raises one additional consideration that should be further explored. History, as a listing of events, critical incidents, and outcomes, can take on a sense of safety by avoiding exactly what people where thinking and feeling. The building of the time line and the emergence of consensus permits exploring the question, "What was it really like to work here?" This question is the foundation for the development of trust and respect, empathy, and the emergence of a cathartic working through of what is often a long history of painful and disorienting workplace experiences. In a sense this amounts to emotional or affective learning that can lay a foundation for considering what needs to be changed in the future. In particular, participants may become sensitized to the human cost associated with the use of presumably rational management methodologies (Allcorn et al. 1996). Organizational splits in the form of in-groups and out-groups may be inspected for their past and present effects on working together and organizational performance.

The Significance of History for Planning and Change

The ability to develop an informed plan of action and get it implemented is often problematic. Organizations are filled with strategic plans on the shelf that were initially developed with an enthusiasm that rapidly waned as efforts to implement the planning encountered organizational resistance to change, unintended consequences, and the need to constantly revise plans to keep them current. No change at all is a very real option for twenty-first-century organizations. It is therefore important to identify the contribution that organizational history makes to overcoming and, better yet, avoiding organizational resistance to change (see Chapter 2).

Throughout the discussion thus far there has been an emphasis on the human side of organizational history. The development of a consensus history that includes how events were experienced by those living through them creates a basis not only for catharsis but also for sufficient empathy to move forward together. In fact, the successful development of the historical time line informed by the SWOT analysis and reconciliation of different points of view provides management and employees with the opportunity to chose to either perpetuate conflict or join together to avoid repeating history. Failure has to be presented as one option that everyone has a stake in avoiding in the future.

Organizational Transformation

Transformation has become a buzzword that sounds good and promises to deliver an outstanding outcome. Transformation is used here to suggest that the effort to rise above what may be a long history of organizational dysfunction is a major challenge for consultants and executives. Calling into question what is and how things work introduces feelings of shame if the organization is less than successful, and fear that if change does occur, the result will threaten "my" position, my relationships with others, my skills and expertise, and even my job. Thus reemerges the problem of resistance to organizational change discussed in Chapter 2. In fact, a long history filled with mythology and mystification is threatened in the sense that accurate reality testing may not support these historically based and distorted world views. There may arise considerable resistance to the process of developing accurate and consensus built reality testing that precedes efforts to determine where we want to be and how to get there. This resistance to knowing and understanding represents an effort not only to hang on to what is familiar, but also to avoid the threats implicit in creating organizational change. In a sense, if one's head is deep enough in the sand, one does not have to worry about the gathering storm on the horizon. In many cases, therefore, it is difficult to work on SWOT, performance audits, and GAP (the gap between what is and what is desired) analyses that are recommended in strategic planning books when accurate reality testing is steadfastly avoided.

At this point, it is important to note that the development of a consensus history that goes before the SWOT analysis represents an effort that, if successful, establishes a process of accomplishing and accepting accurate reality testing. This is essential in locating where we are, where we want to be, and how to span the gap between the two. This process reshapes organizational culture as a concurrent but not explicit part of efforts to strategically plan and problem solve contemporary crises. This approach is a departure from standard discussions of organizational culture in the literature. Goodstein, Nolan, and Pfeiffer (1993, 219) write,

> After the culture requirement has been determined, the degree to which such a culture is present or absent in the organization is typically ascertained in the performance audit phase of strategic planning. [Sometimes], however, the need for a culture change and the awareness of the length of time that such a change would take [are] so apparent that culture-change efforts [are] initiated immediately, rather than later in the planning process. Ordinarily, however, the performance audit would evaluate the organization's current culture, and the required culture would be compared with the present culture during the gap analysis to see how discrepant the two might be and what could be done to bridge the gap.

These authors are to be applauded for their appreciation of the importance of reshaping organizational culture as a part of strategic planning, although there is somewhat of a mechanistic ring to their writing, and shifting organizational culture is much easier said than done. They maintain that "strategy, typically, is limited by and adjusts to the existing culture" (Goodstein, Nolan, and Pfeiffer 1993, 66). How things are and what it is like to work here are a product of history that has shaped organizational culture and employee experience, values, work, and the underlying assumptions about what may be learned and how and what may be known and communicated (Goodstein, Nolan, and Pfeiffer 1993; Schein 1985). These aspects of organizational life, experience, and group and organizational dynamics are so fundamental to the workplace that, if they are not addressed as a part of an effort to change them, the human nature that creates them will compromise efforts for adaptive change in the service of organizational survival. In essence, everyone may collude to go down with the ship.

The fundamental question all of this raises is exactly how to use an organization's history in a way that is beneficial and suitable for all. The methodology suggested here is to use the development of a consensus history and SWOT analyses as a means of negotiating a reality that everyone can "buy into." Implicit within this organizational work is the process of shifting the organizational culture by using this work as organizational development and team building with the outcome being a mutual process of building forward.

The Process of Building Forward

The development of a consensus organizational history by upper management is no easy matter. The consultant or facilitator must be able to open up for discussion much of what was learned during the interviewing process. This requires a tactful, constant press to have the undesirable information heard and addressed. This will most likely succeed within a context of an adequate holding environment where a transitional space and time are created. The importance of this holding environment is underscored by the following passage written by the second most senior executive in a large organization where change was approached in a manner consistent with what is being suggested in this chapter:

> [P]rior to your arrival, our organization's culture was rooted in favoritism, mistrust, deceit, lies, manipulation, and management by fear. A culture based heavily in policies, procedures and memo-driven; a very hostile work environment. Our organization clearly lacked a sense of direction, leadership, and a value structure. Our staff behaviors were those of defensiveness and individualism. . . . Your advice of using the Strategic Planning process as the vehicle in which to launch the culture change process was excellent, while at the same time, developing our vision and mission. (Confidential source)

Although words cannot exactly convey what the consultant or facilitator has to do to achieve the creation of a safe enough context to build a consensus organizational history and SWOT, it is doable. The following is a brief outline of the steps recommended in this chapter.

1. Conduct interviews throughout the organization at all sites. In particular, pay attention to what it is like to work there. This

chapter and Chapter 14 provide considerable information on how to collect this information. This work should preferably be finished before proceeding.

2. Form a task group of upper-level managers including the CEO to spend as much as a day developing a historical perspective using the time-line approach.

3. Meet with a representative cross-section of the organization's employees to develop a SWOT. This can usually be done in one day.

4. Present the employee SWOT to the task group of upper-level managers for their review. They will predictably not agree with what is listed and how it is phrased. They should then be asked to develop their own SWOT analysis. This information should be shared back with the employee group for their reaction in a short meeting. No effort per se should be made at this point to reconcile the two analyses; instead take this opportunity to open a dialogue to promote mutual respect and appreciation that things are different depending on where you are in the organization.

5. Form a strategic planning group that represents a diagonal slice through the organization starting with the CEO and including representatives from departments all the way down to the lowest levels. This boundary-collapsing diagonal slice approach introduces different points of view and historical perspectives into the work of planning, where vision, mission, values, goals, and objectives will be created. Herein lies the process of creating a cultural shift in the organization, from, for example, the caustic one described above to one of greater unity where interpersonal trusts and respect are the foundational assumptions. This work should begin with reconciling the two SWOT analyses.

These steps and the work to accomplish them, it may be readily acknowledged, require considerable skill and patience on the part of the consultant or facilitator to achieve. The process must be constantly adapted to the realities of the moment and requires some courage on the part of the consultant to continually point out denied, rationalized, and forgotten history and events. Diamond (1993, 14–15) writes, "Human behavior in organizations is the outcome of characteristic relational conflicts and patterns between and among participants. It is the result of distinctive organizational identities, which stem from superior–subordinate relationships and collective defenses. These defensive practices are encouraged by traditional organizational norms and values, perpetuating a vicious circle that ensures suppression and denial (or selective attention) at the expense of reflection and personal responsibility." In this regard, this work is not accomplished in a weekend retreat and is most definitely not an off-the-shelf canned approach that implies one size fits all. If it is believed that organizational change must be accompanied by shifts in organizational culture that are compatible with and in support of the new direction, it is essential that the time and effort and the accompanying expense be allocated. Failure to do so turns efforts at organizational planning and change into very often just another marginally successful or failed effort.

In Final Analysis

This chapter has focused on the importance of accurate reality testing that can very often only take place in a safe enough holding environment, which can be said to contain transitional or transformative time and space. Accurate reality testing implies a willingness to inspect past organizational problems, change, leadership styles, and successes and failures. This work is ultimately threatening when many perspectives gathered from throughout the organization are inserted into the mix. Yet it not only offers the promise of shifting organizational culture in the direction of openness and interpersonal trust and respect, but also creates an opportunity to avoid the reemergence of the old culture and resistance to change. Herein lies organizational development, in the sense that organizational splits surface for inspection and what amounts to cathartic healing.

The next chapter goes forward from the consensus-building nature of developing a narrative and looks at organizational diagnosis and intervention. Once the historical narrative and where "we" are today have been established, what needs to be changed, how, and when becomes the challenge. Creating a context for successful organizational change is no easy matter.

14

Organizational Diagnosis and Intervention

[The organizational diagnostic method] . . . should require a student of organizations to fully describe an organization's concept, objectives, plans, its view of itself as well as its relationships with others, and its leadership. It must enable the consultant to understand systems of communications, coordination, guidance, control and support. It must help him to delineate relevant environments and behavior settings. It must be a guide to unfolding the rationale of the organization, explaining its activities, and critically evaluating the organization's adaptive adequacy, followed by a reasoned series of recommendations.

—Harry Levinson, with Janice Molinari and Andrew Spohn,
Organizational Diagnosis (1972)

Thus far, a number of unique aspects of the workplace have been introduced and examined for their relevance in understanding organizational life. Each perspective is anchored in the experiential nature of organizational life. The compound eye contains many lenses for viewing, understanding, interpreting, and responding to a vast array of work experience and organizational dynamics. This compound eye view of the workplace implicitly contains the opportunity to use all of the perspectives in order to see the workplace in much the same way a fly's eye permits a sweeping view of the world around it. When taken together, these perspectives create an opportunity to build a model for organizational diagnosis and intervention. This chapter is devoted to explicating the possibilities. It is not the intention here to exhaust all of the possibilities, but rather direct the reader's attention to the possibility of finding the meaning in organizational experience that exists behind the lenses—an integrated panoramic view of organizational life.

This work is approached by building forward from the content thus far presented. The focus is on developing a survey instrument and/or a semi-directed interviewing methodology based on each of the twelve perspectives. Examples of questions are provided for each. The survey methodology permits the data to be arrayed graphically, facilitating organizational visualization. This chapter concludes with a discussion of how to use these results to reflect back the nature of the organization's culture to management and employees along with suggestions for intervention.

Organizational Diagnosis—In Brief

Organizational diagnosis, if done well, is not as easy a matter as implied by Levinson's words above. It is a difficult and challenging endeavor that requires the utmost professionalism as well as an effective strategy for accomplishing the work. An important consideration in undertaking an organizational assessment and diagnosis is that one's approach must vary based on the size of the organization and the type of business. A coal-mining company that employs thousands of workers is fundamentally different from a telephone marketing organization that employs 250 employees. The same can be said for such factors as the readiness of the chief executive officer (CEO) and top management to embrace a diagnosis, as compared to focusing consultant effort on repairing one problem area in one division, as is too often the case. Organizational diagnosis can therefore be seen as a significant undertaking that will reveal many aspects of leadership style and organizational function. Herein lies the necessity for a professional, clinically oriented approach that is systematic and, most of all, nonthreatening. Organizations willing to develop an organizational diagnosis that may also be viewed as a sophisticated internal assessment stand to benefit in many different ways, as compared to the traditional, narrowly focused interventions most often requested by management. These self-defined and narrowly cast consultation requests are also frequently responded to by regimented approaches to collecting and analyzing data on the part of consultants, who may focus on identifying organizational fat as compared to organizational identity (Diamond 1993).

Interviewing as a Basis for Diagnosing Organizational Problems

Interviewing can reveal a great deal of information and, at the same time, start a process of listening to what employees have to say. In general, a semi-directed interviewing approach permits collecting information on a targeted number of topics while also allowing for learning more about unique points of view and experiences articulated by employees. In particular, stories about how the organization works in practice can be illuminating. They can point to underlying organizational dynamics that are driving organizational events. Interviewing works best when a pledge of confidentially is made. Much depends on how trusting the employees are. Some may still feel that if they say what is on their minds, they will be punished. In these cases, the best response is to point out that the interviewer will hear much the same from others and that what is on the person's mind is likely not attributable to any one individual. It is also often true that when the information is synthesized for feedback to management, it is not likely to be a real surprise to them. Information and stories that might permit management to identify a particular individual must be omitted, and care should be taken at all times to make good on the pledge of confidentiality.

The interview process should start with a detailed organizational chart to permit a selection of interviewees from throughout the organization. Usually everyone in upper management is interviewed. There may be instances in which an individual specifically asks to be interviewed. If the number is not too large, this should be done, not only to hear what the person has to say, but also to demonstrate a willingness to listen. Often, what is said is consistent with what others have to say.

Interviews should be scheduled in hourly increments to permit sufficient time as well as an opportunity for the consultant to reflect and check a few facts with others between interviews. Also useful are group interviews, where it may feel more or less safe for the participants to say what is on their minds. The interview process can be supplemented by the use of a survey.

Extensive interviewing by two or more interviewers introduces the problem of combining information and perspectives. It is not uncommon to find that interviewers focus on collecting information relevant to their personal propensities, which tends to warp what might be learned as well as promote some interpersonal competitiveness as to who has it right. An additional consideration is that interviewers may be assigned certain areas or groups (management as compared to union members) where a strong divergence in information and perspectives can be expected to emerge. These provisos should be heeded in order to maintain integrity in the collection and analysis of data. An observant eye should be maintained on how work is proceeding and watch for the development of conflicts and competition among those participating.

Compilation of the interview data can be equally challenging and usually focuses on locating commonalities in what has been said. A standard format for taking notes is important. The commonalities identified may be recast into general themes that are supported by concrete examples and informative stories. The themes, when combined with history, tell a story that management will react to, further extending its meaning. This work is often best accomplished by one individual who compiles and synthesizes the data for review and discussion with colleagues. This can be challenging if a great deal of information has been collected. However, many times the interview data contain repetition of information and similar points of view. The exception may be informative stories offered by individuals. These can be of value in illustrating particular points and the impact of organizational dysfunctions upon operations.

The agreed-upon synthesis and report are then shared with the CEO, followed by a meeting with the leadership group to review and discuss the results. The process of reviewing the organization's story gleaned from the interviews and any other data collected leads to reflections on the types of problems and opportunities that exist and how to respond to improve organizational performance. Some interventions may seem clear to everyone, while others have to be talked through. It is critical at this point to promote the planning of a systemic approach to organizational change. This approach must be combined with suitable employee participation and a communication process that informs and engages employees, who will be keenly interested to see some results from the interviewing process and how they will be used. Finally, the interview process will have started a respectful listening context between management and employees that should be continued (Stein 1994).

Developing an Assessment Instrument

Developing and using an employee survey can save time as compared to interviews. However, exclusively relying on a survey approach inevitably omits two major strengths of interviewing. First, taking the time to interview employees permits employees to volunteer information that is important but might otherwise go undiscovered. Interviewing also permits follow-up questions that further explore a perspective or factual statement. Many times employees offer important insights that, in order to be fully appreciated, must be further explored. The second omission is that interviewing serves to create a sense of openness and listening that is very often lacking in troubled organizations. The willingness for the organization to invest in the extra time needed to conduct interviews signals a commitment to receiving feedback as well as a willingness to listen to what employees have to say. In a very real sense, interviewing represents the first step in an organizational intervention that lays a foundation for additional listening as efforts to locate problems and plan and implement change ensue (Stein 1994). On the negative side, interview data are difficult to quantify as compared to survey data. In particular, survey data permit one to say that 68 percent of the employees reported that they are pleased with how they are supervised and 22 percent reported that there is insufficient planning before making changes. Survey data are especially useful when it appears that the CEO is a large part of the problem. Many times he or she is more willing to listen to an analysis of a survey than receive a verbal report summarizing interview findings. In sum, quantification does have advantages in terms of speed, low cost, and acceptance. Obviously, a combination of the two serves to provide concrete examples of what the survey shows and a first-hand experience of organizational life as lived by the employees.

There are two common approaches to collecting survey data. One is to have the survey returned to the consultant via the company mail system or the post office, and the other is to ask that employees be convened in groups in a conference room where they complete the survey. Each approach has some advantages and disadvantages. Mailing the survey back gives employees more time to respond and, assuming the survey is anonymous, it offers anonymity, especially if mailed through the postal system. On the negative side, many of the surveys will not be returned and the process takes longer. Convening groups of employees in a conference room has the advantage that it is quick and a survey is received from everyone. Any questions about the survey or its wording can also be addressed at that time. On the negative side, employees may feel that confidentiality is compromised and they have less time to respond in depth by providing lengthy notes and examples that are often volunteered via mail. Regardless of whether an interviewing process or survey instrument or both are used, one must take pains to cover relevant material. The next section provides some of the grist that may compose the interview and survey questions.

An Inventory of Possible Questions

The following questions are organized and informed by the content of each of the foregoing chapters. A number of points about these questions bear mentioning based on the insights of the twelve compound perspectives.

- They are not intended to be comprehensive or fit all situations. They are intended to provide a starting point in developing a survey tool or list of interview questions.
- Some may fit. Some need to be modified for use. Some will not be usable. There are also many additional questions that should be considered but have not been listed.
- Multiple questions are provided that address the same issue but are phrased differently to provoke additional thought. What is not being provided here is a regimented list of questions to put in a survey or to be used for interviews. They must be carefully selected for use.
- How exactly the questions are phrased is important. Care should be given to creating a balance in phraseology between negative and positive questions and statements.
- Balance is a consideration. The number of questions per chapter or section should not vary greatly to avoid a content bias in the results.
- Perfection is not possible. Some respondents will seek clarification, and consideration must be given to how this should be accomplished.
- Confidentiality is important. However, so is capturing enough information to map responses back to the organization and its many parts.
- The interview questions are written in a conversational tone, much like they might be asked.
- Some of the questions may become follow-up questions, given an interviewee's answer.
- Some of the content of the questions is repeated within the lists for each chapter. This underscores the interconnection between what is observed in the workplace and the underlying reasons for why it is found. Care must therefore be taken in terms of interpreting the responses to questions that can appear in more than one list.

- Care should also be given to not create compound survey questions that ask two or more questions. Is planning adequate and implementation effective? This is an example of a compound question. A NO response raises the question, Which is it? Is it not adequate or not implemented effectively, or both? This is not an issue for the interview questions, where clarification can be sought.
- Last, some consideration should be given to collecting demographics that will help to reveal nuances in the data. How long has the person worked for the organization? How long has the person had the same job? What division or section does the person work in? Who is his immediate supervisor? Care must be given to explaining that this is important information to have and that confidentiality is assured.

The survey questions are written as statements that employees can respond to as agree or disagree and a range in between. A five point scale is suggested where 1 is strongly disagree and 5 is strongly agree. The use of a scale acknowledges that the world is most often not an either/or black-and-white experience. The scale also permits relative ease in compiling and analyzing the results.

Chapter 2—Organizational Resistance to Change

The Interview Questions

- What is an example of a change in direction or in how things have been done in your organization?
- Overall, during the past few years, how successful have been efforts to change the organization or processes?
- What seems to be the biggest problem in identifying needed changes?
- What seems to be the biggest problem in planning and implementing change?
- What is a recent example in which a change effort seemed to have major problems?
- What is a recent example of a major success?
- In your opinion, is top management effective at leading organizational change?
- Are there differences within the organization as to how the need for change is determined and how change itself is planned and implemented?

- Would you say that most everyone feels included in the process of making changes?
- To what extent does it seem management hands down a decision to change something without much employee input?
- Would you say the employees are open to making changes?
- When change occurs, do employees understand why it is necessary?
- Do employees understand how changes are to be implemented and when?
- What is an example of an unintended consequence of a change?

Survey Agree/Disagree Statements

- My organization is effective at planning change.
- My organization is effective at implementing change.
- My organization is behind in making needed changes.
- Management is effective at leading change.
- Management is effective at coordinating change.
- Employees usually understand what the nature of the change is.
- Employees usually understand why the change is needed.
- Changes are usually accomplished without creating problems.
- Employees are open to making changes.

Chapter 3—Organizational Fragmentation

The Interview Questions

- How effectively does your division (department, section) work with other divisions?
- Does work seem to be coordinated among divisions?
- Is there a lot of competition between divisions for resources and bragging rights?
- What is an example in which poor cooperation among divisions produced an outstanding result?
- What is an example in which poor cooperation among divisions led to a bad outcome?
- How effectively do all of the layers of management work together?
- Do you think information flows up and down the organization are satisfactory?

- Are there any examples in which the management layers contributed to creating a problem?
- Does a lot of communication, coordination, and work get accomplished by going around the system?
- Are there differences in leadership styles among the divisions?
- How would you describe leadership styles up and down the management hierarchy?
- Do you think most employees trust and respect each other?
- Does management trust and respect the employees?
- Is there a lot of "us versus them"?
- Does it sometimes seem that there are good divisions and bad divisions?
- Are some divisions and managers favorites of top management while others seem to be working under a cloud of disapproval and suspicion?
- Is there a lot of red tape involved in getting work done?
- Does it seem that everyone is working together?
- Do some projects or changes seem to stall?
- Are there problems that just do not seem to get fixed?

Survey Agree/Disagree Statements

- We work well across divisions.
- The layers of management work well together.
- Communication between divisions is good.
- Communication down the organization is good.
- Communication up the organization is good.
- We often get things done by working around the system.
- There is a lot of "red tape" that blocks getting things done.
- Everyone works together just fine.
- There is a lot of "us versus them."
- Some divisions, managers, and employees seem to be the favorites of top management.

Chapter 4—Goals Within the Workplace

The Interview Questions

- Is it clear what the organization's vision and mission are?
- Are there clear goals that direct work?

- Are goals broken down into measurable objectives and clear work assignments?
- Does it often seem that everyone is working on the same goals?
- Do some people seem to have their own goals that are not consistent with organizational goals?
- Are people held accountable for getting the work done?
- Does management seem to say one thing and then do something else?
- It is pretty clear what everyone is supposed to be working on, why, and is that work well coordinated?
- Are there constant changes made to what you are supposed to be working on?
- Does everyone seem to have adequate time and resources allocated to get the job done?
- Who sets the goals?
- How are goals communicated?
- Are there adequate measures of progress on achieving goals?
- Are there instances in which people have been disciplined for not meeting goals?
- How are problems in reaching goals identified and dealt with?
- Does it seem as though some of the goals are out of date?
- Do employees seem to be motivated to reach the goals?
- Are the goals reasonable and achievable?

Survey Agree/Disagree Statements

- Everyone knows what the mission is.
- Clear goals are being set.
- Goals are logically coordinated.
- Our goals provide clear direction.
- Goals are broken down logically into a series of steps and work assignments.
- Everyone is working hard to meet the goals.
- Some people seem to have their own goals.
- The goals and work assignments are being constantly changed.
- Adequate resources are allocated to achieve the goals.
- Adequate time is allocated to achieve the goals.
- It is clear how progress on goals is being measured.
- We are held accountable for reaching the goals.

- Everyone is motivated to work on the goals.
- Problems encountered in accomplishing the goals are promptly and effectively addressed.
- The goals are kept up to date.
- Everyone believes that achieving the goals is good for organizational success.

Chapter 5—Incentives

The Interview Questions

- Are incentives provided to reward good performance?
- Are incentives used to temporarily boost productivity to meet a daily, weekly, or monthly goal?
- Does it feel like you are being manipulated when incentives are used?
- Is it generally felt that managers and supervisors are good at working with employees?
- Are there some measures of productivity everyone knows management is watching?
- Are there instances in which employees have been disciplined for not meeting a performance goal?
- Has the use of incentives produced any unintended consequences?
- Are employees generally self-motivated and seeking to get the job done?
- Are there aspects of work that you would say are demotivators?
- Does management set unrealistic performance goals?

Survey Agree/Disagree Statements

- Employees like the performance incentives program.
- Performance incentives deliver on what management wants.
- Incentives are used to fix the problem of the day or week.
- Managers and supervisors are good leaders.
- Managers and supervisors inspire employees to go the extra mile.
- The measures used to track productivity are good at determining where and when shortfalls occur.
- Everyone is usually more than willing to try to get the job done without being given incentives.
- There are aspects of work that detract from employee motivation.
- Morale is good.

- Incentives have produced unintended outcomes that detracted from organizational performance.
- Management does a good job helping us get the job done.
- Top management is liked.
- Top management is respected.

Chapter 6—Leadership Pathology

The Interview Questions

- Has there been a tendency for top management to take up management fads?
- Do executives, managers, and supervisors tend to insist upon loyalty and following orders and rules?
- How important is it to be seen as a team player?
- Do those in charge solicit and listen to employee ideas and feedback?
- Does it sometimes feel dangerous to speak up and offer ideas?
- Do those in top management blow up or become anxious and overly controlling when problems arise?
- Does the CEO (top executive, manager, and supervisor) have a loyal band of followers who receive special attention?
- How often does it seem people get scapegoated when problems arise?
- Is the CEO and top management accessible and do they listen?
- Is management trusting and respectful of employees?
- Does management seem to be on top of things or ineffective and dysfunctional?
- Is top management respected by employees?

Survey Agree/Disagree Statements

- Being loyal is important.
- Following orders is important.
- New ideas are encouraged by management.
- Management encourages critical thinking.
- It is dangerous to speak out about unsolved problems.
- There is a real possibility of being scapegoated when problems arise.
- Top management is respectful of employees.
- Top management trusts employees to get the job done.
- Micromanagement is a problem.

- Top management is available to listen to employees.
- At times the CEO seems to be out of control.
- At times some in top management seem to be out of control.

Chapter 7—Cultures of Organizational Violence

The Interview Questions

- Would you say it can be dangerous to work here?
- How well does the image of everyone hiding out in a foxhole fit your organization?
- Are you aware of instances in which individuals have been scapegoated or messengers bearing bad news have been fired?
- How important is it to admire and support the CEO and executives here?
- Is there a group of people who are favorites and are treated differentially?
- What happens if the CEO or executives are criticized?
- Do the CEO or executives always have to have it their way?
- Do members of top management tend to see themselves as overly self-important?
- Is the CEO (members of top management) arrogant and indifferent to the thoughts and feelings of others?
- How important is loyalty to top management?
- Does the CEO (top management) assume responsibility for problems when they are encountered?
- Does the CEO (members of top management) try to avoid taking action to fix problems, preferring instead to let others take charge?
- Do people have to leave your organization or are they fired because they have offended someone in upper management?
- How likely is it that supervisors will jump all over employees if something goes wrong?

Survey Agree/Disagree Statements

- Working here can be dangerous.
- People are sometimes severely disciplined or fired for questioning management.
- The CEO tries to control everything.

- Top management tries to control everything.
- Top management is not particularly arrogant and indifferent to what others think, feel, and do.
- No one wants to be around when the CEO and her team show up.
- Top management assumes responsibility for problems.
- Micromanagement is commonplace.
- Top management is always ready to step in to help fix a problem.
- We are not encouraged to think for ourselves.
- Top management is not particularly effective in leading the organization and dealing with operating problems.
- Loyalty and unquestioning support are a prerequisite to keeping one's job.
- There is a group of people who are the favorites and receive special attention and privileges.

Chapter 8—The Human Psyche in the Workplace

The Interview Questions

- Do employees seem to identify with your organization and its mission?
- To what extent does it seem employees change the organization, and what are they doing to suit their own needs?
- Please describe your organization's culture. What is it like to work here?
- Are employees deeply invested in the organization?
- What is the ideal employee like?
- What are some examples of things that happen that are inconsistent with the organization's culture and ideals?
- Do employees tend to change themselves to fit what seems to be expected of them?
- Do employees tend to defend themselves against the organization and how they are managed?

Survey Agree/Disagree Statements

- Employees like the organization.
- Employees identify with the organization and its mission.
- Employees have to adapt themselves to how the organization works in order to get ahead.

- Employees tend to change what they do to better fit with their own desires and expectations.
- The organization really has to be changed.
- There is an ideal way employees should be.
- Employees are willing to make sacrifices for the sake of the organization.
- Employees have to defend themselves from the organization.
- Changing the organization does not seem to be an option.
- Conforming to what is expected is important.

Chapter 9—Selecting In and Out: Creating Organizational Homogeneity

The Interview Questions

- Is there a tendency to encourage everyone to think alike?
- Have there been instances in which people have been disciplined or have had to leave because they offered up different ideas and points of view?
- Are there some areas in which everyone tends to have the same opinions and approaches to work?
- Do some areas seem to have a barrier around them that protects them from outside influences?
- Does management advocate ideas like being a team, where it is understood that it is important to conform and fit in?
- Are there instances in which others have been attacked by management or a group for being different?
- Does the expression "My way or the highway" seem to fit your organization?
- Are some people maligned for deviating from the norm?
- How often do people who do not seem to fit in simply leave?
- Does management say they want new ideas but when these are provided their response make it pretty clear that they are not really interested in the ideas and employee input?

Survey Agree/Disagree Statements

- Conformity is important in order to get ahead.
- People who have different points of view often end up leaving.

- Questioning what is going on and thinking outside of the box can lead to being rejected by others.
- The organization runs on the principle, "My way or the highway."
- Sections of the organization are defensive of their turf and shut out outside influences.
- There are a lot of similarities among managers and employees in terms of their values and what they think.
- Being different is not really tolerated.
- People leave because they do not feel accepted.

Chapter 10—The Surface of Organizational Experience

The Interview Questions

- Does the organization seem to be fragmented where the divisions function as silos that inhibit cooperation and communication?
- How common is it for problems to arise from a lack of communication and cooperation?
- Does it feel as though sometimes there are invisible barriers to working together?
- How open, collegial, and collaborative is your organization?
- Are there a lot of turf issues and struggles for power and control?
- Do employees feel that they are kept from interacting with each other and participating in the larger organization?
- It is sometimes hard to explain why working together is a problem?
- Does it seem as though your division protects you from what is going on within the organization?
- Does your division limit you in communicating and coordinating your work with people in other divisions?

Survey Agree/Disagree Statements

- I am able to communicate freely with anyone I need to in order to get my job done.
- Other divisions limit and block direct communication with their employees.
- Turf issues are not a problem here.
- We work together effectively to get the job done.
- I do not understand why it seems so difficult to work together here.

- I feel that my division does protect me from some of the negative influences in the organization.
- There seems to be a lot of disjointedness and organizational fragmentation that creates problems with the left hand not knowing what the right hand is doing.

Chapter 11—Mysticism in the Workplace

The Interview Questions

- Does the CEO (top-level executives) seem to be larger than life?
- To what extent does the CEO (top management) seem to make intuitive decisions or rely on "gut reactions" not based on a thorough analysis of the situation?
- Does management rely on a hard-to-understand set of ideas or principles to guide decision making and the design of work processes?
- Does management put out reports and analyses that are hard to understand and lack sufficient information to allow one to draw one's own conclusions?
- Have numbers and information been manipulated and distorted to support a particular point of view?
- What are some of the myths about this organization and its leaders?
- How often does it seem that there is a hidden meaning or agenda in what is said or written?
- How easy is it to tell how the organization and its divisions are doing?

Survey Agree/Disagree Statements

- The CEO seems to be larger than life.
- There are some who are thought to have accomplished major feats.
- Decisions are made only after a data collection and analysis process.
- Decisions are frequently "shoot from the hip."
- Intuitive decision making and gut feelings are often relied upon.
- Information about organizational performance is confusing, incomplete, or unavailable.
- It is not uncommon to find that information is manipulated to protect someone or to support a particular point of view.

- Management seems to faithfully rely on approaches and methodologies that have not consistently worked in the past.

Chapter 12—Uncommon Commonality

The Interview Questions

- How effectively led and managed would you say your organization is?
- Does it seem as though the better people often end up leaving?
- In your experience is there very much back-stabbing, maligning, and limiting of what people can accomplish?
- Are there a lot of organizational politics that compromise organizational performance?
- How good are the information systems?
- How good are the databases?
- Is the information that is available used effectively to manage operations?
- Is there a clear sense about where your organization is headed and how it will get there?
- Does it often seem that you cannot be yourself?
- How common is it for people to unquestioningly embrace the organization and what its leaders do?
- Does it often seem as though there are hidden or undiscussable agendas that steer work away from accomplishing the goals?
- How often do you hear others deny and rationalize what is going on?

Survey Agree/Disagree Statements

- Management is effective at leading our organization.
- There are few management problems here.
- We have many outstanding people.
- We are constantly adding new outstanding people.
- There is a brain drain going on here.
- Everyone feels supported in their work by management.
- Everyone feels supported by their fellow workers.
- There is a lot of back-stabbing, interpersonal competition, and unresolved conflict.
- Organizational politics is a problem.
- Our information system is a good one.

- The information that is available permits us to do a good job.
- The organizational vision is clear to everyone.
- The organizational mission is accepted by everyone.
- You have to watch what you say.
- We feel that we are being constantly watched and monitored.
- You cannot really be yourself here.
- Everyone pretty much goes along to get along.
- There are a lot of hidden agendas that are worked much of the time.
- It not uncommon to hear people rationalizing and denying what is going on.

Chapter 13—The Narrative of Workplace Histories

The Interview Questions

- Do you think your organization's history is an important contributor to how you got where you are today?
- Does your history limit your possibilities in the future?
- Are there divisions that have a different historical perspective from others in the organization?
- When history enters the discussion, how easy is it to agree on what it is and how it has affected things?
- What are some of your organization's strengths?
- What are some of your organization's weaknesses?
- What are some of the threats to ongoing organizational success?
- If you were in charge, what would you change?
- Is the organizational planning process doing a good job of determining what you need to do in the future?
- Does everyone feel included in the planning process?
- How are deviations from the plan handled?

Survey Agree/Disagree Statements

- Organizational history has a major influence on where we are today.
- Our divisions tend to see our history differently.
- There is a tendency to rewrite organizational history and its effect on how we got to where we are today.
- It is not always easy to agree on how we got where we are today.

- The organization has considerable strengths.
- The organization has considerable weaknesses.
- We are doing enough planning to make sure we know where we want to be in five years.
- Most people do not feel included in the planning process.
- We are effective at responding to problems that lead to deviations from our plan.

The Graphic Representation

Depending on the results of the survey and the interview process, it might be helpful in communicating the results to array them graphically as a line or bar chart. This approach could be particularly valuable in visualizing results by chapter topic that are either widely disparate or much the same. This approach can be extended to analyzing the results per chapter by displaying responses to individual questions. This is usually informative in understanding the overall results and counterintuitive for major variations. It may also be appropriate to inspect the results on a division-by-division basis for significant variations across the organization. A suggestion when this approach is used is to have each graphic representation accompanied by a table of data used to generate it. Often, employees like one or the other but not both.

Intervention

Organizational intervention is admittedly a vast subject to tackle as a section within a chapter. The twelve chapters, however, do point out important considerations for creating and facilitating organizational change.

The inherent complexities of organizational life have been underscored by the discussion of twelve different perspectives that create a compound eye view of the workplace. All too often consultants, change agents, and transformational leaders focus on one or a few elements of an organization with the hope of making rapid changes that can be demonstrated to have short-run efficacy. In the process they not infrequently degrade organizational morale, systems, processes, and performance, a result that is hard to see in the flurry of activity to cut costs and make changes. Implicit within the content of this book is the need to better understand what is currently going on and why (the diagnosis) before prescribing what may seem like a magic elixir—right-sizing, restructuring, or streamlining processes.

The organizational diagnosis phase, as noted, begins a process of intervention in the sense that renewed or new attention is directed to hearing what employees have to say. It is not uncommon for executives and internal and external consultants who take the time to do the interviewing and collect the survey data to be seen as foci of hope that the organization will change for the better. In the case of substantially dysfunctional organizations, it may come to pass that the consultant(s) assumes an active interim role of leadership where the employees believe that they have been heard and will continue to be heard and look to the consultant to provide direction.

CEOs and senior executives and managers are most often open to receiving feedback from a consultant who has conducted interviews and developed a survey. Care must be taken to do a good job of objectively compiling the information as well as creating a context in which it will be heard. Merely dumping a lengthy report on the CEO's desk does not bode well for organizational change and will almost assuredly only serve to dash the hopes of employees who felt that listening and change were possibilities. Getting the information heard and understood leads to the logical next step, doing something about it. In particular, it might be strongly advocated that employees become involved in the work to avoid what may have been a history of alienating top-down management edicts.

The interventions selected for pursuit represent, if at all possible, a consensus within the organization and with the consultants. The careful process of developing a history and diagnosis that is generally agreed to by everyone makes this possible. The history and diagnosis usually make clear what is to be done, why, and in what order. This is the advantage of "Ready, Aim, Fire." In sum, the time investment in the history and diagnosis makes clear the problems and their likely solutions in an open and communicative context that serves to minimize organizational resistance to change.

A last consideration is a long-term follow-up diagnostic process to once again learn about new problematic aspects of organizational life. If possible, this should be negotiated at the start of the consulting engagement.

In Final Analysis

This chapter has focused on the process of transforming the content of the first twelve chapters into concrete and actionable interview and survey questions. A number of provisos, insights, and suggestions have been offered that should be heeded. In addition, every such effort must be informed by the first-hand knowledge of the organization and its members.

It is sometimes just as important to pay close attention to what has not been said. This book and this chapter have as their ultimate focus appreciating the humanity that organization members bring to work with them every day. This appreciation directs attention away from consulting methodologies driven by numbers and "off-the-shelf" methodologies that are applied to every organization that lies within their path. While these strategies are readily marketable and make consultants a lot of money, one has to recognize that organizational life is often fractured and even laid waste to by these methods, which leave in their wake an organization that must struggle for survival.

Finally, this chapter suggests avenues of reflection for CEOs, executives, managers, and supervisors, and insights into how to better understand organizational experience for all employees. Organizational success in the twenty-first century may well hinge on being able to view the organization through the lens of the compound eye.

The next and closing chapter expands this discussion beyond the boundaries of the workplace while also looking back upon the role of consulting in the workplace. Each of the twelve perspectives that contributes to understanding the workplace also contributes to understanding our lives, families, relationships with others, social groups, and encounters with "organization."

15

The Final Analysis: The Compound Eye's World View

Work has become an important social device for resolving
three major psychological problems: unconscious pressures,
dependency and identity. As an individual reinvests personal
drives in an organization, both the organization itself and the
leadership that represents its power become important aspects
of the person's environment. They define the modes within the
organizational structure through which aggressions may be
expressed and affection obtained or given by promotion,
demotion, transfer, reward, assignment, job definition, and
other methods of control. The organization and its leadership
have an important bearing on how people perceive themselves
as adults—whether they fulfill aspirations of the ego ideal, are
held in esteem, or judge themselves to be a failure.

—Harry Levinson, *Executive* (1981)

This book has looked at the workplace not through a single lens, but many—
the compound eye's world view. These images we see, when assembled
into an integrated world view, reveal the workplace in a different way, one
that illuminates the complexity of work life. These vantage points, when
taken together, provide their user an opportunity to explore work life, history, and culture to achieve an understanding of what exactly it is like to
work within an organization and, just as important, why things are the
way they are. At the same time, no grand unification scheme has been set
forth as to how the compound eye's view of the workplace can be translated into an overarching theory of the workplace or a methodology for
creating a boilerplate, ten-step approach for organizational diagnosis and
intervention. Other lenses may be equally applicable, and no doubt others

are yet to be described. The compound eye suggests that there is no one right way to come to know the workplace, as Micklethwait and Woolridge point out in their book, *The Witch Doctors* (1998). The pursuit of fame and fortune on the part of some has yielded a vast market of soothing and faddish snake-oil remedies. Chief executives officers (CEOs) are prone to grab these remedies as this month's solution to the problem of achieving the goal of profit, earnings for stockholders, and acquiring ever more stock options. The remedy is often accompanied by one or more consultants to implement it. This makes taking a time-out to better understand this process important, and it calls attention to the need for more comprehensive or holistic approaches to organizational analysis and change, such as those being explored in this book.

Organizational Consulting as a Paradigm of Waste

A former career consultant who has since become an executive has provided us with an interesting insight into the consulting world and the workplace in what amounts to a personal confession (see "Confessions of an Ex-Consultant," *Fortune*, October 14, 1996, 134–37). He begins by setting the overarching context, saying this: CEOs are most often average, not the best or the smartest nor the worst at any one area of management. They are generally balanced, not overly analytical, not humanistic, and not highly expert in a functional area. They are generalists who usually know their limitations and compensate for them by hiring consultants who are experts in their areas of weakness. He also notes that consultants are many times more interested in the problem than they are in the solution. As a result, they underestimate the complexity of moving from identifying and defining a problem to fixing it. They do not understand what it means to do the work. It is a lot easier to talk about it than it is to do it. This former consultant also asserts that 75 percent of the consultants that he worked with were deficient and should have been avoided. This observation leads to another. Consulting firms make their money by teaching their young employees that it is their job to cling tenaciously to every client and that they will be rewarded for it. As a result, consultants spend more time thinking about what they are going to sell the client next than dealing with the problem at hand. Expanding the scope of the engagement is the goal, and it is one that is not all that hard to achieve, since there are usually many operating problems and many specialized products and services to sell.

This is a chilling consideration for any would-be employer of a consultant. It also points out that there is a difference between consultation that results in valued outcomes and consultation in which the consultant is employed to compensate for perceived weaknesses on the part of the CEOs and executives who employ her. In working with consultants from large consulting companies, I have observed that they have no problem working on a small component of operations that, if fixed, still does not solve the underlying problem. Worse yet, these consultants know this to be the case and they do it anyway, believing that, at least for a short time, things are better. In sum, trying to help organizations succeed as a whole is not recognized as a viable form of consultation by CEOs nor many times by highly specialized consultants. Additionally, consider that CEOs are interested in protecting their tenure. Getting many of the operating and performance problems out on the table at the same time in one single process is threatening. It seems safer to fix one small aspect of the organization at a time. To be appreciated, then, is that the compound eye's examination of the workplace, when combined with organizational diagnosis, offers management and consultants a different approach to improving organizational performance than the narrow, targeted interventions that compensate for CEO and executive weakness.

It is not easy to understand organizational life. Efforts to do so must be designed to fit the organization and its operating history and context in order to achieve real insights that can lead to adaptive organizational change. Standard or canned approaches do not work as well. Chapter 14 suggests avenues for acquiring the insight and reflective knowledge that are needed to design and implement organizational change. However, the critical feature of asking the suggested questions is that they are joined with an appreciation of the impact that the complexities of human nature have upon the workplace. This is of such great consequence that it merits additional inspection.

An examination of the workplace through the lenses discussed here also suggests that there is no division among them. In particular, a common theme that begins in Chapter 2 and continues throughout the book is that of individual, group, and organizational resistance to change and to the manipulative and dehumanizing aspects of the workplace (goal setting, incentives, and leadership styles). These insights additionally encourage us to examine the roles of human dignity, spirit, soul, and suffering that constitute human nature and in large part the interpersonal, group, and cultural aspects of work and the workplace (Allcorn 2002).

Life in the Shadow of Organization

The twelve perspectives discussed in this book help us understand our lives at work and why our encounter with the workplace may be deficient, frustrating, and even threatening. The twelve perspectives also provide insights into interpersonal and group relations that apply to all types of organizations—religious, social, athletic, or volunteer—and all types of roles that we may have—worker, member, client, customer.

Our Encounter with Organization

It is fair to say that, except for the hermit, we all live in a rich milieu of organizations that directly or indirectly influence, and in some instances dominate, our lives. In addition to the workplace we can add a partial list that includes federal, state, and local government; school districts; advocacy and self-help groups; home owners' associations; large corporations; small businesses; and religious organizations. We are in constant contact with many organizations, and this directs our attention to the inevitability of our encounter with "organization." One need only reflect on this full-body immersion: If our electricity is off, whom do we call? If a product we purchased is defective, how do we return it? If the roads are impassable because of snow, who is responsible for clearing them? "Organization" is perhaps best understood using the compound eye's perspective.

Often, organizations that should change do not. Organizational fragmentation may lead us on an unfulfilling journey into bureaucracy. Governmental goals may be set without much transparency (Chapter 4). To the extent that they are ideologically driven, some are locked out of the process. We are frequently incentivized, manipulated, and subjected to legal and social sanctions (Chapter 5). We are often confronted with leaders (elected or otherwise) who unyieldingly take us in the wrong direction while demanding loyalty and compliance (Chapter 6). We also frequently encounter organizations that have but a single issue or purpose and a membership entirely devoted to it. It may be the case in these organizations that everyone is of the same mind (Chapter 9). We encounter aspects that are walled off from us. When we encounter them, we know that they are there because we can feel their presence (Chapter 10). It is equally true that mysticism is a constant presence, whether it is religious experience or an encounter with a charismatic leader (Chapter

11). We are merely encouraged to accept, believe, and to park our brains at the door. In all of these ways, the content of this book encourages critical thinking about "organization" in our lives.

A Compound-Perspective Workplace Experience

Our places of work cast a long shadow across our lives. How we feel about ourselves, others, our work, and our ability to take care of our families is dominated by workplace experience, as Harry Levinson notes in this chapter's opening quotation. It is therefore important to take a moment to revisit this book's content for its contribution to our individual well-being at work.

The best of organizations do not uniformly or consistently provide their employees with opportunities for rewarding self-experience. Many organizations fall far short, thereby creating stressful, unrewarding, interpersonally divisive, and not infrequently threatening work experiences (Chapter 7). We are all too often left with the problem of trying to change the organization or, failing that, changing ourselves, thereby compromising our integrity. How do we cope with our workplace and our experience of it while maintaining integrity and some sense of being a responsible employee and a productive human being?

There are no easy answers. The content of this book offers its reader perspectives that encourage the development of insights into the workplace, insights that promote reflection, which in turn informs our experience of ourselves and our work. This helps put into perspective the workplace and its effects upon us. Additionally, the book offers validation of self-experience: You are not alone in your experience of your place of work. Others share much the same experience. The ability to create and sustain personal reflectivity is the central focus of this section (Allcorn 2002).

The discussion of organizational resistance to change (Chapter 2) encourages us to reflect upon our experience and, when it is aversive, our response, which may be resistant. Do we not all from time to time receive a directive from a superior or senior executive that we do not respect? In response, we may feel that we are either not going to comply, change the instructions, or, possibly at an extreme, resort to sabotage. Understanding our individual resistances more fully aides us in maintaining intentionality at work as well as our personal integrity. If we feel shut out, disregarded, frustrated, or angry, might we not also righteously feel resistant? These feelings are entirely legitimate; however, acting upon them in the form of resistance also undermines our integrity and self-respect. Thus enters the need for personal reflection. We all have a choice in how we act.

Organizational fragmentation (Chapter 3) directs our attention to how we are divided from each other in many different ways at work. "Us versus them" and "We have it right and they have it wrong" are common workplace themes. Awareness of these themes promotes reflective processes that encourage us to work to span these differences. We do not have to be divided one from the other if we do not want to be. Organizational dynamics that encourage these divisions can be called into question, which is frequently not hard to do since they often introduce demonstrable operating problems. It is equally important to know that we do not have to have these types of feelings. We have a choice.

Goal setting (Chapter 4) may also contribute to negative workplace experience, especially when goals seem inappropriate or are driven top-down. Calling goals into question may not be an option. Resisting them can become the not-so-hidden agenda. Goal setting can be alienating because our knowledge and opinion are essentially dismissed. The workplace is often filled with this type of experience. If we do not agree, what do we do? The answer to this question once again directs our attention to the reflective process. Whatever course of action is selected (resistance or embracing), we need to be aware of our thoughts and feelings and how they contribute to our actions in one way or another. Chapter 4 provides much to think about and incorporate within the reflective process.

Chapter 5 explores facets of the use of rewards (incentives) and punishments (disincentives) in the workplace. They are frequently relied upon to stimulate self-directed work to achieve an organizational goal. It is not uncommon to find, however, that when we pursue the reward, we compromise organizational performance. Chapter 5 makes this clear. The question is, then, how can we responsibly pursue the incentives provided? An ancillary question is, how do we feel about being manipulated by management? Frequently, our feelings about being manipulated determine how we respond. Herein lies yet another opportunity for reflection. We do have a choice regarding how we respond. If we feel alienated, we feel angry. If we feel angry, we may feel justified in optimizing our pursuit of the reward at the expense of organizational performance. Rarely is it the case that rewards and punishments do not introduce the likelihood of organizational dysfunction. If we are to act responsibly and maintain our values and personal integrity, we are obliged to find a way to respond that does not compromise organizational performance.

Leadership pathology is all too common (Chapter 6). The best of leaders are imperfect. It is not uncommon to find marginally effective executives who do not provide adequate direction yet think they do. They may also think that the rules of fair play do not apply to them and that the only problem they have left is rooting out disbelievers or further projecting absolute control. They may be remote managers or micromanagers who trust no one. How we are led and supervised are important contributors to how we experience ourselves at work. Chapter 6 provides insights toward understanding self-experience and our response to management direction. Once again, self-reflection is important if we are to avoid having our self-experience dominated by the pathological aspects of leadership.

Cultures of organization violence (Chapter 7) often flow out of leadership pathology, especially that of the CEO and his support group. Chapter 7 encourages us to reflect not only about leaders but also about the larger experience of work life. What is it like to work here? Organizational culture embodies that experience. Being able to see some of the connections between leadership pathology and organizational culture is helpful in terms of sorting out overwhelming workplace experiences that flood us with many different feelings about ourselves, others, and the organization. The ability to reflect is an essential first step in learning to cope effectively with workplace cultures containing violent tendencies and dehumanizing qualities.

Chapters 8 ("The Human Psyche in the Workplace") and 10 ("The Surface of Organizational Experience") encourage a quality of self-reflection that implies greater personal exploration and understanding of self and self-experience. Our encounter with the workplace affects who we are and who we may become. The workplace also contains many experiences that are hard to recognize and describe. These possess autistic qualities. The ability to identify this omnipresent experience allows us to observe its effects upon us, thereby enabling us to better appreciate our own experience and maintain intentionality in our workplace behavior.

Chapter 9 ("Selecting In and Out") and Chapter 12 ("Uncommon Commonality") direct our attention to a distressing press for commonality in the workplace as well as the fact that most organizations possess the same problems. Being different many times does not pay when management expects loyalty and unquestioning compliance. Those who differ are often asked to leave, or do so voluntarily. This consideration raises the question, why are you still here? The ancillary question is, why do you not feel that you want to stay? Chapter 9 addresses these questions. Chapter 12 raises the problem that the grass is not always greener elsewhere. Why is it that the problems of one organization are so often found in others? It may be sadly the case that it is hard to escape these commonalities by changing organizations. Acknowledging this commonality opens for inspection and reflection our experience of ourselves and of the workplace. It also provides insights into what to look for if a change of jobs is being contemplated.

Chapter 11 introduces the notion that the rational workplace is filled with mysticism to a greater extent than one might expect. Leaders may seem to be bigger than life, and concrete aspects of the workplace may, upon close inspection, have ever-changing properties. Everyone with workplace experience has been exposed to these properties (especially quantitative data) although they may have gone unnoticed or, if observed, blended into business as usual. Appreciating their presence opens them for inspection, which this chapter encourages. It also encourages us to reflect upon our experience of leaders, especially those that seem to have acquired fantastic qualities.

Last, all organizations have a history that affects how they operate in the present (Chapter 13). Appreciating how we got here may not help us avoid making the same mistakes again. It may, however, help us to understand that what is going on and how it is experienced is part of a time line of organizational change. This permits acquiring a broader perspective and insight as to why change is sometimes so steadfastly resisted.

In sum, the chapters of this book give you, the reader, the opportunity to reflect about the workplace and your experience of it and yourself. I suggest here that self-reflection is one of the central elements to workplace survival (Allcorn 2002).

The Future of Organizational Diagnosis and Intervention, and Organizational Dynamics Theory Building

This book has focused on aspects of organizational life that are pervasive. They are experienced on a daily basis but also underappreciated and many times not acknowledged at all. These pervasive aspects of daily life are not particularly recognized as open to elucidation, inspection, and reflection with an eye toward changing organizational life. At the same time, they can be readily documented to exist as a part of a thorough organizational diagnostic process. Anyone who wishes to create a systemic intervention to improve operations, profitability, and employee experience of the workplace must be able to locate and open for inspection and change those aspects of organizational dynamics that are threatening and taboo. The elephant in the room may be said to be standing upon one's foot in some instances. Therefore, this book, and the work of others who strive to make it reasonable and indeed a necessity to explore and understand these aspects of the workplace, opens the door to a larger, more insightful inspection of how things really work. This underscores the importance of the psychodynamics of human nature.

Not long ago, I submitted a paper to a major scholarly journal that argued that most if not virtually everything that we are dealing with in the workplace, and how we deal with it, is an extension of science and management theorizing that took place prior to 1950. The editor of this journal basically agreed with this perspective, but also suggested that something was new. It was the growing use of psychoanalytic theory to explore the workplace. Of course, much of the seminal work did take place prior to 1950. However, it is also true that much of what has developed relative to the workplace has taken place after 1950 and indeed since 1975. This book extends the realm of pre-1950 human relations from a sociological and social psychological perspective to one that is psychoanalytically informed. The first twelve chapters are grounded in human nature and psychology, factors that create less-than-rational workplace dynamics. Human nature is, it has been suggested, the only commonality that accounts for the subject matter of the chapters.

An additional contribution made here is my effort to more intentionally locate and collect these insights so that they can be meaningfully shared by management and employees. A combination of qualitative data collected during interviews informs the development of a survey instrument that can tap and quantify experiential data. The subjective data collected in the interviews provide insights and stories that serve to humanize the data captured in the surveys. All too often, executives leading change and internal and external consultants produce an analysis codified in a report that is politely listened to and then shelved. This does not contribute to organizational change. It is essential to engage top management in a process of inquiry in order to promote reflective practice. Management must be enlisted in the work of change. There is nothing quite as effective as illuminating a survey finding with concrete stories and examples that most often many are aware of but also defensively ignore. In this regard, overcoming resistance to change as discussed in Chapter 2 can be accomplished by working through the human and not-so-rational resistance to change among those in management.

A last contribution this book makes is of a more humbling nature. The twelve lenses described here examine aspects of work life that even the best of interventions may not successfully change. Human nature, it turns out, can be exceptionally resistant to change. People often like it just the way it is, even if it is not perfect. Herein lies a cautionary note for consultants and internal change agents: Success, if achieved, takes patience and persistence and a willingness to acknowledge the humanity of those less open to change. Once again, merely writing it down in a report is not very successful. Requests to prepare a written report should be carefully considered. Very often, a written report encourages management to select but a few of the items mentioned for action; it encourages argument and rebuttal, can be threatening to some, and used as a weapon against others. A report can also end up collecting dust on a bookshelf alongside other reports and recommendations prepared at exceptional expense.

The Final Analysis

If this book has done anything, I hope it has driven home the point that the workplace is filled with the complexity of humanity. Employees, managers, and executives are all striving to somehow make sense of their experience and each other, and lead and work toward making an outstanding product or providing a superior service. Human nature is the commonality that every workplace shares. Learning how to understand it, work with it, and achieve adaptive and timely organizational change is a true challenge in the quest for organizational excellence in the twenty-first century.

References

Adams, Guy, and Danny Balfour. 1998. *Unmasking Administrative Evil.* Thousand Oaks, CA: Sage.

Allcorn, Seth. 1990. "Keep Individuality in Top Management." *Personnel Journal* 69, no. 4: 17–22.

———. 1991. *Workplace Superstars in Resistant Organizations.* Westport, CT: Quorum Books.

———. 1992. *Codependency in the Workplace.* Westport, CT: Quorum Books.

———. 1994. *Anger in the Workplace: Understanding the Causes of Aggression and Violence.* Westport, CT: Quorum Books.

———. 1995 "Understanding Organizational Culture as the Quality of Workplace Subjectivity." *Human Relations* 48, no. 1: 73–96.

———. 2002. *Death of the Spirit in the American Workplace.* Westport, CT: Quorum Books.

———. 2003. *The Dynamic Workplace.* Westport, CT: Praeger, 2003.

Allcorn, Seth. Howell Baum, Michael Diamond, and Howard Stein. 1996. *The Human Costs of a Management Failure: Organizational Downsizing at General Hospital.* Westport, CT: Quorum Books.

Allcorn, Seth, and Michael Diamond. 1997. *Managing People During Stressful Times: The Psychologically Defensive Workplace.* Westport, CT: Quorum Books.

Amado, G. 1995. "Why Psychoanalytic Knowledge Helps Us Understand Organizations: A Discussion with Elliott Jacques." *Human Relations* 48, no. 4: 351–357.

Argyris, Chris. 1983. *Reasoning, Learning and Action: Individual and Organizational.* San Francisco: Jossey-Bass.

Argyris, Chris, and Donald Schon. 1978. *Organizational Learning: A Theory of Action Perspective.* Reading, MA: Addison-Wesley.

———. 1982. *Theory in Practice: Increasing Professional Effectiveness.* San Francisco: Jossey-Bass.

Baum, Howell. 1987. *The Invisible Bureaucracy.* New York: Oxford University Press.

Bion, Wilfred. 1961. *Experiences in Groups.* London: Tavistock Publications.

Blau, Peter, and Marshall Meyer. 1971. *Bureaucracy in Modern Society.* New York: Random House.

Carroll, Lewis. 1999. *Alice's Adventures in Wonderland.* Cambridge, MA: Candlewick Press.

Collins, Jim. 2001. *Good to Great.* New York: HarperCollins.

Colman, Arthur, and Marvin Geller. 1985. *Group Relations Reader 2.* Washington, DC: A.K. Rice Institute.

Covey, Stephen. 1989. *The 7 Habits of Highly Effective People.* New York: Fireside.

Czander, William. 1993. *The Psychodynamics of Work and Organizations.* New York: Guilford Press.

Diamond, Michael. 1986. "Resistance to Change: A Psychoanalytic Critique of Argyris and Schon's Contributions to Organization Theory and Intervention." *Journal of Management Studies* 23, no. 5: 543–562.

———. 1993. *The Unconscious Life of Organizations: Interpreting Organizational Identity.* Westport, CT: Quorum Books.

———. 1996. "Innovation and Diffusion of Technology: A Human Process." *Consulting Psychology Journal* 48, no. 4: 221–229.

Diamond, Michael, and Seth Allcorn. 2003. "The Cornerstone of Psychoanalytic Organizational Analysis: Psychological Reality, Transference and Counter-Transference in the Workplace." *Human Relations* 56, no. 4: 1–23.

———. 2004. "Moral Violence in Organizations: Hierarchic Dominance and the Absence of Potential Space." *Organisational and Social Dynamics* 4, no. 1: 22–45.

Diamond, Michael, Howard Stein, and Seth Allcorn. 2002. "Organizational Silos: Horizontal Organizational Fragmentation. *Journal for the Psychoanalysis of Culture & Society* 7 (Fall): 280–296.

Downs, Anthony. 1967. *Inside Bureaucracy.* Boston: Little, Brown.

Eigen, Michael. 1996. *Psychic Deadness.* Northvale, NJ: Jason Aronson.

Gabriel, Yiannis. 1999. *Organizations in Depth.* London: Sage.

Gerth, Hans, and Charles Mills. 1946. *From Max Weber.* New York: Oxford University Press.

Goodstein, Leonard, Timothy Nolan, and J. William Pfeiffer. 1993. *Applied Strategic Planning.* New York: McGraw-Hill.

Greenberg, Jay, and Stephen Mitchell. 1983. *Object Relations in Psychoanalytic Theory.* Cambridge, MA: Harvard University Press.

Grotstein, James. 1985. *Splitting and Projective Identification.* Northvale, NJ: Jason Aronson.

Guillory, William. 2000. *Spirituality in the Workplace.* Salt Lake City: Innovation International.

Hammer, Michael. 1997. *Beyond Reengineering.* New York: HarperBusiness.

Hammer, Michael, and James Champy. 1993. *Reengineering the Corporation.* New York: HarperCollins.

Hirschhorn, Larry. 1988. *The Workplace Within.* Cambridge, MA: MIT Press.

Horney, Karen. 1950. *Neurosis and Human Growth.* New York: W.W. Norton.

Hummel, Ralph. 1982. *The Bureaucratic Experience.* New York: St. Martin's.

Jaques, Elliot. 1971. "Social Systems as Defense Against Persecutory and Depressive Anxiety. In *New Directions in Psychoanalysis,* ed. M. Klein, P. Heinium, and R.E. Money-Kyrle, 478–498. New York: Basic Books.

———. 1995a. "Why the Psychoanalytical Approach to Understanding Organization is Dysfunctional." *Human Relations* 48, no. 4: 343–349.

———. 1995b. "Reply to Dr. Gilles Amado." *Human Relations* 48, no. 4: 359–365.

Kernberg Otto. 1979. "Regression in Organizational Leadership." *Psychiatry* 42: 24–39.

Kets de Vries, Manfred. 1980. *Organizational Paradoxes.* London: Tavistock Publications.

———, ed. 1984. *The Irrational Executive.* New York: International Universities Press.

———. 1991. *Organizations on the Couch.* San Francisco: Jossey-Bass.

————. 2001. *Struggling with the Demon: Perspectives on Individual and Organizational Irrationality.* Madison, CT: Psychosocial Press.

Kets de Vries, Manfred, and Danny Miller. 1984. *The Neurotic Organization.* San Francisco: Jossey-Bass.

Klein, George. 1976. *Psychoanalytic Theory: An Exploration of Essentials.* New York: International University Press.

Kohn, Alfie. 1993. *Punished by Rewards: The Trouble with Gold Stars, Incentive Plans, A's, Praise, and Other Bribes.* New York: Houghton Mifflin.

Koenigsberg, Richard. 1975. *Hitler's Ideology: A Study of Psychoanalytic Sociology.* New York: Library of Social Science.

Krantz, James, and Thomas Gilmore. 1989. "The Splitting of Leadership and Management as a Social Defense." *Human Relations* 43 (February): 183–204. (See also www.triadllc.com/splitting.doc).

La Bier, Douglas. 1986. *Modern Madness: The Emotional Fallout of Success.* Reading, MA: Addison-Wesley.

Lasch, Christopher. 1979. *The Culture of Narcissism.* New York: W.W. Norton.

Levinson, Harry. 1981. *Executive.* Cambridge, MA: Harvard University Press.

————. 1976. *Psychological Man.* Cambridge, MA: The Levinson Institute.

Levinson, Harry, with Andrew Spohn and Janice Molinari. 1972. *Organizational Diagnosis.* Cambridge, MA: Harvard University Press.

Maccoby, Michael. 1976. *The Gamesman.* New York. Simon and Schuster.

Masterson, James. 1988. *The Search for the Real Self.* New York: Free Press.

Menzies, Isabel. 1960. "A Case Study in the Functioning of Social Systems as a Defense Against Anxiety." *Human Relations* 13: 95–121.

Merton, Robert, Ailsa Gray, Barbara Hockey, and Hanan Selvin. 1952. *Reader in Bureaucracy.* New York: Free Press.

Micklethwait, John, and Adrian Woolridge. 1998. *The Witch Doctors: Making Sense of Management Gurus.* New York: Times Books.

Mitroff, Ian, and Elizabeth Denton. 1999. *A Spiritual Audit of Corporate America.* San Francisco: Jossey-Bass.

Morgan, Gareth. 1986. *Images of Organization.* Newbury Park, CA: Sage.

Ogden, Thomas. 1989. *The Primitive Edge of Experience.* Northvale, NJ: Jason Aronson.

————. 1990. *Matrix of the Mind.* Northvale, NJ: Jason Aronson.

Peters, Thomas, and Robert Waterman. 1982. *In Search of Excellence.* New York: Harper & Row.

Rycroft, Charles. 1973. *A Critical Dictionary of Psychoanalysis.* Totowa, NJ: Littlefield, Adams.

Schein, Edgar. 1985. *Organizational Culture and Leadership.* San Francisco: Jossey-Bass.

Schon, Donald. 1987. *Educating the Reflective Practitioner.* San Francisco: Jossey-Bass.

Schwartz, Howard. 1990. *Narcissistic Process and Corporate Decay: The Theory of the Organizational Ideal.* New York: New York University Press.

Schwartz, Peter. 1996. *The Art of the Long View.* New York: Doubleday.

Shapiro, Edward, and Adrian Carr. 1991. *Lost in Familiar Places.* New Haven, CT: Yale University Press.

Stacey, Ralph. 1992. *Managing the Unknowable.* San Francisco: Jossey-Bass.

Stein, Howard. 1994. *Listening Deeply.* Boulder, CO: Westview Press.

———. 1998. *Euphemism, Spin, and the Crisis in Organizational Life.* Westport, CT: Quorum Books.

———. 2002. "Foreword." In *Death of the Spirit in the American Workplace,* by Seth Allcorn. Westport, CT: Quorum Books.

Stein, Howard, and Robert Hill, eds. 1992. *The Culture of Oklahoma.* Norman, OK: University of Oklahoma Press.

Stern, Daniel. 1985. *The Interpersonal World of the Infant.* New York: Basic Books.

Tansey, Michael, and Walter Burke. 1989. *Understanding Countertransference.* Hillsdale, NJ: Analytic Press.

Tead, Ordway. 1933. *Human Nature and Management.* New York: McGraw-Hill.

vanden Heuvel, Katrina. 2003. "The Coalition of the Rational." *The Nation* July: 17. www.thenation.com/blogs/edcut?pid=822.

Volkan, Vamik. 1997. *Blood Lines: From Ethnic Pride to Ethnic Terrorism.* Boulder, CO: Westview.

Winnicott, Donald. 1965. *The Maturational Processes and the Facilitating Environment.* New York: International Universities Press.

———. 1988. *Human Nature.* Levitt, PA: Brunner/Mazel.

Yankelovich, Daniel. 1978. "The New Psychological Contracts at Work." *Psychology Today,* 11 (May): 46–50.

Zaleznik, Abraham. 1966. *Human Dilemmas of Leadership.* New York: Harper & Row.

———. 1989. *The Managerial Mystique.* New York: Harper & Row.

Zaleznik, Abraham, and Manfred Kets de Vries. 1975. *Power and the Corporate Mind.* Boston: Houghton Mifflin.

Index

Seth Allcorn, Ph.D. is the Assistant Dean and Chief Financial Officer of the Texas Tech University Health Sciences Center School of Medicine. He is the former Associate Dean for Fiscal Affairs for the Stritch School of Medicine, Loyola-Chicago and former department of medicine administrator at the University of Missouri and the University of Rochester. He has worked on a part and full time basis as a consultant to organizational change for twenty years.